Triple Bottom Line Risk Management

Triple Bottom Line Risk Management

Enhancing Profit, Environmental Performance, and Community Benefits

Adrian R. Bowden

Malcolm R. Lane

Julia H. Martin

John Wiley & Sons, Inc.

New York • Chichester • Weinheim • Brisbane • Singapore • Toronto

Library of Congress Cataloging-in-Publication Data

Bowden, Adrian R.
    Triple bottom line risk management : enhancing profit, environmental performance, and community benefits / Adrian R. Bowden, Malcolm R. Lane, Julia H. Martin.
        p.   cm.
    Includes bibliographical references and index.
    ISBN 0-471-41557-X (cloth : alk. paper)
    1. Risk management.   I. Lane, Malcolm R.   II. Martin, Julia H., 1962–
III. Title.
    HD61 .B66   2001
    658.15′5—dc21   2001017827

Printed in the United States of America.

10 9 8 7 6 5 4 3 2 1

To the rest of the "Gang of Five"

CONTENTS

FOREWORD

I would like to believe that this book is the result of a continuing process of innovative improvement that we have been fostering in our firm for many years.

In 1991, I was the chief executive officer of Woodward-Clyde, an environmental engineering consulting firm that is now part of the large, New York Stock Exchange–listed, URS Corporation. At that time I was working closely with Steve James, who had the global role to disseminate throughout our company innovative technology developed by Woodward-Clyde. During a visit to Australia, Steve was promoting a very comprehensive computer database called ERMIS (Environmental Risk Management Information System). ERMIS had been developed in Switzerland and the United States for a large French client in the automobile parts manufacturing sector. When Steve arrived in Australia, he was asked to contact Adrian Bowden in our Melbourne office, who would assess the potential of the system and possibly could become responsible for introducing it to the Asia-Pacific region.

Adrian accompanied Steve on one of his first presentations to a major client in Melbourne. Steve gave a polished and comprehensive demonstration of ERMIS that left the client representatives extremely impressed. The presentation showed that through ERMIS the client could readily access large volumes of environmental data (i.e., soil tests and groundwater analyses), link the data to compliance requirements, and flag the required management actions. ERMIS introduced the concept of environmental risk being the product of the probability of an environmental event occurring by the cost of remediation. ERMIS also used a relatively simple method to describe the uncertainty of remediation costs as probabilistic cost distribution rather than single deterministic numbers.

After the presentation, Steve asked Adrian what he thought of the prospect of providing ERMIS to the client. Adrian felt the model required too much data (at the time comprehensive environmental data were usually not available for most sites around the world), and even large corporations were not ready for ERMIS. Maybe in ten years. Adrian believed, however, that many of his clients had a clear need for a simpler tool that would use the same approach but that could be more appropriately applied to sites with incomplete environmental information.

The next day Steve and Adrian gave a modified presentation to a multinational mining company. Steve concluded the presentation by making the point that the ERMIS concept could be used in a much-simplified form to suit a wider range of conditions. The corporate risk manager for the mining company was in the audience and was facing the immediate challenge of restructuring the company-wide, third-party environmental insurance strategy in a cost-effective manner. The next day the mining company engaged Woodward-Clyde to develop a prioritized risk profile of third-party liability (both sudden and gradual) for all of its 36 sites worldwide. This assignment was successfully completed in a short time using available information and a relatively simple spreadsheet model. This project was the first time that environmental risk profiles had been applied to obtain third-party insurance.

Since that time Adrian and his colleagues have refined the method substantially, and its capability has been greatly expanded to the point where it has been shaped into a very useful approach to business risk management we refer to as RISQUE method. This method forms the core of a totally new, very successful business (Business Risk Strategies, a division of URS). The RISQUE method has now been applied by the staff at Business Risk Strategies to a wide range of applications. The method has been used to the immense benefit of a large number of diverse clients around the world.

In recognition of their contributions to the development of innovative practice, Woodward-Clyde/URS awarded both Steve James and Adrian Bowden the Yves Lacroix Prize in 1992 and in 1996, respectively.

The story of the RISQUE method and Business Risk Strategies is a good example of how an embryonic concept, when seeded in fertile ground and nurtured in the right environment, can develop into a viable business in its own right.

Jean-Yves Perez
Executive Vice President and Director
URS Corporation

ACKNOWLEDGMENTS

The authors are very appreciative of the unreserved support that URS Corporation (formerly Woodward-Clyde) has given for initiation and development of the new business that is the subject of this book. All of the projects described in the case histories were performed by Business Risk Strategies (a division of URS). We are fortunate that URS is committed to providing an environment that encourages new ideas and ways of integrating them into the triple bottom line.

The case studies are published with kind permission of the following URS client organizations: Ok Tedi Mining Limited; Water Corporation of Western Australia; LandCorp; Eglinton Estates; Woodsome Management; Meridian Energy Limited; Boral Recycling Pty Ltd.; Waihi Gold Company; and Metrowater. The client organizations contributed immensely to each of the projects and demonstrated a willingness to apply new technology and to venture into uncertain territory.

Steve James was responsible for seeding the business initiative by introducing the concept of quantifying difficult risk events and providing backup resources during the early stages of business development. Steve, together with Jim Schaarsmith, also contributed substantially to the discussion of corporate reporting and SAB 92. Dale Cooper provided very constructive criticism that has added considerable value to the RISQUE Method.

Many colleagues gave significant assistance with projects, marketing opportunities or business development support. These people are: Martin Howell, Tom Farrell, Jean-Yves Perez, Jim Miller, Simon Lee, Leanne Gough, Andrew Firth, Harry Grynberg, Warren Pump, Jeff Smith, Stephen Hancock, Merv Jones, John Gillett, Victoria Sedwick, Dan Predpall, and Alan Gale.

We acknowledge the time and experience given by the following individuals: Bob Goodson, Steve Raab, Brian Fox-Lane, Tasio Cokis, Frank Kroll, Frank Marra, Ross Yearsley, Bob Mackie, Willie Ng, Kathy Mason, Rob Fisher, Alison Brown, Colin Stevens, Manapouri Power Station staff, Ken Voigt, Marshall Lee, and the staff and advisers of OTML.

INTRODUCTION

Risk management increasingly appears as a key theme in conferences and literature targeted at a wide range of public and private sector businesses—no longer is it the primary domain of the insurance industry. Surprisingly, the growing attention given to "risk" does not appear to be inspired by the profit-enhancing opportunities that risk management practices offer; rather it is driven by apprehension associated with a negative perception of risk.

This negativity is reinforced by publicized cases of imprisonment of corporate directors for regulatory compliance breaches, losses incurred by insurance underwriters through coverage of environmental incidents, and an increasing incidence of shareholder and broader community protests against perceived complacent and arrogant corporate behavior. Unfortunately, this preoccupation with the adverse consequences of risk events impedes recognition of the usefulness of risk management processes to optimize business practices and demonstrate corporate responsiveness.[1]

Businesses that want to be sustainable in the twenty-first century would be better advised to adopt the philosophy that risk management is a process of continuous improvement "directed towards the effective management of *potential opportunities and adverse effects*"[2] (emphasis added). From an opportunistic viewpoint, successful management of business risk has vast potential to improve the so-called triple bottom line, the social, environmental, and financial accountability of a business.[3] For example, the Institute of Chartered Accountants[4] suggests that well-executed risk management practices can potentially deliver the following types of benefits to a company:

- A process for engagement of stakeholders and improving stakeholder relations
- Greater likelihood of achieving business objectives
- Increased likelihood of change initiatives being achieved
- More focus internally on developing and implementing best practice standards
- Lower cost of capital
- Better basis for strategic direction setting

- Achievement of competitive advantage
- Reduction in management time spent "fire-fighting"
- Fewer sudden and unwelcome surprises

Our professional observations support that advice, and in this book we describe an approach that can be used to assess and quantify business risks in a way that they can be addressed proactively in a company's business management strategy. The RISQUE method (*r*isk *i*dentification and *s*trategy using *q*uantitative *e*valuation) is a multifaceted approach that is designed to help business managers make informed, defensible risk management decisions as part of a triple bottom line management strategy.

We have developed the RISQUE method by listening to our clients' needs and trying to develop ways to apply our broad experience to a wide range of industrial sectors and business management challenges. Our collective 60 years of consulting experience in working with multidisciplinary teams has revealed that managers responsible for making business decisions frequently have difficulty in making the best use of the often complex, highly qualified, technical information provided by their internal and external advisory experts.

The RISQUE method originated from an idea that Steve James, in his capacity as a senior business strategist for Woodward-Clyde (now URS Corporation), introduced in 1992. Since then we have applied the method (and its forerunner) to many challenging new applications. These applications have included: water supply and wastewater asset management; quantification of the financial risk of acquisitions; prioritizing management of environmental issues and development of environmental risk management strategies; formulation of financial assurance strategies for landfills and mines; estimation of mine rehabilitation costs; financial benefit-cost analyses of mine tailings management options; economic analysis of landfill postclosure management strategies; and financial reporting of contingent liability.

AIM OF THIS BOOK

The aim of this book is to inform readers of current risk management approaches and to demonstrate that a rational, quantitative method (the RISQUE method) is a sound, defensible, transparent process that is very useful for development of risk management strategies.

The RISQUE method is a risk management process that has been specifically developed in response to the recognized need to translate complex, technical, triple bottom line information into financial terms. It incorporates a quantitative risk assessment process that translates the so-called intangible or nonquantifiable environmental and social risks, such as community outcry, business reputation damage, legal culpability, and environmental impacts, into financial measures that can be used to develop risk treatment strategies. The broad application of the RISQUE method is illustrated through a series of case studies.

By the end of this book, readers should:

- Appreciate the general concept of risk in relation to their business
- Understand the commonly used risk assessment techniques, together with their advantages and disadvantages
- Have a basic understanding of the methodology, assumptions, advantages, and disadvantages of the quantitative RISQUE method
- Have identified how the RISQUE method can be applied to specific areas within their business to reduce negative risk and increase opportunities
- Know what specialist risk assessment skills to seek to assist development of risk management strategies
- Feel equipped to implement a risk management process that will demonstrate commitment to triple bottom line management

WHO SHOULD READ THIS BOOK

This book is intended for those professionals working in the private and public business sectors who are:

- Making decisions based on complex factors, such as multiple sites or multi-faceted events
- Responsible for ensuring that appropriate risk management processes are in place to demonstrate due diligence
- In the process of acquiring or divesting capital assets
- Required to negotiate performance bonds and financial assurances with regulatory agencies
- Structuring corporate insurance strategies
- Selecting options that require financial analysis of benefit and cost
- Determining the value of a business and its contingent liabilities

Those who would find the book useful are:

- Business managers involved in strategic planning through to operations
- Policymakers
- Regulators
- Consultants
- Students of business management and applied technology

BOOK STRUCTURE

Part One outlines the need for risk management, describes the role of risk assessment in the risk management process, and discusses current risk assessment approaches.

Chapter 1 ("Risk Management Process") provides background information on the nature of risk and discusses the risk management process and where risk assessment, a fundamental component, fits into the process.

Chapter 2 ("Why Use Anything Other Than Quantitative Risk Assessment?") reviews the commonly used risk assessment practices (qualitative, semiquantitative, and quantitative) and discusses their relative advantages and disadvantages.

Part Two ("RISQUE Method") introduces the quantitative RISQUE method and discusses development of risk treatment strategies.

Chapters 3 through 8 describe in detail the quantitative, five-stage RISQUE method. These chapters describe (using examples) how the information derived using this method can be arranged, related to common business indicators (e.g., net operating income, benefit-cost ratios, return on assets), and used to develop strategies to manage and reduce business risk.

Chapter 9 ("Benefits of the RISQUE Method") reminds us of the advantages over other approaches and reiterates the benefits that application of the RISQUE method can provide to business managers.

Part Three describes eight case studies where the RISQUE method has been used, to demonstrate its applicability across a wide range of business activities and events. The case studies should provide many pointers to enable readers to generate ideas where the RISQUE method might be applicable to their own business. The introduction contains synopses for all case histories so that readers can quickly assess which ones they would like to study in detail.

The case studies presented in Chapters 10 through 17 provide examples of situations where the following questions have been addressed:

- *"Project Selection":* How can we select and justify the best option? (Ok Tedi, Papua New Guinea, mine waste management options)
- *"Acquisitions":* How much additional liability could we be acquiring? (Acquisition of large power generation assets, United States)
- *"Quantifying Intangibles":* How can we account for "nonquantifiable" events? (Total community benefit cost analysis of land development opportunities at Alkimos, Western Australia)
- *"Community Safety":* How can personal injury be used as a measure of risk and compared with accepted levels of societal risk? (Risk associated with a tourism venture in Fiordland, New Zealand)
- *"Financial Assurances":* What is a realistic financial assurance to place for operation of a sanitary landfill? (Establishment of a financial assurance strategy for a large municipal landfill, Australia)

- *"Indemnity in Perpetuity":* How much do we need to set aside for future liabilities? (Establishment of postclosure monetary bond for Waihi gold mine, New Zealand)
- *"Corporate Reporting and Insurance":* How can we comply with reporting requirements, and what is the best insurance structure considering our risk profile? (Mining and mineral processing plants, United States and Asia-Pacific region)
- *"Asset Management":* What asset management strategy gives us the best return? (Auckland, New Zealand, sewage pumping stations risk assessment)

At the end of the book, there is a glossary that defines the technical terms used in the book.

We hope that this book will provide readers with ideas that they can use to improve their business risk assessment processes and to formulate well-informed and defensible risk management decisions that satisfy corporate objectives to increase profit, improve environmental performance, and enhance community benefits: the triple bottom line.

Notes

1. Corporate responsiveness describes the way in which companies address their corporate responsibilities, that is, their legal, social, economic, and environmental obligations to the communities in which they operate.
2. Standards Association of Australia, *AS/NZS* 4360: *Risk Management*. Strathfield, NSW: Standards Association of Australia, April 12, 1999.
3. J. Elkington, *Cannibals With Forks. The Triple Bottom Line of 21st Century Business*. Oxford: Capstone Publishing Limited, 1999.
4. Cited by M. Vincent, "Creating the Pathway for Corporate Change. Executive Briefing," *Corporate Risk*, September 2000, p. 33.

Part One
RISK MANAGEMENT

1

RISK MANAGEMENT PROCESS

Business risk is a condition involving exposure to events that would have an adverse impact on a company's objectives. Business risk is therefore a combination of the likelihood of an event occurring and the magnitude of its consequences.

The term "business risk" covers the full range of risks faced by today's companies that have potential to affect the triple bottom line. A company's business risk portfolio may include events with potential for impacts on the organization's investments, income, staff and local community welfare, occupational health and safety, the natural environment, company reputation, technological capability, security, political environment, property, and legal liabilities.

The scope of business risks is broad—risks may arise from a range of sources, as demonstrated by the following five examples.[1] Depending on the activities in which a business is involved, the number of risks may be reduced or expanded.

1. Strategic risk is the risk of planning failure. Strategic risks may include:
   - Poor marketing strategy
   - Poor acquisition strategy
   - Unexpected changes in consumer behavior
   - Political and regulatory change
2. Financial risk is the risk of failure of financial control. Financial risks may arise from:
   - Treasury operations
   - Lack of counterparty and credit assessment
   - Fraud and its control
   - Systemic failure
   - Poor receivables and inventory management
3. Operational risk is the risk of human actions, either willful or by omission. Examples include:
   - System mistakes
   - Unsafe practices

- Employee routines
- Willful destruction

4. Commercial risk is the risk of business interruption. Commercial risks may arise from:
   - Loss of key personnel
   - Supplier failure
   - Legal issues and compliance
5. Technical risk is the risk of failure of physical assets. Examples include:
   - Equipment failure
   - Infrastructure breakdown
   - Fire and physical impact
   - Explosion and/or sabotage
   - Pollution
   - Natural events

Business risks arise from the occurrence of risk events—those events that might reasonably be considered to have the potential to occur over the lifetime of a business. For example, a large storage tank fire, in a well-operated fuel tank farm (with a 50-year design life), would not be expected to occur over a 30-year period, if safety measures have been implemented to decrease both the likelihood of a fire and the magnitude of the consequences. Nevertheless, there remains a very low likelihood that a large fire actually will occur within that time frame, and therefore this eventuality should be considered as a risk event worthy of assessment.

For the purposes of risk quantification, the magnitude of the risk is calculated as the mathematical product of the likelihood of the risk event occurring and the consequences. A risk event may pose a high risk because it is likely to occur frequently, although the consequences may not be substantial in financial terms. A risk event also may pose a high risk if it has a low likelihood of occurrence but the consequences will be substantial in financial terms. A risk event that poses an "extreme" risk to the business will represent both a high likelihood of occurrence and substantial financial consequences.

It is important to recognize from the outset that identification and characterization of risks is an inherently subjective process that may be highly influenced by the personal beliefs, training, and experience of the individuals who make judgments about the risks.

For example, the risks posed by the presence of a large water storage dam are likely to be perceived quite differently by a civil engineer as compared with a crop farmer living downstream of the dam. Similarly, the operational risks posed by a gold mine are likely to be perceived differently by the company's corporate financial controller compared with the company's on-site environmental manager.

Given the intrinsic subjectivity of human perspectives, it is unrealistic (and risky) to expect one or two experts or company managers to be able to develop a comprehensive and balanced profile of a company's business risks.

WHY MANAGE RISK?

Although many managers use risk management principles both formally and informally in their day-to-day work, prudent managers will adopt a structured approach to risk management to ensure that risks are identified and addressed in a consistent manner. In order to perform risk assessment and to develop a risk management strategy, business managers need to understand the concept of risk and the risk profile that businesses face.

Some business activities are inherently complex or challenging, and particular attention to risk management is warranted, irrespective of their scale. In large projects there may be substantial potential losses unless the project activities are managed carefully. Such projects often involve unbalanced cash flows, requiring large initial investments before any returns are gained. Other smaller projects or activities also may be inherently risky because they involve unusual or nonroutine activities. Such activities are new technology, work in unfamiliar locations, unusual legal or contractual arrangements, and/or special consideration of issues (political, economic, or financial aspects; sensitive environmental, social, or safety issues; or regulatory or licensing conditions).

The commercial and legal consequences of failure to adequately identify, understand, and manage risks can be substantial. Increasingly, due diligence clauses in legal statutes, corporate governance requirements, and corporate social responsibility principles require companies to identify and manage their risks. For example, the Australian Stock Exchange requirement for disclosure of corporate governance practices (in accordance with rule 4.10.3) includes a requirement to define the "Board's approach to identifying areas of significant business risk and putting arrangements in place to manage those risks."[2]

Adverse consequences of inadequate risk management practices can include[3]:

- Costs of sanctions (fines, imprisonment, personal liability of directors and managers)
- Civil claims (common-law damages)
- Legal costs in defending criminal and civil actions
- Statutory and common-law cleanup obligations
- Natural resources damages claims
- Direct lender liability
- Adverse publicity
- Loss of staff morale

- Increased insurance premiums
- Increased establishment costs (seed investment)
- Increased financing costs
- Future liability to provide indemnification agreements and warranties
- Revocation of regulatory licenses and permits

Clearly, these adverse consequences are not in the commercial interests of organizations that want to demonstrate that they are responsible and sustainable investments for shareholders. Identification and assessment of business risks therefore play an important role in both strategic and operational decision making.

All business managers usually attempt to identify strategic and operational risks for those aspects with which they are familiar. Most organizations have some level of risk management in place, although commonly the measures focus on their core areas of operation and are aimed at reducing negative impacts on the financial bottom line.

For example, every gold mining company is exposed to variation in gold price, a fundamental operational risk to that business. As a matter of course, the astute financial controller typically has access to reliable knowledge of the likely price variations and their timing, and takes action to reduce the risk. A commonly applied risk management action is to place hedging contracts. This action reduces the risk to an acceptable, or practical, level, although there is likely to be some degree of residual risk that the hedging contracts will be ineffective.

Unlike their comprehension of the familiar or obvious "core" risk (e.g., the gold price), business managers often have less understanding of the risk events associated with other operational aspects of their businesses, even though the events may present considerable financial exposure. For the gold miner, such events could include, for example, adverse community reaction to a change in mine operations that company management had anticipated to have a negligible social impact. Such risks may not be recognized or may be underestimated because they are "unfamiliar" to the company decision-makers.

This differentiation between "familiar" and "unfamiliar" is important because collectively these risks make up the entire business risk profile. To perform a comprehensive business risk assessment and develop a whole of risk management strategy, business managers need to understand the concept of risk and their organization's risk profile.

Residual risk is that which remains beyond the identified, managed risks. An organization's risk acceptance is determined by how much residual risk it is prepared to carry. While the assumption is that the level of residual risk is acceptable, experience suggests that this is often not the case. Most organizations do not have an understanding of the magnitude of their residual risk, and therefore the firms cannot objectively determine whether the level is acceptable.

The lack of understanding of residual risk has been accepted largely because organizations have not had the tools with which to quantify its magnitude. Utilization of an appropriate risk management process is an effective way to make the external knowledge base more accessible.

WHAT ARE THE APPLICATIONS OF RISK MANAGEMENT?

The risk management process consists of a continually reviewable cycle of risk criteria formulation, risk assessment, risk reduction, and review. It is a logical process that provides for systematic identification, analysis, and evaluation of risks in order to lead to development of an appropriate risk treatment strategy. The process enables risk treatment actions to be formulated based on the source of the risk and on the components of risk (likelihood and consequence). The application of this process can ensure that:

- All risks of relevance to the success of the business are identified
- Identified risks are understood, in terms of the range of potential consequences they represent and their likelihood of occurrence
- Assessment is undertaken of individual risks relative to the other risks to support priority setting and resource allocation
- Strategies for treating the risks take account of opportunities to address more than one risk
- The process itself and the risk treatment strategies are implemented cost effectively

This process can be applied to all stages in the life cycle of a business or project. Examples of the applicability of this process include:

- *Prefeasibility appraisal of a proposal:* Strategic decisions must be made, often on the basis of limited market and technical information, to reject the proposal, to postpone it, or to proceed with more detailed feasibility studies.
- *Marginal projects:* A decision may be required as to whether or not to undertake a project, when the return calculated on the basis of the best estimates of capital requirements and cash flows is close to the target rate of return.
- *Volatility:* When a business activity involves unusual risks or uncertainties or potentially volatile market prices, there may be a wide and unpredictable range of possible rates of return. Risk assessment can provide a financial measure of this uncertainty.
- *Options analysis:* Strategic decisions may be necessary when choosing between alternative business opportunities for a project or concept that has already been justified at an earlier prefeasibility or feasibility stage.
- *Tactical decisions:* Risk assessment may be appropriate for tactical decisions when developing detailed plans or specifications for an approved concept.

- *Operational safety improvements and technical hazard reduction:* Specialized risk assessment is critical when implementing potentially hazardous projects and for the systematic review of risk treatment options.
- *Exit strategies:* When planning for decommissioning of an operation nearing the end of its life, risk assessment may be used to determine the appropriate remediation, closure, or divestment options.

WHAT IS THE RISK MANAGEMENT PROCESS?

The generally accepted approach to risk management comprises a series of steps, as depicted in Figure 1.1 and listed below:

Step 1. Define the context and risk management criteria

Step 2. Identify the risks

Step 3. Assess the significance of those risks

Step 4. Identify, select, and implement risk treatment options

Step 5. Perform monitoring, review, and corrective actions

Each step offers a convenient milestone for reporting, review, and action. Each subsequent step is dependent, and builds, on the work completed in the previous step, providing an evolving understanding of the issues and development of progressively more robust risk management actions.

The following subsections describe each of those steps and their interrelationships.

Step 1: Define Context and Risk Management Criteria

The objectives of this step are to:

- Establish the organizational context within which risk assessment is to take place
- Specify the main objectives and outcomes required
- Identify a set of criteria against which the identified risks can be evaluated
- Define a set of key elements for structuring the risk identification and assessment process

Context. The purpose of defining the business context is to ensure that there is a clear understanding of the responsibilities and accountabilities at each level in the organization and to identify where ambiguities or weak links may exist that may compromise the organization's ability to manage its risks. The context is used to develop an understanding of the organization's commitment to, and capability of,

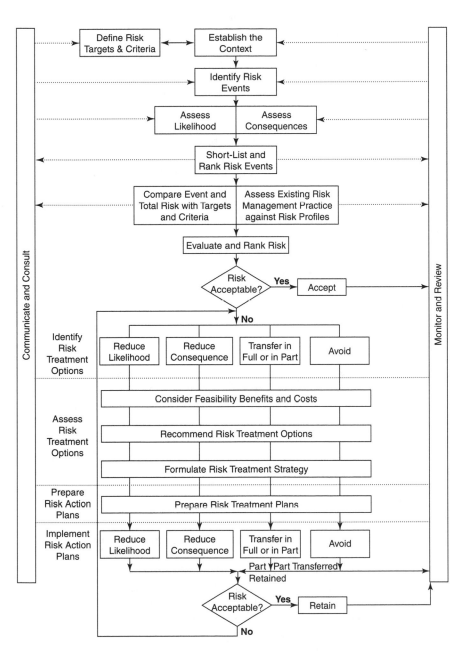

Figure 1.1 Overview of the risk management process.

deciding if a risk is acceptable or not and forming the basis of options for risk treatment.

Definition of the context within which the business operates, or a project will be conducted, should consider, as a minimum:

- The company's operations
- The company's policies, goals, and objectives
- The scope and measurable performance objectives of the project or activity
- A description of the stakeholders to be taken into account
- The company's level of control over its business risks, including political and legal aspects of the company's operations, stakeholder requirements, legal obligations (e.g., due diligence, corporate governance), and financial aspects (e.g., financial opportunities and penalties)

This information may be gained from:

- Examination of strategic and operational documents, such as annual reports, divisional and unit objectives, performance targets, and productivity achievement
- Review of organizational charts and determination of individual management responsibility
- Interviews with individuals and groups
- Researching benchmarks from similar operations

Stakeholders may introduce business risks because they have perceptions about the acceptability of the business activities that differ from those of the company managers. For example, some stakeholders may disagree with the approach to financial investment taken by the managers. As a consequence, the company may encounter unexpected opposition or resistance to its plans.

Analysis of the stakeholder interests should be framed by the following three questions:

1. Who are the stakeholders?
2. What are their issues of concern?
3. What degree of influence do they have over the project or business?

Stakeholders may be defined as those individuals, groups, or organizations that may affect, be affected by, or perceive themselves to be affected by a decision or activity of the company or are affected by aspects of a company's project or activity.[4] In this regard, the company's stakeholders may include:

- The company, its shareholders, and staff
- Customers for the products or services provided by the business
- Users, including management, staff, and operators of the delivered project

- Principal suppliers, contractors, and subcontractors
- Regulatory licensing and approval authorities
- People who may be affected by the company's activities, such as those living near the company's facilities
- The government and community leaders who may be affected by project activities or associated employment or to other opportunities
- Special interest groups, such as indigenous landowners and heritage and environmental groups

The stakeholders in the company's activities potentially represent a broad cross-section of the community. The demands of the stakeholder environment may therefore be diverse and in conflict with each other. Stakeholder expectations should be viewed as a dynamic influence, which may shift in response to the actions of the organization and societal perceptions of the company, its industry sector, and ethical, environmental, and other such issues.

Objectives and Outcomes. Performance objectives will be dependent on the business objectives and the phase of the project cycle or business activity. For example:

- In the planning stages of a project or activity, the requirements are often related to corporate policy, including growth and rate of return targets.
- Technology criteria and stakeholder acceptance of the activity or project may be important in the design stage.
- In the bidding stage, contractual issues and value for money become important considerations.
- In the delivery, operation, maintenance, and marketing stages, criteria are likely to be more specific, such as: cost control—ensuring the activity is completed within the available budget; schedule control—ensuring the activity is completed within the specified time frame; and performance quality control—ensuring the delivered outcome is suitable for its intended purpose.

Risk Criteria. Risk assessment involves comparing the predicted levels of risk against defined risk management performance targets. For decision-making purposes it is desirable to have a set of criteria against which risks can be evaluated to determine whether a risk is acceptable or requires treatment to reduce it. Where practicable to do so, these criteria should be developed when establishing the risk management context and reviewed once the risk assessment outputs are available.

For example, an accepted industry approach to the control of hazards to people, plant, production, and the environment is the elimination or minimization of each risk to as low as reasonably practicable (ALARP). In terms of public safety, for example, the ALARP criterion may be defined in terms of a specified probability of loss of life.

Scoping the Risk Assessment. An important consideration in conducting a program of risk assessment and strategy development is to ensure that the results of the process are not compromised by a lack of time, finance, or negotiating expediency. In many cases, issues are not addressed sufficiently early, with the result that companies are taking risks that they would not if they had a better knowledge and appreciation of the possible consequences.

For example, the integration of a risk assessment approach with the planning process of an organization facilitates the efficient gathering and analysis of information. It also allows the critical success factors to be set pragmatically and adjusted as business imperatives change. The quality and relevance of each success factor and the specific focus of each performance measure is substantially enhanced when the risks in achieving each are identified, analyzed, and treated concurrently with their development.

Scoping of the risk identification and assessment process is therefore an important exercise to ensure that the subsequent analysis is neither too broad nor too narrow.

Step 2: Identify the Risks

The risk identification process involves three key elements:

1. Identification of risk events
2. Estimation of likelihood of occurrence
3. Description of the consequences

This step involves formulation of a comprehensive list of risk events that might affect each element of a business or activity. Risk is analyzed by considering estimates of likelihood and consequences in the context of the existing or proposed control measures (in the case of a new project or activity). Existing management and technical systems and procedures for controlling risk should be identified first. The effectiveness of these controls will influence the estimates of likelihoods and consequences in the subsequent analysis.

Risk identification should draw on various sources of information, including past experience, modeling, and expert judgment. Methods and information sources that may be used to generate a register of risk events include:

- Brainstorming
- Similar projects or activities
- Checklists
- Specialist studies, such as hazard and operability (HAZOP) studies, and construction safety studies
- Historical records for similar or related projects

- Previous experience, either specific to the type of activity under assessment or more general experience with large or complex activities, similar technologies, similar geographic locations, or similar contractors and suppliers
- Industry best practice and experience, including relevant benchmarks and standards
- Relevant published literature and research reports, including appropriate actuarial information such as failure modes or equipment reliability
- Product brochures, technical manuals, and audit reports
- Test marketing and market research
- Experiments and prototypes for technical risks or areas in which more empirical information may be useful
- Economic or other models to provide the basis for specific and general risk assessments, including, for example, cash flow and sensitivity models
- Expert commercial and technical judgment, from the project team and appropriate internal and external advisers

For each listed risk, the following information should be collected and documented:

- A brief description of the risk event
- The possible causes and consequences for each feasible event
- The main phases of the project or business activity in which the risk is most likely to occur
- The critical success factors likely to be affected if the risk occurs
- An analysis of the likelihood of occurrence of the risk and its impacts if it does occur
- The position or department responsible for managing the risk

The output of this step is a register of risks and their key characteristics.

Step 3: Assess Significance of Risks

The next stage in the risk management process is the analysis and evaluation of the registered risks. The term "risk assessment" collectively refers to the steps of risk analysis and risk evaluation. The aim of risk assessment is to partition risks into prioritized groups that assist in the development of a risk management strategy.

As defined by Australian and New Zealand Risk Management Standard 4360: 1999, risk analysis is a systematic process to determine how often events may occur and the magnitude of the likely consequences.[5] The risk analysis process generates a set of risk factors, levels, or quotients that are used to set risk treatment priorities.

Risk evaluation is the process used to determine risk management priorities by comparing the level of risk against predetermined standards, target risk levels, or other criteria established as part of the strategic and organizational context analysis.

Step 4: Identify, Select, and Implement Risk Treatment Options

Following prioritization of risks, options for treatment and mitigation of the risks are examined and benefit-cost analysis or other analyses can be performed to select the preferred risk treatment options or strategies. In this step the most beneficial risk treatment option is chosen, the option that will reduce the risk to an acceptable level and/or treat or transfer the risk (also referred to as laying off risk). Treatments are commonly chosen on the basis of relevance, effectiveness, and cost.

The following categories of risk treatment options may be applied to develop a risk treatment strategy:

- *Risk transfer or sharing:* For example, insurance, where for an annual premium a third party accepts the risk and thereby reduces the operation's exposure to the full scenario consequence; or contractual arrangements where the risk is transferred or shared with another party or parties
- *Risk reduction:* The implementation of systems or physical works that reduce the likelihood of occurrence, the consequence, or both, such as rapid response systems, installation of detection systems, and engineering works
- *Risk acceptance:* Where the business is prepared to pay for the consequence of the risk event if it occurs

Typically, the strategy formulation exercise reveals that addressing a limited number of the riskiest issues first lays off most of the risk and that the remainder can be addressed by activities such as political lobbying and risk communication.

Once selected, risk treatment strategies are implemented through risk action plans that define the detail (who, when, and how).

Step 5: Performance Monitoring, Review, and Corrective Actions

The final steps that complete the process cycle are establishment of mechanisms to measure the level of implementation effectiveness of the risk treatment controls. Typical monitoring mechanisms include:

- Internal and external audits
- Regular investigations
- Regular reporting and review
- Organizational management reviews

This stage may be used as a check to ensure that the intended risk reduction measures actually have been implemented—for example, to check that a new refinery has been built to the intended design and to verify that actions from previous risk studies have been incorporated into the plant design and construction. The process also monitors for the emergence of new risks as part of the process of continual improvement to minimize risk exposure.

It is also important to acknowledge the presence and character of residual risk in this process. Residual risk is the risk that is still present after the risk treatments have been applied. If the residual risk is not acceptable to the company, it needs to be managed and reported and additional risk treatment measures must be implemented, such as formulation of contingency plans.

Risk treatment through the continuing implementation of the steps of the risk management process is a living process, performed to progressively lower the level of company exposure in balance with the accrued benefits.

BENEFITS OF THE PROCESS

Risk management is the systematic application of management policies, processes, and procedures to the tasks of identifying, analyzing, assessing, treating, and monitoring risk. The aim of the risk management process is to reduce exposure to the consequences of risk events to levels that are considered acceptable by the business.

In these days of increasing fiduciary responsibility, business managers need to adopt a rational, defensible method to determine the manner in which risk management dollars are spent. From a business management viewpoint, there is a need to understand the consequences of risk events in financial terms, so that provision can be made for their prevention or occurrence—risk management is as much about risk acceptance as it is about risk minimization.

Through a process of risk assessment, business managers are able to separate acceptable and unacceptable risk events and to derive information that assists in the development of a risk management strategy. The following chapters demonstrate how application of properly conceived quantitative risk assessment techniques can enable the so-called nonquantifiable or intangible risks to be assessed to derive financial decision-making information suitable for formulation of integrated triple bottom line management strategies.

Notes

1. List obtained from M. Vincent, "Creating the Pathway for Corporate Change, Executive Briefing," *Corporate Risk,* September 2000, p. 33.
2. Australian Stock Exchange Listing Rules, Rule 4.10.3, Item 7, Appendix 33, List of Corporate Governance Matters.
3. List obtained from J. H. Martin, "Petroleum Exploration and Production—What Are the Environmental Obligations of Joint Venture Participants?" *APPEA Journal, 37, part 1* (1997): 738–745.

4. A. B. Carroll, *Business & Society. Ethics and Stakeholder Management*, 3rd ed., Cincinnati: South-Western College Publishing, 1996.
5. Australian and New Zealand Risk Management Standard 4360: 1999, herein referred to as AS/NZS 4360, is an industry standard that has been developed to provide guidance to organizations to identify, assess, and manage their organizational risks in a transparent and consistent manner.

2

WHY USE ANYTHING OTHER THAN QUANTITATIVE RISK ASSESSMENT?

The aim of the risk management process is to reduce the exposure to the consequences of risk events to levels that are considered acceptable for the business. Risk management as a process needs to consider risk first and then make decisions based on the assessed risk. This process allows risk treatment actions to be selected on the basis of the nature of the risk and its components, namely likelihood and consequence.

Risk assessment is an important step in this process as it provides an understanding of the risks and the basis for defining acceptable and unacceptable risk events. Corporate governance reporting requirements commonly require business managers to demonstrate management of their organization's risk exposure at acceptable or practical levels. However, often managers do not appreciate how risk assessment methodologies can be used to analyze their organization's risk profile and select cost-effective options for risk treatment.

In particular, the use of quantitative techniques to assess business risks has been limited, despite the recognized need to report liabilities in financial terms. Given the widespread availability of relatively affordable, high-powered portable computers and user-friendly spreadsheet software, it is surprising that many managers seem reluctant to adopt a quantitative approach to assessing their business risk profile.

This reluctance may be attributed partly to the commonly expressed belief that the complexity and costs of risk assessment techniques increase as they become more quantitative.[1] This chapter presents an overview of three general types of risk assessment:

1. Qualitative
2. Semiquantitative
3. Quantitative

The overview covers their relative strengths and weaknesses in relation to assessment of business risks. It is argued here that by using modern methods, properly conceived quantitative risk assessments can not only be carried out very simply and economically, but have substantial advantages over qualitative approaches, which tend to be very restrictive in application.

QUALITATIVE RISK ASSESSMENT

Qualitative risk assessment is most frequently used to obtain a general or screening level indication of business risks. The qualitative risk assessment technique uses descriptive terms to define the likelihoods and consequences of risk events. These are usually presented as a risk matrix. The qualitative terms are tailored to meet the needs of the specific application under evaluation. The qualitative risk matrix generates results that differentiate risk events on a relatively crude basis, such as high, medium, and low, for example.

Table 2.1 provides an example of qualitative descriptions of likelihood.

Table 2.2 shows an example of a set of qualitative terms for describing consequences.

The descriptions in Tables 2.1 and 2.2 clearly show that considerable subjectivity in interpretation can occur and that this could vary substantially from one risk analyst to another.

Table 2.3 shows a typical risk matrix that could be produced by combining the qualitative likelihood and consequence tables of Tables 2.1 and 2.2. A risk class for a given risk event is selected by reading across and down the matrix using the assigned likelihood and consequence descriptors.

The qualitative risk assessment method offers the following advantages:

- It is quick and relatively easy to use. Provided that the assessment is well structured, the risk events can be considered in turn and the broad consequences and likelihoods can be identified.
- Users can gain a general understanding of comparative risk between risk events. The matrix can be used to separate the risk events into risk classes.

Table 2.1 Qualitative Descriptions of Likelihood

Level	Descriptor	Description
A	Almost certain	Is expected to occur in most circumstances
B	Likely	Will probably occur in most circumstances
C	Possible	Might occur at some time
D	Unlikely	Could occur at some time
E	Rare	May occur only in exceptional circumstances

Note: Derived from AS/NZS 4360

Table 2.2   Qualitative Descriptions of Consequence

Level	Descriptor	Description
1	Insignificant	No injuries, low financial loss
2	Minor	First aid treatment, on-site release immediately contained, medium financial loss
3	Moderate	Medical treatment required, on-site release contained with outside assistance, high financial loss
4	Major	Extensive injuries, off-site release with no detrimental effects, major financial loss
5	Catastrophic	Death, toxic release off-site with detrimental effect, huge financial loss

Note: Derived from AS/NZS 4360

The method also has a number of disadvantages:

- It is imprecise. Risk events that plot within the same risk class can, in fact, represent substantially different levels of risk.
- It is difficult to compare events on the same basis. Risk events cannot be compared on a common basis, such as dollar value or serious injury/death.
- Comparison between risk classes can lead to inconsistencies. Selection of the derived risk classes is qualitative and is done by visual interpretation of the risk matrix. No process ensures that the A1 (high) risk class on Table 2.3 represents approximately the same risk as, for example, the E5 risk class, which has also been nominated as a high-risk event.
- There is rarely clear justification of any process used to weight the risk based on severity of consequences. Table 2.3 is clearly biased toward high consequences, as nine of the risk classes are considered low to moderate and 16 of the classes are high to extreme. The bias may be justified, but the rationale used to assign risk classes is usually not transparent.

Table 2.3   Qualitative Risk Analysis Matrix

Likelihood	Consequences				
	1 (Insignificant)	2 (Minor)	3 (Moderate)	4 (Major)	5 (Catastrophic)
A (almost certain)	High	High	Extreme	Extreme	Extreme
B (likely)	Moderate	High	High	Extreme	Extreme
C (possible)	Low	Moderate	High	Extreme	Extreme
D (unlikely)	Low	Low	Moderate	High	Extreme
E (rare)	Low	Low	Moderate	High	High

Note: Derived from AS/NZS 4360

- There is poor differentiation between risk events. Risk profiles generated from the analysis consider a limited number of risk classes. For example, only four risk classes are derived using the matrix shown in Table 2.3. This may be acceptable in cases where only a limited number of events is being considered, but in most applications the assessment evaluates a substantial number of risk events. Development of a prioritized list of actions is therefore difficult if 20 or 30 events all lie within the same risk class.

- The method uses emotive descriptive terms. Traditionally, "risk" has been perceived to have a negative implication, and therefore risk assessment is associated with analyzing what can go wrong and the adverse consequences of such events. The use of emotive terminology, such as "catastrophic," to describe a class of risk reinforces this perception and makes it difficult for risk communicators to present risk assessment findings to stakeholders openly, without causing unnecessary alarm and anxiety.

- The method provides a very simplistic definition of risk events through the combination of several consequences that may arise from a single event. For example, a single risk event, such as an explosion at an industrial facility, could potentially cause extensive injuries (major consequence), release of a contaminant that can be immediately contained on-site (minor consequence), and cause high financial loss due to public reaction (moderate consequence). Considering the range of potential consequences, it is difficult to assign a truly representative combined consequence to an event that could be considered major or perhaps even catastrophic.

- There is very limited application to quantitative financial analysis of risk treatment options. Output from qualitative risk assessments usually cannot be incorporated into other quantitative tools, such as benefit-cost analysis, that are used to derive financially defensible risk management strategies.

To some extent, qualitative risk assessment achieves one of the objectives of risk assessment—to separate acceptable and unacceptable risk events—but the method is limited in its suitability to achieve the other objective—to provide information that assists selection of appropriate risk treatment actions.

SEMIQUANTITATIVE RISK ASSESSMENT

Semiquantitative risk assessment is used most commonly to derive a more detailed prioritized ranking of risks than can be derived using qualitative risk assessment. This type of risk assessment takes the qualitative approach a step further by attributing values or multipliers to the likelihood and consequence groupings. Semiquantitative risk assessment methods may involve multiplication of frequency estimates of likelihood with a qualitative scale representation of consequence.

The likelihood column of Table 2.4 shows an example of application of a set of annual frequency-of-occurrence values to the qualitative likelihood classes shown in Table 2.1. The values that are assigned to define the frequency classes can be

Table 2.4 Semiquantitative Risk Matrix

Likelihood	Consequences				
Annual Frequency	1 (Insignificant)	2 (Minor)	3 (Moderate)	4 (Major)	5 (Catastrophic)
0.5 (almost certain)	0.5	1	1.5	2	2.5
0.1 (likely)	0.1	0.2	0.3	0.4	0.5
0.01 (possible)	0.01	0.02	0.03	0.04	0.05
0.001 (unlikely)	0.001	0.002	0.003	0.004	0.005
0.0001 (rare)	0.0001	0.0002	0.0003	0.0004	0.0005

subjective and variable, according to specific circumstances and the time frame that is relevant to the risk events under assessment.

The values used to describe the consequences usually reflect the relative magnitude of the consequences and, as such, are not absolute measures. The semiquantitative risk matrix of Table 2.4 shows the relative risk values that would be derived by replacing the qualitative descriptions of consequence with numbers to provide some relativity.

The semiquantitative approach can be taken a step further by applying multipliers to the scales of consequences to create greater differentiation between the risk classes. For example, on a relative scale, the risk analyst may consider that the consequences of a major injury (as described in Table 2.2) are twice as great as those derived from moderate injury. In this case a multiplier is applied so that the estimated risk associated with a major injury reflects the degree of difference between the two consequences.

The consequence columns of Table 2.5 show an example of application of a relative set of multipliers to the qualitative injury consequences shown in Table 2.4. The semiquantitative risk matrix of Table 2.5 shows the relative risk values that would be derived by replacing the qualitative descriptions with the relative scale multipliers.

Table 2.5 Semiquantitative Risk Matrix with Weighting Multipliers

Likelihood	Consequences				
Annual Frequency	Multiplier 1 (Insignificant)	Multiplier 2 (Minor)	Multiplier 5 (Moderate)	Multiplier 10 (Major)	Multiplier 100 (Catastrophic)
0.5 (almost certain)	0.5	1	2.5	5	50
0.1 (likely)	0.1	0.2	0.5	1	10
0.01 (possible)	0.01	0.02	0.05	0.1	1
0.001 (unlikely)	0.001	0.002	0.005	0.01	0.1
0.0001 (rare)	0.0001	0.0002	0.0005	0.001	0.01

The semiquantitative risk assessment method offers the following advantages:

- It is quick to apply. No additional time is required to perform a semiquantitative, as compared with a qualitative, assessment, provided that the assessment is well structured.
- It can provide a reasonable understanding of comparative risk, although the quantified aspects of the relationships are relative rather than absolute.
- There is reasonable differentiation between risk events. Risk profiles generated from the analysis consider an expanded number of risk classes. For example, 17 risk classes are derived using the matrices shown in Tables 2.4 and 2.5. This may be acceptable in some applications where the assessment evaluates a relatively small number of risk events.
- There is less use of emotive, descriptive terms for risk classes.

The method also has some shortcomings:

- It is imprecise. Events that lie within the same risk class can represent different levels of risk.
- It is difficult to compare events on the same basis, although in some cases it is possible.
- It is not possible to ensure that two events that are assigned the same risk value represent similar risk.
- It provides a very simplistic definition of risk events, by combining several consequences that may arise from a single event.
- The method has limited application to quantitative financial analysis of risk treatment options. Semiquantitative risk assessment offers advantages over qualitative assessment by being better able to separate acceptable and unacceptable risk events. However, like qualitative analysis, the output from semiquantitative risk assessments usually cannot be incorporated into other quantitative tools, such as benefit-cost analysis and financial modeling, that are used to derive financially defensible risk management strategies.

QUANTITATIVE RISK ASSESSMENT

Quantitative risk assessment is used across the full range of risk applications, from deriving preliminary, first-pass separation of risk events, to much more comprehensive assessments. The comprehensive assessments can derive detailed risk profiles for priority ranking, estimates of the potential costs that may be incurred due to risk events, input to structural finance models, and as a basis for benefit-cost analysis.

Quantitative risk assessment takes the basic risk assessment approach (of deriving an expression of risk from the product of likelihood and consequences) to its full extent by attributing absolute values to likelihood and consequences.

Estimates of likelihood are made in terms of event frequency (e.g., annual frequency or frequency over the period of a specified project) and/or probability of occurrence.

Estimates of consequence can be made using any consistent measure, selected according to the nature of the application. For example, engineering risk assessments often measure risk in terms of frequency and number of potential lives lost, while financial controllers may measure risk in terms of frequency and cost (expressed as dollars or some other currency).

It is important to note that the numerical value of risk derived from quantitative risk assessment is the product of an occurrence probability and some numerical measure of consequence. So while, for example, the risk value derived from the financial controller's risk assessment is expressed as dollars, this measure is not an absolute dollar value, as we would commonly understand the term to mean. To remind readers that we are in fact referring to a mathematical derivation when we use the term "risk," we prefer to call it the "risk quotient."

In the context of quantitative risk assessment involving consequences expressed in financial terms, the risk quotient is equivalent to the commonly used term "expected cost" or "expected value."[2]

Where the risk quotient is expressed in dollars per annum, for example, the "expected cost" is more appropriately described as the annual sum that would be required to be paid in perpetuity to account for the frequency of occurrence of the risk event over an infinite period of time. Since all business activities take place within a very limited time period, in a relative sense, it would be unrealistic for a business manager to consider that the financial exposure to risk was equivalent to the "expected cost" of an event. The business manager would experience a very unpleasant surprise in the event of that risk event occurring, particularly if its likelihood of occurrence was very low.

The concept of an insurance premium to cover the consequential cost of a risk event is effectively equivalent to "expected cost." Insurance underwriters reduce the exposure to the risk of a low-frequency risk event by spreading the cover and obtaining annual premiums over a large number of insureds. In the hypothetical case of an insurer operating on a nonprofit basis, revenues from a large number of premiums for a given insurance line should, over time, be the same as disbursements paid for successful claims. The action of spreading risk over a large number of customers is equivalent to spreading exposure to risk over a long period of time.

Household insurance illustrates how the concept of risk (or risk quotient) is related to likelihood and consequence. For example, an insurance premium of $440 to cover the replacement cost of $25,000 for a private car represents the risk to the underwriter and is equivalent to the risk quotient. These numbers reflect the situation that, on average, the underwriter expects that each person insured will require replacement of the $25,000 vehicle every 50 years. Alternatively, each year one in 50 people insured will require replacement of their car.

Car insurance is considered around twice as risky as private house (building only) insurance where an annual home insurance premium of $200 represents less than one half of the risk of a car. The $200 premium provides replacement cost cover of $150,000. Here, the underwriter expects that on average, each person insured will require replacement of their home every 950 years, or each year one in 950 people insured will require replacement of their home.

The process of quantification of the risk quotient is fundamental to the RISQUE method (which is described in detail in Part Two). The risk quotient is derived in the RISQUE method to differentiate, on a comparative basis, between risk events using a consistent measure of risk and to identify those events that pose the most risk.

Figure 2.1 shows an example risk profile generated by the RISQUE method. In this example, the events in the figure are ranked in order of decreasing risk, which assists with prioritization of events as part of the risk management process. The relevant risk quotient value on the vertical axis is calculated from the product of the likelihood of occurrence and the cost if the event occurred. This figure shows that the risk quotients of all events are directly comparable (e.g., the first event presents approximately twice as much risk than the third event).

Uncertainty associated with quantifying consequences can be readily incorporated into the calculations using Monte Carlo simulation (such as Crystal Ball™ or @Risk™) to input costs as probability distributions rather than as a single value.

The profile of Figure 2.2 shows the uncertainty associated with the cost occurrence of each risk event (as indicated by the difference between the costs at the selected confidence levels that were obtained from a Monte Carlo simulation). This profile can be used to decide whether immediate action would be most appropriate or whether more study of an event may be required prior to taking action.

For example, in Figure 2.2 the estimated optimistic (50 percent confidence level) occurrence cost of the riskiest event (acid rock drainage) is around $2,000,000, but the conservatively high, or pessimistic, estimate (95 percent confidence limit) is substantially greater at around $6,000,000. The large difference in the estimated costs at the selected confidence levels indicates a great deal of uncertainty in the estimate. The degree of uncertainty suggests that further study would be advisable prior to carrying out any potential risk management action.

For the second most risky event (excessive noise), the difference between the optimistic and pessimistic cost estimates is relatively small (around $250,000). In this case the business manager might decide that the estimated cost range of the noise event is within reasonable limits and that no further study is required.

The profile of Figure 2.3 helps the business manager developing a risk management strategy to demonstrate and evaluate value for money—that is, the risk costs that can be laid off by up-front expenditure on activities or infrastructure designed to prevent occurrence of the events.

Figure 2.3 shows that a conservative estimate of the cost to prevent the two riskiest events from occurring is considerably less than a conservative estimate of the costs if the events were to occur. On the basis of this information, the business manager may decide simply to perform the prevention works. Conversely, the prevention cost of the seventh riskiest event (respirable dust) far exceeds the estimated cost of the event occurring. In this case the most appropriate action may be

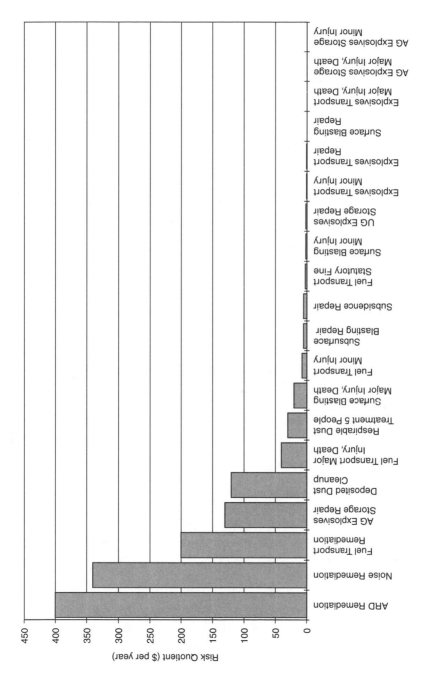

Figure 2.1 Example risk profile showing risk events ranked in order of decreasing risk quotient.

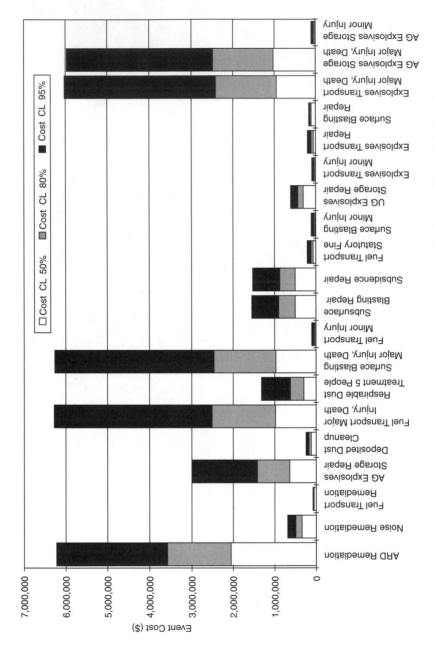

Figure 2.2 Example exposure profile of risk-ranked events showing the cost at three levels of confidence if the event occurs.

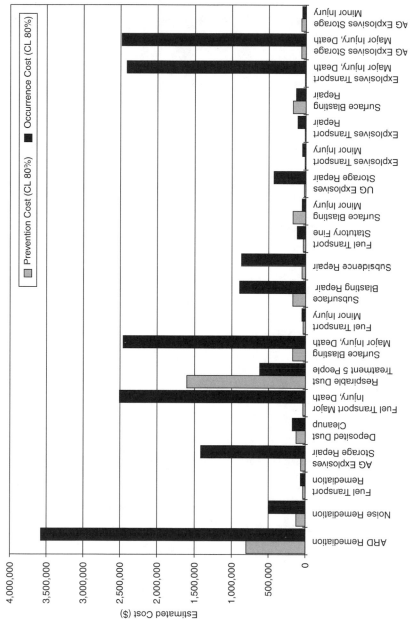

Figure 2.3 Example exposure profile showing a comparison of the cost to prevent each event from occurring with the cost if the event occurs.

to transfer the risk, through insurance, rather than carry out capital works to prevent the event from occurring.

Figure 2.4 shows how the results of quantitative risk assessment also can be used to perform benefit-cost analysis. For example, when considering whether to proceed with a gold mine extension, the expected ultimate cost of the project needs to be compared with the projected returns or revenues to determine whether the mine extension is viable.

It is difficult to assess the ultimate extension cost because it consists of two types of cost, base cost and risk cost. The "base cost" is the cost of infrastructure, operation, and other committed costs over the life of the project and is readily determined using cost estimation tools. The "risk cost" is the cost of the consequences of those risk events that occur over the project life. The risk cost component can be estimated using quantitative risk assessment to determine expected occurrence costs.

Figure 2.4 shows an example of the information provided for a typical benefit-cost analysis for a mine. The total cost on the horizontal axis on Figure 2.4 is comprised of the base cost of $600 million (shown by the heavy vertical line) and three points that show the effect of adding estimates of risk cost at three increasingly conservative levels of confidence (optimistic, planning, and pessimistic).

Figure 2.4 shows that the estimated total project cost (using the pessimistic estimate of risk cost) of $1.2 billion is high, at double the project base cost, and not substantially less than the expected project benefit of around $1.6 billion. The pessimistic benefit-cost ratio of approximately 1.3 may tend to discourage the more conservative mine planner. However, the figure also shows that a conservative yet

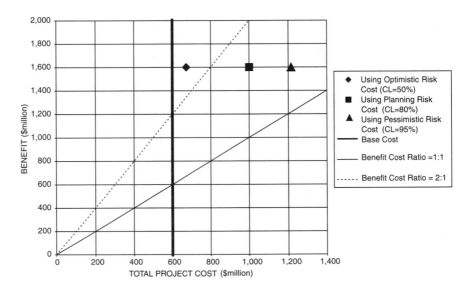

Figure 2.4 Proposed mine extension benefit-cost relationships showing the correlation between base cost, risk cost, and benefit gained.

reasonable mine extension cost estimate (using the planning risk cost) is around $1 billion, which would yield a more attractive benefit-cost ratio of 1.5.

This example demonstrates how information provided in this manner can usefully be applied to decision making, regardless of the conservatism of the decision-maker.

The advantages of using a quantitative risk assessment approach may be summarized as follows:

- Can be performed quickly if required for a preliminary indication of relative risk.
- Can provide a clear understanding of comparative risk.
- Process directly accounts for severity of consequences and the rationale used is transparent.
- Provides good differentiation between events. Risk profiles generated from quantitative analysis differentiate on the basis of real numbers.
- No use of emotive terms to describe classes of risk.
- Precise definition of risk events. Events are presented as true values of risk.
- Easy to compare events on the same basis.
- Events that display the same risk quotient present the same risk.
- Can include complex events through event tree analysis, by combining several consequences that may arise from a single event.
- Extensive application to strategy development. Output from quantitative risk assessments can be used to develop comprehensive risk management strategies.
- Can include usually "unquantifiable" events, provided a systematic approach is used. For example, the consequences of decreased public amenity in relation to access to a beach area can be quantified as the cost of transport to an alternative location and the cost of uplifted land value forgone.

Quantitative risk assessment demonstrably achieves both of the objectives of risk assessment: It separates acceptable and unacceptable risk events and provides information that assists in the development of a risk management strategy. In this regard, of the three general types of risk assessment (qualitative, semiquantitative, and quantitative), the quantitative technique offers substantial advantages over the other two approaches.

QUANTIFYING "NONQUANTIFIABLE" EVENTS

Development and application of appropriate quantitative risk assessment tools has become more imperative with the increasing corporate recognition of the role of triple bottom line reporting as a measure of business sustainability. Triple bottom line representation of business risks in corporate reports, by definition, requires the quantification of the organization's financial, environmental, and social risks, so that the effectiveness of risk treatment actions can be measured and reported in a transparent manner.

In order to communicate financial, social, and environmental risks in corporate reports—for example, to satisfy stock exchange reporting requirements—the risks need to be expressed in financial terms. However, practitioners often confront a stumbling block when attempting to transform the various technical expressions of multifaceted risks into a common language and a common denominator as a basis from which they can be collectively analyzed and evaluated.

Financial assessments of business risks can essentially be divided into those that have a market value (e.g., provision of services, products, etc.) and those that do not. Methods for estimating financial losses with market values are well established, and the process is relatively straightforward in regard to events such as property damage, loss of revenue, and some aspects of environmental remediation and consequential loss. However, financial business liability, associated with social and political events, is often perceived to be difficult to quantify. Social and environmental risks, such as degradation or loss of amenity, and community outcry are often regarded as "nonquantifiable" or "intangible" and are therefore perceived to be unsuitable (other than in a qualitative or semiqualitative manner) for incorporation into financial assessments of consequential impact.

Nevertheless, incidents like the Brent Spar disposal controversy have clearly demonstrated that community outcry can manifest itself as consequences that appear on the company's financial statements.[3] Therefore, such consequences must be considered if the company is to be assured that it has conducted an adequate assessment of its business risks.

For example, social consequences associated with such risks as a gas pipeline failure and supply discontinuity and an accidental oil discharge may include[4]:

- Social and emotional disruption to users of the affected areas
- Disruption to customers
- Social and legal events associated with compensation claims
- Community outcry and associated political backlash caused by inconvenience and/or pollution
- Statutory fines, prosecutions, and/or changes to operating license conditions

Categories of economic loss for the community for which the company may be held responsible may include:

- Loss of customers' ability to produce products and services during the period of disruption, for example, income from electricity generation
- Loss of asset value, for example, the value of land, infrastructure damage, amenity values such as recreational uses, and community values
- Consequential losses, for example, due to pollution of property or other resources from oil discharges

We believe that all of the so-called nonquantifiable risks can be expressed in quantitative financial terms. The key to assessing these risks in financial terms is to approach the problem with a holistic understanding of the potential scenarios and to focus on defining the consequences.

For example, in the Brent Spar disposal controversy, the "risk" was a socially unacceptable disposal method.[5] A primary consequence was community rejection and outcry. The secondary consequences arising from the outcry were product boycotts that reduced product sales and public protests that disrupted business trade. The Royal Dutch/Shell corporation experienced business discontinuities and loss of trade, resulting in losses of several million dollars.[6] In addition, the corporation was required to invest time and resources in a restrategizing process that involved extensive stakeholder consultation as well as ongoing organizational changes to improve its corporate image.[7] From this example, we can see that the primary consequence in itself is not readily measurable in financial terms. However, the secondary consequences can be calculated easily using traditional accounting tools.

BENEFITS OF QUANTITATIVE RISK ASSESSMENT

During the formulation of business management plans, managers are rarely able to be certain of the financial consequences of potential future risk events, but by using forecasting techniques, such as risk assessments, it is possible to make a reasonable estimate by characterizing the organization's risk profile.

Risk assessment techniques can assist decision-makers to develop an understanding of the consequences and likelihood of occurrence of risk events, so that appropriate financial provisions can be made to reduce the company's exposure. However, it is important that decision-makers choose a risk assessment technique that is suited to their application and information needs and that it is an informed choice based on an understanding of the relative strengths and weaknesses of the available risk assessment methodologies. Decision-makers who will use and rely on the results of a business risk assessment must be comfortable with the process used in order to have confidence and trust in the findings.

In general, the more sophisticated the risk assessment technique, the more detailed will be the information produced by the assessment process. Traditionally, assessment of social and environmental business risks has been limited by the constraints of qualitative and semiquantitative techniques, but new quantitative risk assessment tools have been developed to overcome some of the shortcomings of those methods.

The RISQUE method is one of those tools. It uses a quantitative risk assessment approach to assess risks and present the findings in a form that is of direct use in the development of a risk treatment strategy. The method readily lends itself to identification of gaps and deficiencies in the risk management practices of organizations.

Notes

1. This is expressed, for example, by Standards Association of Australia. *AS/NZS 4360:1999 Risk Management.* Strathfield, NSW: Standards Association of Australia, April 12, 1999.
2. See, for example, E. J. Vaughan, *Risk Management.* New York: John Wiley & Sons, 1997.
3. Brent Spar is a large buoy, which was used by Shell Expro (an operating company of the Royal Dutch/Shell Group) between 1976 and 1991 to store oil extracted from the Brent Field, which is offshore northeast Shetland in the United Kingdom. Shell Expro investigated options for disposal of the buoy at the end of its functional lifetime. Owing to its structural weakness and the risk of structural failure if it was brought ashore for disposal, Shell Expro focused on the possibilities of dumping the buoy at sea. Dumping in the shallow waters of the North Sea was rejected on environmental grounds, but disposal in the deeper waters of the North Atlantic was adopted as Shell Expro's favored option. The British government duly approved this option. However, a large-scale community outcry campaign ensued, primarily orchestrated by the environmental nongovernmental organization (NGO) Greenpeace. Finally, in response to the intense public pressure, Shell Expro revoked its decision to dump the Brent Spar at sea and embarked on a multipartite stakeholder consultation program to determine a more socially acceptable disposal option.
4. A. R. Bowden, J. H. Martin, and J. Mitchell, "Strategic Business Risk Assessment—An Approach for Financial Characterisation of Social and Environmental Risks." *APPEA Journal* 40 (2000): 605–616.
5. A. Neale, "Organisational Learning in Contested Environments: Lessons from Brent Spar." *Business Strategy and the Environment* 6(2) (1997): 93–103.
6. J. Grolin, "Corporate Legitimacy in Risk Society: The Case of Brent Spar." *Business Strategy and the Environment* 7(4) (1998): 213–222.
7. J. H. Martin, "Corporate Social and Environmental Responsibility—The Upstream Petroleum Sector in South-East Asia with Particular Reference to Thailand." Unpublished Ph.D. thesis, The Australian National University, Canberra, Australia, September 2000.

Part Two
RISQUE METHOD

3

OVERVIEW OF THE RISQUE METHOD

The RISQUE method is a risk management process that involves assessment of risk and development of risk management strategy using predominantly financial measures. The method has been developed in response to the recognized need to translate complex, technical information into financial terms and to quantitatively assess the so-called nonquantifiable environmental and social business risks.

Figure 3.1 presents a flowchart of the RISQUE method process. The flowchart is consistent with the risk management process depicted in Figure 1.1 (see Chapter 1).

The RISQUE method offers a systematic methodology that is defensible with respect to current world best practice, complies with existing formal standards,[1] and is consistent with the Canadian Risk Management Standard.[2]

The steps involved in the RISQUE method are not new; neither are its quantitative techniques, which have been in use for some years. However, the method is unique in its application of techniques to quantify risks associated with aspects such as community outcry, business reputation, legal culpability, and environmental impacts and in its generation of financial expressions of risk, risk profiles, and benefit-cost relationships.

This brief introduction provides an overview of the general concepts and processes used by the RISQUE method and is followed by detailed description of the method in Chapters 4 through 8.

At the end of each chapter, key elements of the RISQUE method are illustrated by reference to an example dam risk assessment by a water utility. The example is based on an actual project with real risk events, but the names and location have been changed. For the sake of simplicity, a shortened list of risk events is used.

It should be noted that the example was chosen from a wide range of potential business applications, any one of which would have made a good example. When following the example risk assessment, readers should apply some lateral thinking and use the principles demonstrated to generate analogies with their own area of activity.

ROLE OF STAKEHOLDERS

A defining feature of the RISQUE method is the inclusion of stakeholder representation throughout the process. Figure 3.1 shows the relationship between the RISQUE method process and the roles of key stakeholders (the project manager, community representatives, and specialist technical experts) and the risk analyst.

The "project manager" is the "client" or the person responsible for commissioning or championing the risk management process for a given business activity or a project. The management position this person holds in an organization can be anything from chief executive officer to a manager of a specific site activity, depending on whether the objective of the process is to assess strategic or specific operational risks. For simplicity, we have used the generic term "project manager" to refer to that person.

The RISQUE method requires substantial buy-in from the organization requiring the risk assessment. Project managers making decisions on the basis of information gained from risk assessment need to be fully involved with the process that generates that information. The project manager is therefore expected to be closely involved in all stages of the process.

The risk analyst is the technical specialist engaged to guide the risk assessment process and perform the quantitative analysis. The risk analyst has two key responsibilities:

1. To ensure that the process and technical aspects of the risk assessment are appropriate and correct
2. To assist the project manager to communicate the results effectively and efficiently to the end users

The expert panel is a critical resource in the RISQUE method. The adage "garbage in, garbage out," which is often glibly used with reference to mathematical modeling studies, is very pertinent to quantitative risk assessment. The strength and ultimate success of any application of the RISQUE method depends heavily on the accuracy and completeness of the risk information that is used as the basis for risk modeling. The risk information is drawn from the expert panel.[3] The quality of information is therefore dependent on the skill and knowledge level of the expert panel and, to a lesser extent, on the ability of the risk analyst to effectively guide the panel through the process.

A truly expert panel (consisting of people who genuinely understand the business and the range of potential risk events deriving from the activities) always provides the best available information on specific events and is unlikely to omit major events from consideration. To date, no third-party reviewers of the RISQUE method have substantively disagreed with the opinions and data provided by an expert panel.

The reputation of individual members of an expert panel is often important to the credibility of the risk assessment. In high-profile assessments of risk, which, for example, break new ground or involve far-reaching political decisions, decision-makers are more likely to act on the recommendations of an eminent

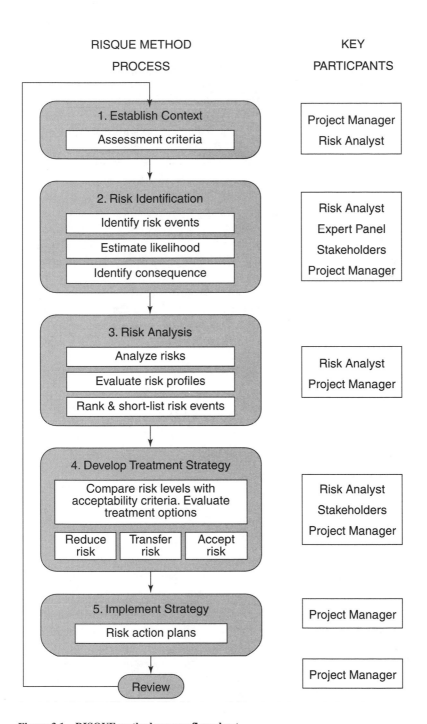

Figure 3.1   RISQUE method process flow chart.

panel. Such panels usually consist of a combination of nationally or internationally recognized experts and regionally based experts who understand the potential ramifications of local activities.

The use of an expert panel is fundamental to quantitative risk assessment because inputs to risk modeling (i.e., likelihoods of occurrence and magnitude of consequences) based on actuarial information are rarely available for many risk events. Substantial actuarial data are available for only a limited range of events. For example, with respect to the performance of boilers, where standards and conditions can be universally controlled, the likelihood of a boiler explosion for a specified size of pressure vessel can be looked up in relevant tables.

In other cases, some actuarial data may be available but cannot be applied directly to most potential risk events. The likelihood of a ship taking out a bridge span or the probability of a toxic release to the environment depends on locally specific circumstances and practices. The combined knowledge and experience of panel members is required to take account of past events and conditions in other places and circumstances and to apply that knowledge to the specific event under consideration within the setting where the activities are undertaken.

As discussed in Chapter 1, the composition of the stakeholder group also will vary on a project-specific basis. Identification and representation of stakeholder interests should be based on the considerations outlined in that chapter.

RISQUE METHOD STEPS

As depicted in Figure 3.1, the RISQUE method of risk assessment and formulation of risk management strategy proceeds as a staged process:

Stage 1. Establish the context
Stage 2. Identify the risk
Stage 3. Analyze the risk
Stage 4. Formulate a risk treatment strategy
Stage 5. Implement the risk treatment strategy

Stage 1: Establish the Context

In establishing the background to the risk management process, the nature of the activities and potential impacts are assessed. This allows the stakeholders to be identified and leads to formulation of the risk management aims and structure. The scope of the risk management process is then defined. In addition, initial criteria against which risk is to be evaluated may be established.

The project manager and the risk analyst usually jointly define the contextual scope and considerations for the risk assessment process.

Stage 2: Identify the Risk

The risk identification process involves utilizing a good understanding of the project for which the risk assessment is required to guide an appropriately skilled expert panel to identify and characterize the key risk events. For each event, the expert panel is guided through an event-tree approach to define the likelihood of occurrence, the consequences if the event occurs, and the potential time scale of occurrence. Documentation of the panel findings usually takes the form of a risk register, a description of each risk event, and a diagrammatic event tree.

The risk analyst facilitates risk identification by the expert panel (e.g., representatives from the project manager's organization and selected specialist consultants) in consultation with community representatives.

Stage 3: Analyze the Risk

For the RISQUE method, risk analysis involves quantifying and modeling the probabilities and consequences for each substantive risk event. A specific selection of techniques is applied in the risk model to derive prioritized profiles of risk quotient and to estimate the potential cost (the risk cost) that may be incurred in the future due to the occurrence of risk events.

Typical outputs of the risk analysis process include:

- Estimates of risk cost at optimistic, pessimistic, and conservative yet realistic (planning) levels of confidence
- A risk profile, which shows each risk event ranked in order of decreasing risk
- An exposure profile, which shows the range of consequential cost for the ranked risk events

The risk analyst, usually in consultation with the project manager, performs the risk analysis.

Stage 4: Formulate a Risk Treatment Strategy

Formulation of a risk treatment strategy utilizes the results of the risk analysis process to define and evaluate options for action plans to treat key risk events. Various measures of risk and risk cost are compared with risk management costs and business elements such as project cost and project revenue. The benefits, in relation to risk reduction, of implementing the action plan are estimated by modifying and rerunning the risk model. The benefit-cost relationships are reviewed and, if acceptable, the risk treatment strategy is accepted.

The risk analyst and project manager, often in consultation with other stakeholder representatives, develop the risk treatment strategy.

Stage 5: Implement the Risk Treatment Strategy

Implementation of a risk treatment strategy can involve actions such as risk transfer through insurance or contractual agreements, further investigations, establishment of rapid response systems, installation of detection systems, engineering works, lobbying, and community consultation. The project manager is responsible for implementing the risk treatment strategy.

The stages of the RISQUE method are described in detail in Chapters 4 through 8. Each stage of the RISQUE method offers a convenient milestone for reporting, review, and action. Each subsequent stage is dependent, and builds, on the work completed in the previous stage, providing an evolving understanding of the characteristics of risk events and progressively more robust management practices.

Notes

1. Standards Association of Australia, *AS/NZS 4360:1999 Risk Management.* Strathfield, NSW: Standards Association of Australia, April 12, 1999.
2. The Canadian Standard (CSA-Q850) is under consideration for adoption within the regulatory framework of a number of federal government departments in both Canada and the United States.
3. The RISQUE method relies on the use of the Delphi approach, which is a technique for obtaining an independent opinion on a topic by consulting with subject-matter experts.

4

STAGE 1: ESTABLISH THE CONTEXT

Establishment of the context for a quantitative risk assessment is critical because it defines the objectives and scope for the risk assessment process. The series of tasks that comprise this stage of the process are described in this chapter.

TASKS

Obtain Organizational Commitment

Any organization making key decisions on the basis of risk assessment needs to be fully involved with, and committed to, the risk management process in order to defend and be comfortable with decisions arising from the process.

In due diligence matters, one school of thought believes that due diligence assessments need to be performed by entirely independent parties in order to be defensible to external reviewers. Even if this is the case in some instances, the policy does not translate to the risk assessment aspect of due diligence.

It is not defensible or appropriate to conduct an independent risk assessment on any aspect of a business. If the experts responsible for evaluating risk events do not have access to the complete range of available information, then the conclusions of such an independent assessment generally do not coincide with local experience and judgment. On the few occasions where independent risk assessment has been carried out, the findings were not trusted or used for decision-making and risk reduction. In addition, the project managers felt that considerable time and expense had been wasted.

The following example demonstrates the value of appropriate involvement of local knowledge in the risk assessment process. The operator of a large base metal mine engaged a highly credentialed, global engineering company to conduct an independent risk assessment of the engineering aspects of the mine operation. Independence was considered desirable to ensure credibility to the shareholders.

The consultant was given virtually unrestricted access to the mine site and mine engineering records. In order to ensure independence, the consultant was prevented from discussing any technical aspect with mine personnel.

The risk assessment report was duly completed and handed to the mine operator. Unfortunately, the report was not well received. In the opinion of mine operations staff, the report authors did not adequately understand and take into account the real problems associated with mining operations at the site (which is characterized by over 40 feet [12 m] of rainfall per annum, repeated earthquake activity, and unstable terrain leading to frequent landslides). As a consequence, the mine operator rejected the conclusions of the risk assessment.

It is probable that if the external consultant had been provided with the benefit of firsthand experience from operations staff and had blended that information in with its global, first-rate technical experience, the report would have taken the disputed aspects into consideration. In that case the risk assessment conclusions are more likely to have been useful to the client.

Fortunately, as a result of this learning experience, the mine operator developed an understanding of the importance of buy-in and subsequently became actively involved with all forms of risk assessment at the site while ensuring that the integrity of the assessments was maintained.

Define the Nature of the Project

This task describes the activity that is being carried out, or is proposed to be carried out, and how it interacts with the wider environment (social, political, environmental, infrastructure, etc). During this task the type of risk events that could occur and their principal consequences are identified.

Identify Who Is Affected

The stakeholders are those people who could potentially affect or be affected by the project or activities. Most activities could potentially involve many types of stakeholder. Key stakeholders are frequently local communities, management and employees of the organization, regulators, contractors, and customers. Stakeholders in a broader capacity include politicians, nongovernmental organizations, banks, and insurance companies.

Define the Risk Management Aims

The overarching aim of risk management is to reduce exposure to risk usually by development of a risk treatment strategy. Specific risk management aims can be relatively simple, such as knowing by how much to reduce a bid price to account for acquired risk, or identifying the riskiest events facing an organization. The aim also can be challenging, such as selecting a preferred option from a complex range of alternatives or determining a project structure that minimizes risk without compromising project viability.

Secondary risk management objectives also need to be determined. Such objectives may be to gain a clear understanding of corporate risk expressed in dollar terms, perform a defensible and documented assessment, follow a transparent and auditable process, provide feedback to design, clearly demonstrate due diligence, and identify cost-effective actions.

Identify Who Will Use the Results

During the process of developing risk treatment strategy, knowledge of the end users' needs, abilities, and style preferences enables those performing the risk assessment to adapt their conclusions to suit interested parties. The people responsible for ensuring that the risk assessment is carried out within an organization therefore need to communicate frequently with the end users to ensure that maximum benefit will be achieved.

Within organizations, risk assessments can be carried out over a wide range of activities—for example, from detailed technical assessment of asset risk to events of business-wide significance. Business risk assessments frequently are aimed at addressing major business events. In such cases, the requirement to conduct a business risk assessment within organizations is driven by decision-makers at senior management and board levels, who will use the results to make strategic business decisions. Senior management gives authority to a project manager (frequently operations management) to ensure the assessment is carried out in an appropriate and timely manner.

Define the Risk Assessment Structure

Setting the structure of a risk assessment is a key task that the risk analyst must perform very early in the process in order to adequately define the required scope of work, identify the resources required to perform the risk assessment, and produce outputs for application in development of the risk treatment strategy. This task is probably the most demanding one required of the risk analyst and usually draws on the analyst's entire range of experience, expertise, and innovation.

The first step in defining the structure is to gain from the end users an accurate perception of the risk assessment aims and expected outputs.

The risk analyst must develop a clear initial understanding of the project activities and their potential impacts. The analyst usually does so by consulting with managers, operators, and specialist consultants; by reading relevant documentation; and, ideally, by inspection of site conditions and surrounding activities.

The risk analyst develops the risk assessment structure by working back from the outputs required by the end users. The outputs determine which methods and procedures are appropriate, which in turn dictate the nature and extent of information required and how the information is to be obtained.

At this stage it is possible to assess the range of disciplines needed on the expert panel and for the business manager to compile a preliminary list of panel experts.

Define the Scope of Additional Work

Preliminary evaluation of the risk events, the potential impacts of the activities, and the stakeholder composition usually reveals information gaps that need to be filled prior to the formal risk identification process. The business manager and the analyst establish the scope and timing of these studies and give priority to commissioning and completing the additional studies.

Timing of the Risk Management Process

Organizational deadlines, such as board meetings or the risk management system review cycle, often set the timing of the reporting of the results of risk assessment. Corporate reporting requirements or regulatory review can set external deadlines.

When designed and performed in a systematic and defensible manner, the completion of the risk management process can take considerable effort by many contributors. Adequate time and/or resources must be allocated for timely completion of the risk management process.

The schedule should include time for:

- Briefing the organization management and the expert panel in the process that will be followed
- Expert panel preparation of relevant information
- An initial panel meeting
- Collection and incorporation of information identified at the initial panel meeting
- A follow-up panel meeting
- Risk modeling
- Review by the business manager organization
- Strategy development
- Reporting.

Depending on the nature and extent of the risk assessment portion of the risk management process, the time to complete could range from four weeks to six months. Most business risk assessments take around three months to complete.

Establish Initial Criteria

Prior to performance of an initial risk analysis, it is usually possible to establish only preliminary criteria against which risk will be evaluated. During the initial revolution of the risk assessment-plan-do-review cycle, it is usually not realistic to attempt to conform to predetermined criteria, such as those set by formal (but not regulatory) standards. Risk reduction and management is an iterative process that ultimately aims to conform to high standards. There must be recognition that risk reduction needs to focus initially on higher-risk events and progressively address lower-risk events until standards-based criteria can be met. Until that time, the criteria need to be set at realistic levels and move progressively toward more stringent or standards-based criteria.

WATER UTILITY EXAMPLE

The following water utility example demonstrates application of the steps in the context definition stage.

The organization (the Utility) that required the risk assessment was a water utility in the northeastern region of the United States. The Utility supplied potable and irrigation water to approximately 100,000 people distributed over an area of 3,000 square miles (5,000 square kilometers). The Utility owned 14 water supply dams, five of which were classified as large dams.

A preliminary investigation of one of the five priority dams indicated that its factor of safety was of concern. The dam engineers considered that there were several potential ways in which the dam could fail (failure types), leading to different rates and volume of uncontrolled release of water.

The dam was located upstream of a regional town, substantial agricultural development, and some light industrial activity. The Utility recognized that if the dam were to fail, there would (depending on how the dam failed) be varying degrees of potential for loss of human life, environmental impairment, infrastructure damage, revenue losses, and harm to its community image.

A large number and a diverse range of people could have been affected directly by dam failure. The key stakeholders were the residents of the regional town, downstream farmers, industrial workers, local road users, recreational lake users, the Utility customers, dam operators, employees and management of the Utility, emergency service workers, the environmental regulator, and insurance and financial organizations. Broader-scale stakeholders were other water authorities, local and federal politicians, the media, and suppliers to the local community and customers.

The Utility needed to reduce the financial exposure to risk as a result of dam failure. It required a business risk assessment of the dam to guide formulation of a business risk reduction strategy. The Utility also required a rigorous, quantitative risk assessment that used a consistent process which, if appropriate, could later be applied to the remaining dams. The Utility wanted the risk assessment to consider all aspects of financial risk only; it excluded loss of life, which was the subject of a separate evaluation, from the risk assessment scope.

The headworks manager was the end user of the risk assessment results. The results were intended to be used to develop a cost-effective strategy to reduce the risk to levels that were considered acceptable at the time. The risk assessment project manager for the Utility was a senior engineer.

The risk assessment was structured to generate financial risk profiles based on possible failure types. It was decided to use two expert panels. An Engineering Panel was required to review dam break studies to determine the likelihoods and modes of failure and also to define the nature of the water release (the flood-wave characteristics, inundation areas, warning time, etc.). A Consequences Panel consisting of specialists in selected areas (e.g., community, environmental, infrastructure, corporate, agricultural economics) was required to consider the consequences of the various potential water releases.

The planned risk modeling was to develop event trees based on likelihood and consequence information generated by the panels. The risk model would generate profiles of risk quotient that could be used later to develop and evaluate, in advance, the beneficial impact of the risk reduction strategy.

Some additional evaluation of the flood characteristics and inundation areas needed to be completed to better define the potential impacts of uncontrolled release.

The Utility required the risk assessment to be completed within four months and the financial criteria to be determined after performance of the risk analysis.

5

STAGE 2: IDENTIFY THE RISK

Three basic steps are followed in the systematic identification of risk events. They are:

1. Select an expert panel
2. Conduct a panel workshop
3. Document the panel conclusions

SELECTION OF AN EXPERT PANEL

The RISQUE method uses an expert panel to identify the nature of potential risk events. The organization that commissions the risk assessment is ultimately responsible for selection and acceptance of panel members. The organization usually seeks assistance from its staff, the risk analyst, and its existing body of consultants to define the most appropriate panel composition in terms of skills and experience.

The organization needs to have a high degree of trust in the judgment and skill of panel members. The decision-makers need to be confident that the decisions they will make are based on information that can be relied on and reflect an understanding of the way in which the organization does business and the environment in which the business activities are carried out. Consequently, the expert panel may include internal and external technical experts, company operations staff, and contractors who are familiar with the design, operation, and monitoring of the project or activity.

The technical disciplines and experience of panel members need to cover the full range of expertise that was identified during the task of defining the project structure when setting the context of the risk assessment. The panel composition should be flexible and not considered to be immutable. Ongoing panel discussions frequently reveal risk events that require additional expertise; in such cases new members need to be found and added to the panel.

Similarly, a panel may be considered excessively large because too many people have similar skills and experience. It is inefficient use of time to have a group of experts filling a role that could be done by one person. In addition, experience has shown that if several experts get together, they can spend considerable time discussing relatively minor, technical points. In both of these cases, the organization needs to select a single individual to fill the role.

The following anecdote is provided as an example of a flexible panel structure: A panel was established by a water utility to identify financial risk events associated with rationalization of assets. During the preliminary stage, to identify the key events, the panel consisted predominantly of operations water engineers. After considerable discussion on operational aspects of the event tree, the panel was unable to put a dollar value on the consequences (which they recognized as severe) if water delivery within a specific urban network was interrupted for a period exceeding 15 hours. After substantial discussion, the uniform response of the operations engineers to the question was that "all hell would break loose from Corporate."

The risk analyst who was facilitating the workshop requested that the corporate legal specialist attend and provide an opinion. Within a few minutes, the corporate specialist was able to provide a graphic account of the public and political response; the measures that would need to be taken (which were predominantly implementation of a costly public relations program, and substantial overdesign of remedial works on affected facilities to ensure that the problem would not arise again); and the substantial financial resources that would need to be applied to manage the consequences of the delivery failure.

Consequentially, the utility decided to reduce the panel in size and expand the skill base. Four engineers were removed from the panel; the legal specialist, the corporate financial manager, and the community relations manager were added.

Most individuals chosen for a panel are usually supported by an organization with its own diversity and depth of knowledge, which the panel member can draw on if necessary. Each individual on the panel should be encouraged, as appropriate, to utilize backup resources and to consult with colleagues within the field. In many respects, the quality of resources available to the panel is a defining quality.

A final point on panel selection. A successful panel is one that can function efficiently and in a timely manner. Generally, the larger the number of panel members, the more difficult it becomes to have a fully functional panel. All panel members must be committed to their involvement in the process, make themselves reasonably available for meetings, and properly respond to requests and communications.

In summary, experience has shown that the risk assessment process is best performed using an expert panel in a workshop situation, facilitated by a risk analyst. This type of forum allows interactive discussion between those people involved in various aspects of the project, which rarely takes place otherwise. The forum promotes comprehensive evaluation of the project or business activities and usually provides a profound understanding of the risk event scenarios and their potential consequences.

THE PANEL WORKSHOP

Background to the Panel Workshop

The panel process identifies and provides an understanding of key risk events, particularly their likelihoods of occurrence and their consequences. The ultimate goal of the panel workshop is to quantify risk event likelihoods and consequences using the collective judgment of the workshop participants.

In order to achieve the aim of the panel workshop efficiently, the panel needs to understand the broad risk assessment process and the role of the panel in the process.

The panel needs to be aware of the scope of the risk assessment so that panel deliberations remain focused on relevant events and do not enter into excessive detail. In most instances, particularly during initial stages of the workshop, the facilitator allows the panel substantial latitude to ensure debate is not stifled and so the panel can recognize, when it is pointed out, that the discussion has gone too far or wide.

The panel members also need to understand that their responsibility is to provide information that, on the basis of their experience, is the best available information, regardless of the remaining uncertainty. The RISQUE method is designed so that the integrity of the data is retained when others (the risk analyst and the client organization) use the information during the risk analysis stage. The panel needs to understand that it is not responsible for how the information is used.

If panel members are not confident that the process is sound, then they may not be prepared to have their name associated with the assessment and withdraw from the process. An alternative response is that panel members may feel the need to be excessively conservative and provide only information of which they are certain. This situation does not utilize their full range of experience and expertise to provide best estimates and severely limits the usefulness of the information provided. Panel members knowledgeable in their discipline readily recognize the substantial benefits of the process and understand the level of judgment required to be provided.

For panel members to provide the best available information, they must have access to all relevant information held by the client organization. This information should be provided in advance of any panel workshops.

People attending the panel workshop also should be aware that the panel process is not a democratic process per se. Many risk events have a wide range of potential causes and effects. When assessing specific events, often several experts from different disciplines must jointly identify the entire nature of the event. However, quantification of the likelihood of a social impact, for example, must be performed by the relevant community expert. In assessing the probability, the community expert may seek specific advice or clarification from other experts around the table, but it is not appropriate for other panel members to expect to "vote" on matters where specific expertise is available. Panel members are therefore responsible for the veracity of information within their own fields of expertise.

Once panel members understand their role in the process and the overall aims of the workshop, they need to be informed of the specific goals of the workshop. The panel should be shown examples of the ultimate panel outputs that will be used in the risk modeling process. The panel should also be provided with specific pro-forma sheets that are to be used as checklists or data sheets. Pro-forma sheets are extremely useful as documented, primary sources of information, for ensuring that all the relevant information is collected, and for identifying areas where there are data gaps.

These background aspects should all be addressed during an introductory session of a panel workshop. If this is done, then the main business of the panel workshop (to identify and quantify risk events) can be undertaken with purpose.

Identify and Quantify Risk Events

The risk identification and quantification process involves the following key elements:

* Development of a preliminary list of risk events
* General description of risk scenarios
* Development of event trees
* Estimation of probabilities of occurrence
* Estimation of magnitude of consequences

Development of a Preliminary List of Risk Events. The aim of this process is to generate the preliminary list of risk events for analysis. This process is essentially a brainstorming exercise. Development of the preliminary list of events should not involve detailed discussion of the events themselves. The risk analyst needs to ensure that the discussion remains focused on developing the list. However, panel members should be encouraged to think beyond their normal fields or expertise, which assists with recognition of additional expertise that eventually may be required on the panel (or made available to the panel).

The process quickly generates common understanding of the nature and range of potential risk events and leads to crystallization of ideas, so the preliminary list of events usually does not take the panel long to develop. Usually, most (often around 95 percent) of the substantive risk events are identified in this first round of evaluation. The preliminary list should include all conceivable events, even those events that some panel members may intuitively consider to be very low-risk events. If an event is raised, it should be included on the preliminary list.

The list of events for consideration in the risk assessment should not be considered final at any stage during the risk assessment process. Ongoing evaluation frequently reveals risk events that had not previously been identified. As new events arise, they must be added to the list.

The complete list of preliminary events must be documented. The preliminary list of events becomes a checklist for subsequent, more detailed panel consideration. It is recommended that the panel also sort the events into groups of similar events. This procedure is not compulsory, but it frequently points to duplication or overlap of events.

General Description of Risk Events. Description of the risk events provides the basis for development of the event trees. The panel must systematically review each event on the preliminary list.

For each event, relevant panel members need to describe the initiating event, how likely the event is to occur, and ways in which the event could be initiated. The panel also needs to describe the potential chain of impacts that could occur and that lead to the end consequences.

The consequences should be described in some detail, particularly in relation to aspects such as: who would be affected; what would be the nature of any damage; how extensive the consequences would be; for how long the impacts would be felt; and how a dollar value could be estimated.

The panel also should identify how impacts within an event may be interlinked and whether there could be any correlation with other risk events.

The descriptions of all events considered must be documented so that there is clear understanding of the panel's opinion of all events, the panel findings are defensible, and the descriptions can be used directly to generate the event trees. On completion of full descriptions of all events on the preliminary list, it is then possible to reduce the list of events to those that are relevant to the scope of the risk assessment.

After the panel has described the nature of the events, the client organization may consider that some of the identified events have such a low likelihood of occurring that they should be excluded from further consideration. Similarly, the consequences of other events may be considered to be relatively low and therefore not material to the risk assessment.

It is necessary at this point to define thresholds of likelihood and consequence in order to differentiate between those events that should be included and those that should be excluded from the assessment. The client organization is solely responsible for deciding the thresholds because the organization needs to be comfortable that all substantive events have been identified and included in the assessment.

The organization may decide to exclude any event that, in its view, has a "negligible" chance of occurring or if it is inconceivable either that a risk event will occur or that the organization would be held responsible for the consequences of an event. The likelihood threshold is the frequency below which the organization considers that a risk event has negligible chance of occurring. With respect to consequences identified during a business risk assessment, organizations need to define a dollar threshold that is material to the business.

The consequence threshold is frequently defined as a financial cost that could marginally be absorbed by the usual operational contingency. As a guide, the threshold for a risk assessment of a business line within an organization may be, for example, $100,000. In contrast, the consequence threshold for an organization-wide business risk assessment could be $2 million.

If any event falls below either the defined likelihood threshold or consequence threshold, it should be excluded from the risk assessment. However, such events should always be reincorporated into the assessment if subsequent investigation indicates that both of the thresholds could be exceeded.

The panel should create a final list of events that will be included in the risk assessment, and a description of each event. In addition, it should create a list and description of events excluded from the assessment, together with the reasons for exclusion.

Development of Event Trees. A key component of understanding risk events is the use of the event-tree approach to establish the full range of potential substantive outcomes that could follow each risk event. The fundamental principle of the event-tree process is to unravel a relatively complex event to derive a sequence of simpler component events, whose probabilities and consequences have a better prospect of being estimated using available data or judgment.

Event-tree analysis can range from very complex to relatively simple analysis. A complex event tree would contain an exhaustive map of all of the potential impacts deriving from a single trigger event, including all of the branches where there is potentially no impact. On more complex event trees, conditional probabilities are assigned to each branch of the tree and the sum of the probabilities of each branch is equal to one.

Since risk assessment primarily evaluates the chance of consequences occurring, it is usually sufficient to include only those pathways on the event tree that result in substantial consequences. Thus, a relatively simple event tree can be created that is extremely valuable, covers an appropriate level of detail, and accurately represents the available information.

Event trees offer additional benefits to quantitative risk assessment because they are instrumental in providing transparency to the process. It is always helpful to document graphical representation of the event trees. In addition, the event-tree format is ideal for unambiguous data entry into a risk model.

During the panel process, the panel needs to consider each risk event systematically in the manner described earlier. Discussion and development of an event tree for the first one or two events invariably takes considerable time. However, once the panel has practical experience with the process and develops an understanding of the nature and level of information required, the process becomes much quicker. It is usually most efficient if the panel can incorporate quantification of likelihood of occurrence and consequences concurrently with development of the event trees.

Figure 5.1 shows a mining example of a simple event tree. This event tree shows the impacts and consequence pathways derived from 11 initiating (or trigger) events. In this example, 20 risk events were identified. Four events were potentially able to occur as a result of the first listed trigger event, a vehicle accident during transport of fuel on-site, resulting in a spill of fuel. Two of the potential events involve environmental damage, and the other two events could result in personal injury (both minor and major injury). The consequences of environmental damage were considered to be remediation (essentially clean-up costs) and the possibility of receiving a fine from the regulatory agency.

Construction of event trees aid in the process of quantifying so-called "nonquantifiable" events (which is discussed in Chapter 2). For quantitative business

ISSUE	Annual Freq	IMPACT	Prob	IMPACT	Prob	CONSEQUENCE	Prob	Average Cost ($)	High Cost ($)
Fuel transport accident	0.04	Fuel spill	0.1	Environmental damage	1	Remediation	1	50,000	75,000
						Statutory fine	0.01	60,000	200,000
			0.1	Personal injury	0.1	Minor injury	0.9	20,000	100,000
					0.1	Major injury, death	0.1	1,000,000	6,000,000
Explosives transport accident	0.002	Explosion	0.01	Personal injury	0.85	Minor injury	0.9	20,000	100,000
					0.15	Major injury, death	0.1	1,000,000	6,000,000
			0.01	Property damage	0.2	Repair	1	50,000	200,000
Aboveground stor. explosion	0.001			Personal injury	0.0001	Minor injury	0.8	20,000	100,000
					0.0001	Major injury, death	0.2	1,000,000	6,000,000
	0.001			Property damage	0.2	Repair	1	650,000	3,000,000
Underground stor. explosion	0.001			Property damage	0.005	Repair	1	300,000	600,000
Deposited dust off-site	1			Property damage	0.01	Cleanup	0.1	120,000	250,000
Respirable dust off-site	0.001			Personal injury	0.1	Treatment 5 people	1	300,000	1,200,000
Surface blasting	1	Fly rock	0.001	Personal injury	0.1	Minor injury	0.8	20,000	100,000
					0.1	Major injury, death	0.2	1,000,000	6,000,000
			0.001	Property damage	0.001	Repair	1	100,000	160,000
Subsurface blasting	1	Vibrations > 10 mm/s	0.0001	Property damage	0.1	Repair	1	500,000	1,500,000
Subsidence	0.00001			Property damage	1	Repair	1	500,000	1,500,000
Noise	1	Exceeds limit	0.01			Remediation	0.1	340,000	680,000
Acid Rock Drainage	0.002			Environmental damage	0.1	Remediation	1	2,000,000	6,000,000

Figure 5.1 Event Tree; mining example showing 11 initiating events that ultimately lead to a set of 20 consequences.

risk assessment, event-tree analysis promotes a systematic and logical thought process that clarifies cause-and-effect relationships and greatly facilitates the ultimate discovery of a financial consequence.

The Alkimos case study in Chapter 12 shows how dollar values can be derived for formerly "nonquantifiable" consequences of corporate decisions and then used to support decisions on the basis of enhanced community benefit. In that example, the panel that considered the social benefits of relocating the proposed Alkimos treatment plant identified greater community diversity as a beneficial consequence of relocation. At that point there was some difficulty in translating "community diversity" into a dollar value. The facilitator used the event-tree process to extend the cause-and-effect panel discussion to derive financial consequences. The panel concluded that greater community diversity would lead to increased localized employment, which could readily be expressed as a benefit in dollar terms. Furthermore, more local employment would reduce pressure on transport infrastructure development, which also could be expressed as reduced cost. In addition, the panel determined that community diversity would lead to a healthier, more vibrant community, which could be expressed as reduced cost of public healthcare.

Estimation of Likelihood of Occurrence. Quantitative estimation of the likelihood of occurrence can be based on several sources. Actuarial information is available for a minority of events (e.g., traffic accident frequency). Empirical observations (e.g., flood and earthquake frequency) for some naturally occurring events are useful sources for estimating frequencies. Most estimates of likelihood, however, are based on the application to a specific event of experience gained from a large number and wide range of comparable situations.

When basing estimates on experience, it is useful for the facilitator to provide the panel with a tabular guide to estimating probabilities. Such tables relate descriptions of likelihood to a range of numerical annual likelihoods or probabilities. While there are differences among guides, if all panel members use the same guide, a greater opportunity for consistency of likelihood estimation over all of the events considered usually results. Tables 5.1 and 5.2 show examples of two guides that have been used on different projects.

The aim of risk assessment is to evaluate exposure to risk events over a given time. Therefore, the estimate of likelihood used needs to be expressed as a fre-

Table 5.1   Example Guide to Quantification of Likelihood

Likelihood of Occurrence	Annual Likelihood	
	(per year)	*(years)*
Negligible	$<1 \times 10^{-6}$	<1 in 1,000,000 years
Very Low	1×10^{-6} to 1×10^{-4}	1 in 1,000,000 to 1 in 10,000 years
Low	1×10^{-4} to 1×10^{-2}	1 in 10,000 to 1 in 100 years
Moderate	1×10^{-2} to 1×10^{-1}	1 in 100 to 1 in 10 years
Significant	$>1 \times 10^{-1}$	>1 in 10 years

Table 5.2   Example Alternative Guide to Quantification of Likelihood

Qualitative Description	Order of Magnitude Annual Probability	Basis
A. Certain	1 (or 0.999, 99.9%)	Certain, or as near to as makes no difference
B. Almost certain	0.2 – 0.9	One or more incidents of a similar nature has occurred here
C. Highly probable	0.1	A previous incident of a similar nature has occurred here
D. Possible	0.01	Could have occurred already without intervention
E. Unlikely	0.001	Recorded recently elsewhere
F. Very unlikely	1×10^{-4}	Has happened elsewhere
G. Highly improbable	1×10^{-5}	Published information exists, but in a slightly different context
H. Almost impossible	1×10^{-6}	No published information on a similar case

quency, that is, the probability of an event occurring within a specified time frame. The frequency can be expressed as an annual likelihood or, alternatively, as the likelihood of occurrence over the anticipated life of a project.

Financial modelers of most new projects usually select a time frame of between 10 and 20 years as realistically reflecting the project financials; however, in many cases substantially longer time frames are selected. The client organization must select the project time frame that it feels is appropriate for the risk assessment being carried out. The selected time frame should be provided to the panel prior to estimation of event likelihoods.

In many cases the initiating event is expressed as a frequency and subsequent events along the event tree are expressed as probabilities (the chance that the event will occur, assuming the initiating event has occurred). The overall likelihood that a specific end consequence will occur is obtained as the product of all of the contributing likelihoods along the event-tree branches from the initiating event.

End users usually want the panel to come up with single estimates of probability. The estimates should be considered as central estimates. There can be substantial uncertainty in likelihood estimates. A single estimate is generally appropriate, provided assessment of sensitivity of model results to probability of occurrence is undertaken.

The mining example event tree depicted in Figure 5.1 shows that the panel estimated that the likelihood of a fuel transport traffic accident was 1 in 25 years (0.04 per year). If there was an accident, then there was a 1 in 10 (0.1) chance that there would be a substantial fuel spill. In the event of a substantial fuel spill, the panel felt that environmental damage would definitely occur (probability equals 1 or 100 percent) and that environmental remediation would be required (probability equals 100 percent). However, the panel also concluded that in the event of environmental damage, there was only a 1 in 100 chance that the company would receive a penalty from the regulatory authority.

The overall annual likelihood that a fuel transport accident will occur leading to remediation is 0.004 per year (the product of the contributing probabilities: 0.04, 0.1, 1.0, and 1.0). Similarly, the likelihood of a fuel transport accident leading to a fine is 0.0004 per year (or 1 in 2,500 years).

Estimation of Magnitude of Consequences. The cost of each of the end consequences needs to be estimated for all events. A measure of uncertainty in the estimations also should be sought for each event. The uncertainties with this type of assessment are associated with predicting the scale of the impacts if a risk event occurs and uncertainty related to accurately costing the consequences when a risk event occurs. A probabilistic costing approach, where costs are expressed as probability distributions, is used to account for inherent uncertainty of the consequences of risk events.

For consequential costs, panel members should be asked to provide two estimates of cost that reflect the uncertainty and range of potential costs. Panel members should be provided with a clear understanding of how to visualize the cost estimates that they will provide. The first cost to be estimated by the panel is the median cost, that is, the best or most likely estimate. The median cost estimate is the 50 percent confidence-level estimate, that is, there is a 50 percent chance that the indicated cost will be exceeded. The 50 percent confidence level estimate also can be referred to as the 50th percentile cost estimate.

The second cost estimate required is a very conservative estimate that indicates a high end cost but not the highest conceivable cost. The conservatively high cost should be considered as one that is high but realistic and would be expected to be exceeded in only 5 percent of similar cases. This is the 95 percent confidence level estimate, or the 95th percentile estimate. The spread between the two selected confidence levels provides a measure of uncertainty, which is a critical input to the quantitative risk assessment process.

Panel members should be aware of how the costs will be assumed in the risk model to be distributed on the basis of the two cost estimates that they provide. If the panel has no specific knowledge or preference on the distribution of cost, a log normal distribution with attributes defined by the median and the 95th percentile value is adopted as a standard.

The log normal distribution closely reflects most cost distributions. This distribution assumption is appropriate because:

- It includes only positive values.
- It is skewed to the right. (It has a long tail at the high cost end of the distribution.)
- It is a smooth curve with a recognizable central tendency (it has one peak) identified as the median.

- Although the cost has no theoretical upper limit, it is constrained in practice by the 95th percentile value.

Graphical representations of the cost distributions derived from the expert panel can be generated using spreadsheet software. The distribution graphs should be reviewed in detail by the appropriate experts, to confirm that they represent the intended distributions, at least for the high-cost events.

In most risk assessments, risk modeling needs to account for the time value of money. The final task of the panel, for each risk event, therefore is to indicate the potential timing of that event. In many cases, risk events have the capacity to occur at any time; this should be clearly stated by the panel.

However, external influences control the occurrence of many events. For example, an air discharge event at a power generation facility may not be relevant under existing licensing conditions. However, if the license becomes subject to renewal and review in eight years, at that time it is possible that the regulator will tighten environmental controls. If the regulations are made more stringent, discharges could potentially fall outside newly established license limits. The panel also should indicate the potential timing of those events that, for specific reasons, have an identifiable window of opportunity for occurring.

DOCUMENTATION OF THE PANEL CONCLUSIONS

Full documentation of the key panel findings is required, mainly as reference documentation that becomes very important during subsequent review stages and when developing a risk management strategy. Furthermore, the documented information ensures transparency of process and the origin of inputs to the risk model.

At the completion of this stage, the panel has identified all relevant risk events, their consequences, their likelihood of occurrence, and their potential timing, and has fully documented the outcomes of the panel deliberations. The information then can be used as input to a range of quantitative techniques in order to produce outputs suitable for development of risk management strategy, as described in Chapter 6.

WATER UTILITY EXAMPLE

The following water utility example demonstrates application of the steps in the risk identification stage.

The Engineering Panel (six people) consisted of four specialist engineers in the fields of geotechnology, embankments and structures, hydraulics and hydrology, and mechanical and electrical; the Utility dam manager; and the Utility project manager.

The Consequences Panel (eight people) consisted of experts in the fields of infrastructure engineering, agricultural economics, dam engineering (also a member of the Engineering Panel), community relations, hydrogeology, Utility corporate, ecology, and the Utility project manager.

The following 16-point list shows the identified range of engineering risk events and the nature of the resultant consequences:

1. Probable Maximum Flood (PMF), overtopping, ample warning, breach of main embankment, moderate flood wave, 150-square-mile (240 sq km) inundation area, moderate loss of life

2. PMF, piping, breach of main embankment, ample warning, moderate flood wave, 150-square-mile (240 sq km) inundation area, moderate loss of life

3. PMF, embankment instability, breach of main embankment, ample warning, moderate flood wave, 300-square-mile (240 sq km) inundation area, moderate loss of life

4. Major flood, overtopping, breach of main embankment, ample warning, minor flood wave, 300-square-mile (240 sq km) inundation area, low loss of life

5. Major flood, piping, breach of main embankment, ample warning, minor flood wave, 300-square-mile (240 sq km) inundation area, low loss of life

6. Major flood, embankment instability, breach of main embankment, ample warning, minor flood wave, 300-square-mile (240 sq km) inundation area, low loss of life

7. Earthquake, cracked embankment, breach of main embankment, little warning, large flood wave, 150-square-mile (120 sq km) inundation area, high loss of life

8. Earthquake, embankment batter slip, breach of main embankment, little warning, large flood wave, 150-square-mile (120 sq km) inundation area, high loss of life

9. Earthquake, outlet tower collapse, little warning, no flood wave, local inundation, minor loss of life, long-term out of service

10. Earthquake, turbine pump station collapse, little warning, no flood wave, local inundation, minor loss of life, long-term out of service

11. Earthquake, spillway bridge collapse, vehicle accident, minor loss of life

12. Geotechnical instability, breach of main embankment, little warning, large flood wave, 150-square-mile (120 sq km) inundation area, high loss of life

13. Piping failure, breach of main embankment, little warning, large flood wave, 150-square-mile (120 sq km) inundation area, high loss of life

14. Guard gate mechanical or electrical failure, little warning, no flood wave, local inundation, minor loss of life, long-term out of service

15. Turbine pump station mechanical or electrical failure, little warning, no flood wave, local inundation, minor loss of life, short-term out of service

16. Geotechnical failure of upstream embankment, roadway collapse, vehicle accident, minor loss of life

The following discussion provides a full description of the first listed event (embankment overtopping during a Probable Maximum Flood event), the nature of the subsequent releases from the dam, and the range of potential consequences on the wider environment.

The PMF is potentially the highest conceivable flood that could occur in the catchment and has an extremely low likelihood of occurring. During a PMF event, the flood spillway would not be able to pass the entire flood flow and the water in the pond behind the embankment would overtop the embankment. During overtopping, it is most likely that erosion of the embankment would occur, leading to a major breach of the embankment. A very large additional volume of water would be suddenly released through the breach.

The water released would form a moderate, 30-ft- (10 m) high flood wave within the confines of the valley for a distance of 8 miles (13 km) below the dam. Over the wider floodplain areas, the flood wave would then progressively decrease in height to around 3 ft (1 m) at a distance of 50 miles (80 km) downstream. The area expected to be flooded is approximately 90 square miles (235 sq km).

It is likely that, during such a major flood event, rising water levels would be observed and there would be ample warning that the embankment would be overtopped. Despite the warning, however, it is anticipated that substantial physical damage and moderate loss of life would occur.

The full range of potential consequences of the release is: loss of life, house and farm property damage, livestock loss, crop losses, small business revenue losses, industry revenue losses, debris clean-up, riparian vegetation damage, fauna damage (from low temperature or oxygen deficient water), infrastructure damage, accessibility loss, lake amenity loss, utility revenue loss, adverse community reaction, and dam repairs.

The event tree in the Water Utility example case was derived by combination of the event trees developed by the engineering panel and the consequences panel. The example event tree considers the events that could lead to a sunny-day failure and the consequences that could occur.

The combined event tree, shown in Figure 5.2, is typical of many risk assessment event trees, which in effect consist of two event trees. This figure demonstrates that a set of different initiating (or trigger) events can potentially have sequences of independent consequences that can all lead to a single risk event, in this case a sunny-day failure and catastrophic release of water.

In the example, the engineering panel considered that two initiating events, earthquake and full storage conditions, could potentially follow five pathways that all lead to a breach of the embankment and sunny-day failure. The rate and volume of water released during a sunny-day failure would be catastrophic. The consequences panel recognized 14 major consequences and their financial implications that could follow a sunny-day failure of the embankment.

Figure 5.3 shows the likelihoods that the engineering panel attached to each branch of the engineering portion of the sunny-day failure event tree of Figure 5.2. The event tree shows that the estimated frequency of an earthquake of sufficient size (magnitude 6 or higher) is very low, at 9×10^{-5} per annum (or around 1 in

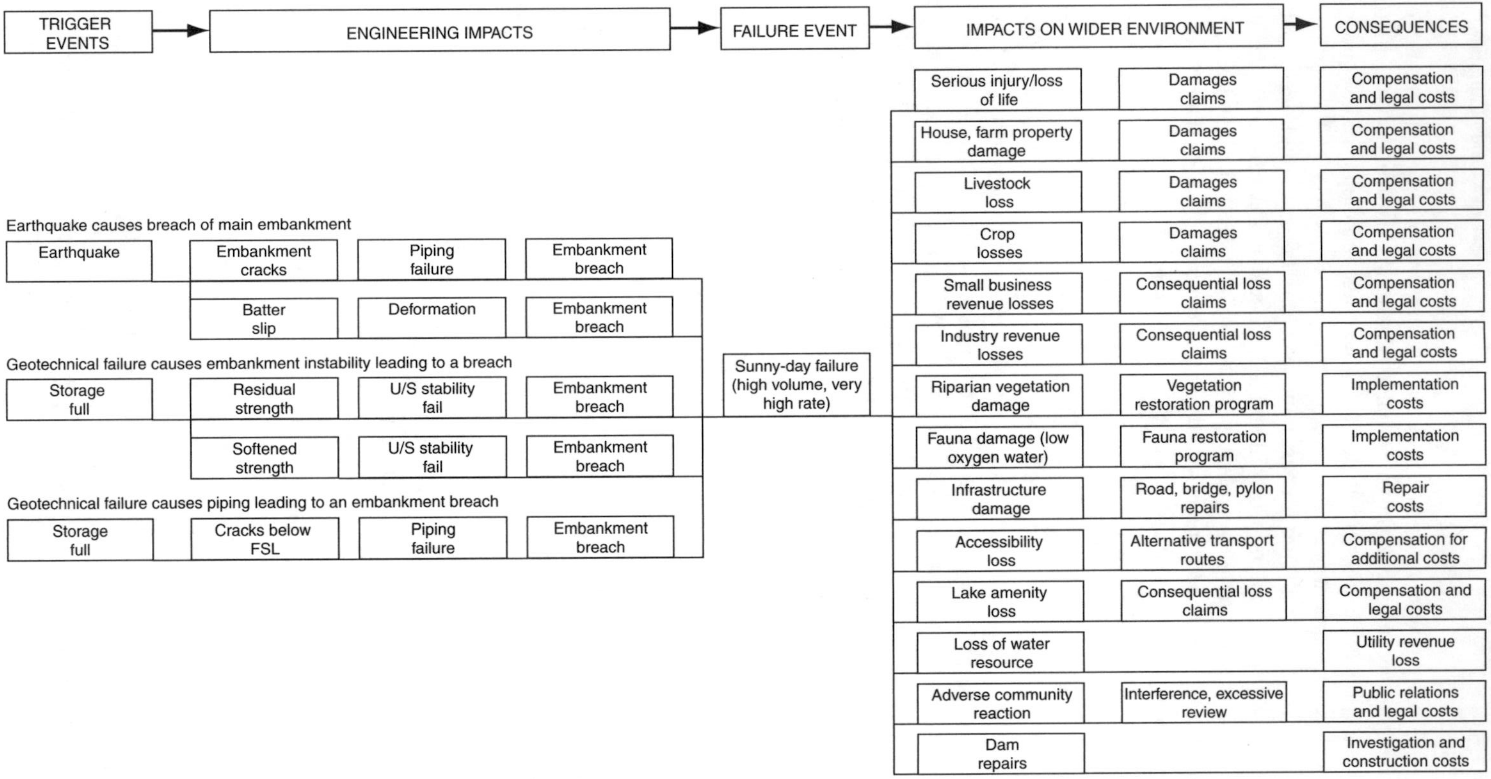

Figure 5.2 Dam failure event tree showing the range of events that could initiate a sunny-day failure and the resultant consequences.

SUNNY-DAY FAILURE TRIGGER EVENTS

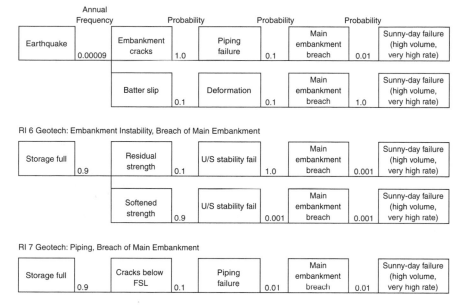

Figure 5.3   Engineering component event tree showing the sequence of impacts, and their probabilities, if an initiating event occurs.

11,000 years). Following the first branch of the event tree, the panel considered that if such an earthquake were to occur, then cracks would form (likelihood is 100 percent) in the embankment. Consequently, the relevant panel expert concluded that there would be a 1 in 10 chance that piping would form within the crack network. If piping were to occur, the expert assessed that there would be a 1 in 100 chance that the piping would be sufficiently extensive to cause the embankment to collapse.

Figure 5.4 shows samples of the 50 and 95 percent confidence level cost estimates provided by the consequences panel and graphical representations of the cost distributions derived from the panel information. The samples show cost estimates associated with infrastructure damage and adverse community reaction that were potential consequences of a sunny-day failure.

All graphical distributions were provided to the appropriate panel members for review and to confirm the nature of the distributions.

Sunny-Day Failure

Sample Issue	Cost Item, CL 50%, CL 95% of log normal distribution	Assumption Central Value
C10 Infrastructure damage	Bridge $1m – $3m	1
	220kV pylons $1m – $2m	1
	Roads $1m – $3m	1
	Board sackings $1m – $2m	1
C14 Adverse community reaction	Excessive ops checks $1m – $2m	1
	Review all storages $10m – $15m	10
	PR campaign $1m – $3m	1
	Legal defense $1m – $4m	1

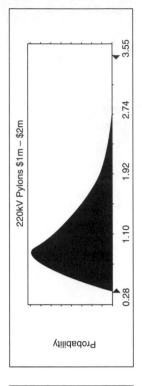

220kV Pylons $1m – $2m

Probability

0.28   1.10   1.92   2.74   3.55

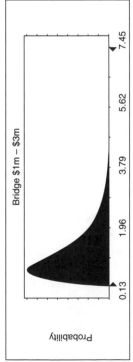

Bridge $1m – $3m

Probability

0.13   1.96   3.79   5.62   7.45

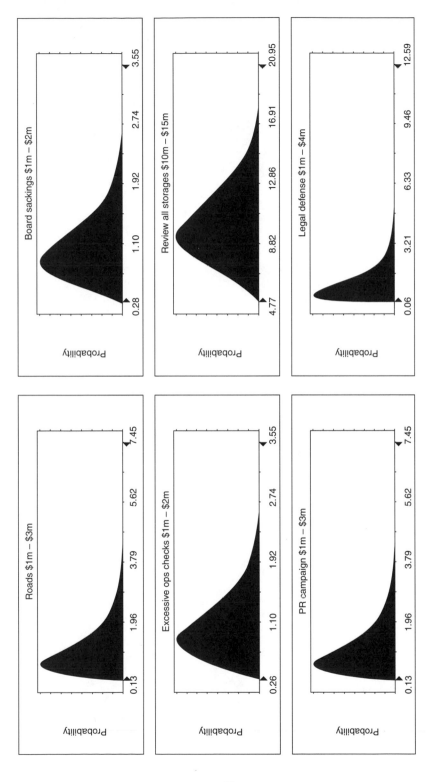

Figure 5.4 Panel outputs and the related cost distributions generated from the panel's "median" and "high" cost estimates.

63

6

STAGE 3: ANALYZE THE RISK

Risk analysis using the RISQUE method involves quantification and modeling of the constituent probabilities and consequences for each identified risk event.

The aim of risk modeling is to process the likelihood and cost information for each risk event (derived from the panel process). Risk modeling derives a quantitative understanding of the characteristics and distribution of risk associated with the situation under evaluation. A number of techniques are applied to derive ranked and proportional profiles of risk quotient and to estimate the potential cost (the risk cost) that may be incurred in the future due to the occurrence of risk events.

QUANTITATIVE MODELING TECHNIQUES

Spreadsheet models are the most appropriate tools for incorporating risk modeling into the RISQUE method. All risk models discussed in this book were created in Microsoft Excel™ spreadsheets. Probabilistic calculations in the analysis were performed using the Crystal Ball™ simulator, which is a commercial add-on software package to Microsoft Excel™. The simulation software computes spreadsheet solutions for at least 2,000 trials, using the Monte Carlo sampling strategy. Simulation using Crystal Ball™ is used in the risk models to not only treat costs as probability distributions but also to permit random distribution of events over specified time intervals. The @Risk™ software package is also an appropriate alternative for performing the probabilistic calculations.

The techniques that have been applied in the RISQUE method have been selected for their suitability to:

- Define risk events in financial terms, so that some provision can be made that accounts for their likelihood of occurrence and consequences
- Account for uncertainty in the likelihood of occurrence of a risk event
- Account for uncertainty in the magnitude of the consequences of a risk event

Outputs of the modeling process express the risk relationships between the events, show the magnitude of combined risk presented by all of the events, and indicate a reasonable estimate of cost that could be incurred due to the occurrence of risk events (risk cost).

Typical outputs of risk modeling include:

- Estimates of risk cost at three predetermined levels of confidence. The different levels are usually representative of a low (optimistic) cost, a conservative yet realistic (planning) cost, and a high (pessimistic) cost.
- A risk profile that shows each risk event ranked in order of decreasing risk quotient. Risk profiles are essentially prioritization tools.
- An exposure profile, which shows the range of consequential cost for the ranked risk events. Exposure profiles are helpful in assessment of whether direct risk management action or further study of an event is more appropriate.

This section describes the main aspects of the risk modeling process and key elements of RISQUE method models. Detailed discussion of specific risk modeling techniques is not provided here. Each application of the RISQUE method requires that case-specific conditions and information be taken into account. For this reason, each RISQUE method model needs to be specifically designed to integrate the unique elements of the situation under consideration with the modeling processes that apply to a wide range of conditions. Therefore, each risk model is different and cannot be constructed according to a set prescription. However, a range of insights into risk model development can be gained from the case studies that are presented in Part Three.

MONTE CARLO SIMULATION

Monte Carlo simulation is a very useful tool for dealing with uncertainty. Monte Carlo simulation is particularly useful in business risk assessment for incorporating uncertainty of magnitude of consequences. Many project managers have heard of this simulation technique but are reluctant to consider its use as a routine analytical tool. To these managers, the term "Monte Carlo simulation" conjures an image of a sophisticated and complicated process, which they would most likely not understand and therefore would not use as a trusted decision-making tool. Monte Carlo simulation is, however, not as difficult to understand or use as it might seem.

What Is Monte Carlo Simulation and How Does It Work?

Monte Carlo simulation is a statistical technique that uses random numbers to account for uncertainty in a mathematical model. Monte Carlo simulation is universally available as commercial spreadsheet add-ins, such as the Microsoft Excel™ add-ins Crystal Ball™ and @Risk™.

Monte Carlo simulation recognizes variables within a calculation as probability distributions rather than single numbers. For example, a network manager considering the purchase of a computer (estimated price $1,600) and color printer (estimated price $1,000) for the business would expect to pay $2,600 in total. In reality, when purchasing the equipment, the budgeted cost may be more or less than the actual purchase price, depending on where the purchases were made. Considering the computer and printer prices as single numbers does not account for variation of price in the market.

In the market, the computer price could average $1,600, but the range could vary from $1,100 to $2,100. Figure 6.1 shows a graph of the computer price in 20 stores. The figure is essentially a probability distribution of computer cost. The graph shows that the distribution is uniformly bell shaped and that the most common price (in four stores) is $1,600. If it is assumed that the computer will be purchased at any of the stores on a random basis, then there is a 4 in 20 (or 20 percent) chance that the computer will cost $1,600. The lowest price of $1,100 is available only in one store; therefore, there is a 1 in 20 (5 percent) chance that the price will be $1,100. Similarly, there is a 5 percent chance that the price will be $2,100. Judging from the computer cost distribution, it can be seen that there is a 75 percent chance that the cost will not exceed $1,700 (the price is more than $1,700 in five out of 20 shops).

Figure 6.2 shows the cost distribution for the printer. The printer cost distribution is not uniformly bell shaped but is skewed heavily toward the higher end of the cost range. This figure shows that the printer cost could vary from $500 to $1,600, with the most common cost being $800. Considering the price in all 20 stores, the average printer price is $1,000 and there is a 75 percent chance that the cost will not exceed $1,200.

Taking note of the cost distributions of the computer and printer, the chance that the network manager will pay the lowest combined price of $1,600 or the highest combined price of $3,700 is considerably lower than the chance of paying around the average combined price. In this example, Monte Carlo simulation calculates the combined cost of the two items not as single numbers but as cost distributions. The results are expressed as a range of possible outcomes together with the likelihood of each outcome.

Within the modeling software, the Monte Carlo simulation is complex; however, the overall process is simple. Monte Carlo simulation essentially considers

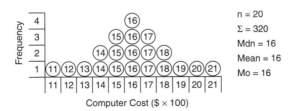

Figure 6.1   Computer cost distribution represented by a set of numbered balls.

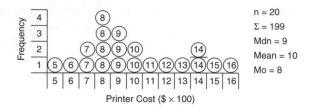

Figure 6.2   Printer cost distribution represented by a set of numbered balls.

the cost distributions in the office computer equipment example as numbered balls inside lottery barrels. The computer barrel would therefore contain one $1,100 ball, one $1,200 ball, one $1,300 ball, two $1,400 balls, three $1,500 balls, and so on. It is therefore three times more likely that a $1,500 ball would be drawn from the barrel than a $1,100 ball, for example. In adding the two costs, the computer randomly pulls out a ball from each barrel, calculates the combined cost, and remembers the result. The balls are replaced and the process is repeated, usually many times. Using this approach, the output of Monte Carlo simulation appears as a frequency distribution.

Table 6.1 shows Monte Carlo simulation forecast values for a small number (30) of trials. In this example, for the first trial the printer price was $800 and the computer cost was $1,700, deriving a combined cost of $2,500.

Figure 6.3 shows the results of the Monte Carlo simulation in graphical form. The figure shows the frequency of each possible cost for the printer and computer.

Table 6.1   Office Computer Equipment Example—Forecast Values from 30 Trials

Trial Number	Printer ($)	Computer ($)	Printer and Computer ($)	Trial Number	Printer ($)	Computer ($)	Printer and Computer ($)
1	800	1,700	2,500	16	800	1,300	2,100
2	700	1,500	2,200	17	900	2,000	2,900
3	1,400	2,100	3,500	18	1,000	1,500	2,500
4	1,500	1,800	3,300	19	900	1,600	2,500
5	600	1,600	2,200	20	1,400	1,200	2,600
6	1,500	1,700	3,200	21	800	1,200	2,000
7	1,000	1,500	2,500	22	900	1,600	2,500
8	900	1,500	2,400	23	1,100	1,400	2,500
9	1,600	1,900	3,500	24	500	1,800	2,300
10	900	1,300	2,200	25	600	1,400	2,000
11	600	1,500	2,100	26	900	1,600	2,500
12	1,000	1,500	2,500	27	1,500	2,000	3,500
13	1,000	1,600	2,600	28	1,000	1,900	2,900
14	1,400	1,300	2,700	29	900	2,000	2,900
15	1,500	1,700	3,200	30	1,600	1,200	2,800

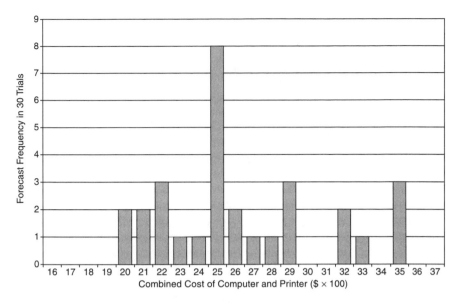

Figure 6.3   Monte Carlo output for computer plus printer after 30 trials showing the frequency of occurrence for each number and the uneven nature of the distribution.

It shows that several possible costs did not occur during the limited number of trials and that the simulated range was $2,000 to $3,500, which is narrower than the potential range of $1,600 to $3,700. The graph also shows that the most common cost derived was $2,500, which occurred in eight of the 30 trials. This figure also indicates the probability of exceeding a given cost. For example, the cost in 24 (80 percent) of the trials was less than $3,200; therefore, on the basis of these 30 trials, the likelihood of exceeding a cost of $3,200 is 20 percent. Thus, on the basis of 30 trials, there is a 20 percent chance that the network manager will pay more than $3,200 for the printer and computer and negligible chance that the total cost will exceed $3,500.

Only 30 trials were performed in the preceding example. While the frequency chart of Figure 6.3 provides an indication of the cost distribution (particularly central values), the forecast distribution has substantial gaps and does not include costs from the entire range of possible outcomes. The results from 30 trials clearly show that the distribution based on a limited number of trials is strongly affected by random chance and is most likely not representative of the combined cost if a larger number of trials were undertaken. Figure 6.4 shows the example Monte Carlo simulation frequency chart for 2,000 trials. It shows a much smoother distribution that also covers the entire range of possible outcomes.

As a general rule, greater precision in outcome (particularly toward the tails, or ends, of forecast distributions) can be obtained by performing larger numbers of trials. For example, if 100 trials are performed, then on five occasions it is expected that numbers would be generated that exceed the 95 percent level of confidence

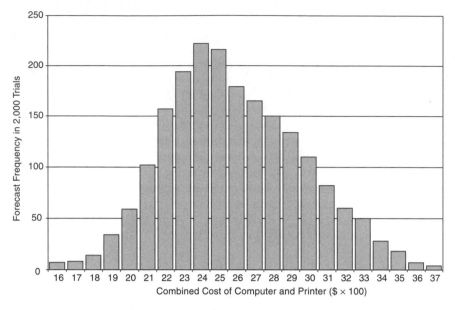

Figure 6.4 **Monte Carlo output for computer plus printer after 2,000 trials showing the frequency of occurrence for each number and the even nature of the distribution.**

limit (i.e., a probability of 5 percent of being exceeded). In this case, the five forecasts generated may cover a wide and uneven range of values. Alternatively, if 1,000 trials are performed, then it is expected that approximately 50 values would exceed the 95 percent level of confidence, which would provide more precise information to interpret the potential cost at the high end of the range.

On the basis of 2,000 trials, there is a 20 percent chance that the network manager will pay more than $2,900 for the printer and computer, and there is a 0.65 percent chance that the total cost will exceed $3,500.

In this book, 2,000 trials are usually used in the examples provided.

Application of Monte Carlo Simulation to Risk Analysis

Quantification of risk involves numerical estimation of likelihoods and consequences. There is considerable uncertainty in estimation of potential consequences for most risk events. As stated earlier, Monte Carlo simulation is particularly useful in business risk assessment for incorporating uncertainty with respect to magnitude of consequences.

Consider the potential consequences of a transport union blockade on a chemical manufacturer resulting in temporary shutdown of the plant. Under union embargo circumstances, there would be direct loss of revenue (not including subsequent loss of market share) from lost production for some period. Assuming that the unit value of production is set by contract (constant), then potential direct revenue losses would vary depending on the stage in the production cycle during the shutdown period and on the duration of the break in production. The losses would be estimated by multiplying the known product value by the rate of lost production (variable) by the duration of production loss (variable).

Competent production managers should readily identify uncertainties associated with the rate of lost production. They should be able to define the most commonly achieved (the median) production rate, together with the production rate achieved for specific percentages of operating time (i.e., production at various levels of confidence). The production rates then can be input to the Monte Carlo simulation model as a reasonably clearly defined probability distribution.

On the other hand, industrial relations officers are unlikely to have comprehensive performance data that will allow as precise an estimate of the probability distribution applicable to duration of the embargo period. They will have to base an estimate on factors such as union attitude, company responsiveness to demands, and duration of stoppages elsewhere. These officers might estimate, for example, that the most likely expected stoppage duration is around 10 days and that there is a low (approximately 5 percent), but not extremely low, chance that the duration could exceed 20 days. Under these circumstances, the stoppage duration estimates could reasonably be defined by a log-normal probability distribution that can be input to the Monte Carlo simulation model.

After deriving the inputs for estimation of the value of lost production, the Monte Carlo simulation model would be used to calculate the outcomes for a large number of trials. The potential dollar value of lost production would be determined for any desired level of confidence.

Conservatism and Levels of Confidence

The level of confidence that is used for financial planning purposes depends on the conservativeness of the ultimate decision-maker. For example, a highly conservative manager would tend to reserve a cost estimate at very high levels of confidence of around 95 to 99 percent (i.e., the costs have very low likelihoods, 1 to 5 percent, of being exceeded).

Operations managers are generally more tolerant of risk and prefer not to reserve funds that may never be called on and that could otherwise be put to good operational use. Operations managers therefore are more likely to reserve a cost estimate at lower levels of confidence (65 to 85 percent), which are considered to be conservatively high but not so excessive that business is restricted.

The use of probability distributions and Monte Carlo simulation to describe consequences has additional value. In cases where estimates of cost are based on single values, many experts will be involved in deriving the entire suite of costs. Each estimate from each person reflects that person's level of conservatism. If most of the experts feel that they need to be conservative, then the end result of adding all of the contributory costs is a highly inflated estimate of cost. As a consequence, when the decision-makers (i.e., board members) add a margin reflecting their own level of conservatism, the excessively conservative result can needlessly kill a potentially viable business project.

Where Monte Carlo simulation is used, the probability distributions contain all of the experience, knowledge, and degree of uncertainty that has been relayed by the individuals on the expert panel. The probability distributions utilize expert opinion but do not utilize judgment based on the conservatism of individual experts. For this reason, the integrity of the expert information is retained throughout the analysis where Monte Carlo simulation is applied, while the level of conservatism that is applied to the result rests, rightfully, with the ultimate decision-makers.

CALCULATE RISK QUOTIENT

The risk quotient for each event is calculated directly in the model by multiplying likelihood and cost.

Likelihood

The probabilities obtained from the expert panel are worked into an event-tree format and input directly to the risk model. The frequency of each event is calculated by multiplying the frequency (annual or over a set period, such as the selected project life) of the trigger event by the product of all of the subsequent probabilities along the entire branch of the event tree.

Cost

The cost of occurrence of each event identified by the panel can be input to the model at any level of detail and complexity, depending on the nature of the situation being modeled, the degree of precision required (usually relatively low for preliminary evaluations), and the availability of information.

In some cases, the panel experts may have to rely heavily on their judgment based on experience in other situations; therefore, a precise, detailed estimate of cost is not possible or defensible. Under these circumstances the risk event cost estimate that is input to the model will be in the form of a log-normal distribution characterized by the median and 95 percent confidence-level estimates provided by the panel.

In other cases, the cost estimate may involve a complex calculation based on, for example, a schedule of rates and quantities, together with probability distributions to represent each component in the costing.

Incorporation of the time value of money is a very important aspect of cost estimation for many situations. Many applications of the RISQUE method are concerned with evaluation of the financial exposure over the duration of the project period that has been selected. Under these circumstances the potential timing of risk cost expenditure needs to be taken into account and can make a substantial impact on the viability of a project.

Most business decisions are based on financial models that express money as net present value (NPV). NPV is the net present value of an investment over a period of time, calculated using a discount rate and a series of future payments and incomes. Project managers usually require that the risk modeling results are incorporated into the financial business model; therefore, the risk model results must often be provided in NPV dollar terms.

In such cases, the panel opinion on when risk event could possibly occur needs to be input to the risk model. Project managers must select the discount rate used to calculate NPV. The discount rate selected needs to reflect the nature and attitude of the business under evaluation and should be defensible.

In some cases project managers may not be able to reveal the corporate discount rate due to the need for confidentiality. Under these circumstances, risk analysts can select and use an alternative discount rate that is acceptable to the project managers. The latter should be able to assess the impact of using the alternative rate instead of the corporate rate.

Most risk models are constructed to include a schedule of exposure to the consequences of risk events in order to take into consideration potential timing of future expenditure or income. The risk model can handle estimation of the time value of money in several ways.

In some cases, the conservative assumption can be made in the model that the risk event occurs at the earliest possible time. The assumption is reasonable where the potential time range over which the event can occur is relatively short, say one to four years. The assumption becomes much more conservative where the risk event could occur at any time over, say, a 20-year period.

Similarly, a much less conservative assumption can be made that the event occurs at the midpoint of the time period. This assumption usually is not sufficiently conservative for most project managers, particularly if many of the risk events could occur at any time over the project period.

Where necessary, more complex risk models have been designed to overcome the limitations set by the above types of assumption. The model structure allows each risk event to occur at random over the time frame specified by the panel. Where the consequences of a risk event involve expenditure of ongoing costs, such as capital and operating costs, the exposure is calculated as NPV and that value (the current dollar value) is assumed to occur at random over the appropriate time frame.

The occurrence cost of each risk event is computed in the risk model, and the costs can be expressed at any selected level of confidence.

Risk Quotient

Deriving an estimate of risk expressed as a probability distribution is relatively straightforward. However, probabilistic expressions of risk quotient would not help decision-makers gain an understanding of risk. (Indeed, probabilistic expressions of risk quotient would be potentially confusing.) In the RISQUE method, quantitative estimates of risk quotient are used for comparative purposes only; consistently derived, single-point estimates of risk quotient therefore can be meaningfully applied to risk assessment.

For each consequence, the RISQUE method can calculate risk quotient in two alternative ways: (1) use a best estimate and (2) use a conservatively high estimate of consequence. The simplest (and often the most appropriate) way is to multiply the total likelihood of a risk event occurring by the estimated cost at the 50 percent confidence level, provided by the panel. This alternative derives an expression of risk that most closely represents a "best-estimate" approach.

Risk analysts also can use a probabilistic method to determine a conservative estimate of consequence (say the 80 percent confidence level) and multiply the conservative cost estimate by likelihood to derive a more conservative expression of risk quotient.

GENERATE RISK PROFILES AND MAPS

Risk profiles and risk maps show the relationships between risk events and how the total risk is distributed across the risk events. They permit differentiation of events, first on the basis of risk quotient, then on the basis of the component parts: likelihood and/or cost. Risk profiles and maps can be produced in various forms to demonstrate the relationships between risk events. Finally, risk profiles and maps provide inputs for risk analysis.

Ranked Risk Profiles

Ranking risk events in order of decreasing risk quotient and then graphically plotting the results creates ranked risk profiles. Ranked risk profiles clearly indicate relationships, such as the relative magnitude of risk quotient for each event, and show which events are the riskiest, and those that are the least risky. Ranked risk profiles are extremely useful in prioritizing risk events. Figure 2.1 is an example of a ranked risk profile produced for the mining example.

Proportional Risk Profiles

Proportional risk profiles are derived by expressing risk as a proportion of the total risk presented by all risk events. Proportional risk profiles show how much risk each event, or a group of events, contributes to the total risk presented by all risk events. Proportional risk profiles indicate which events contribute to most of the risk and which do not contribute significantly to total risk. Proportional risk profiles are useful for differentiating between events, particularly with respect to identification of the impacts on total risk of risk reduction measures for specific risk events. Figure 6.5 is an example of a proportional risk profile produced for the mining example.

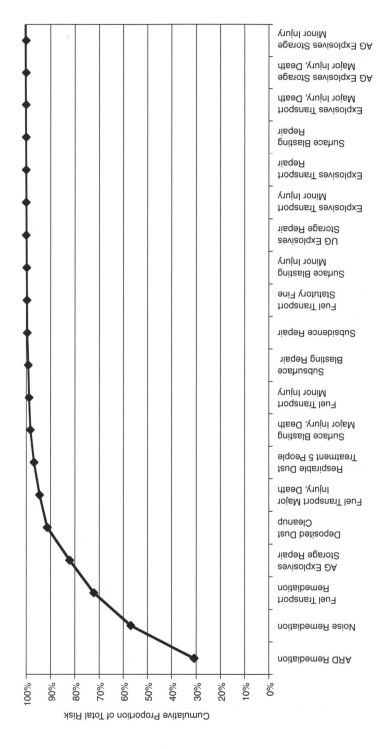

Figure 6.5 Cumulative risk profile showing the progressive increase in risk as each event is included.

Exposure Profiles

The RISQUE method uses calculated risk quotient for strictly comparative purposes. Although the risk quotient is expressed in monetary value over time (i.e., dollars per year), the actual risk quotient usually does not provide a practical indication of the financial exposure that could be incurred by each risk event over the life of a business.

Unlike risk profiles, exposure profiles show the financial exposure that would be derived from occurrence of each risk event. Exposure profiles usually are ranked in order of decreasing risk quotient. Financial exposure profiles usually express the estimated cost at three levels of confidence (optimistic, pessimistic, and planning), so that the amount of inherent uncertainty contained within the estimate is easy to recognize.

Risk Maps

Risk maps are graphs that show the probability of a risk event occurring plotted against the consequences (e.g., financial cost or lives lost). The location of the point on the risk map where the values intersect is equivalent to the risk quotient. Risk maps usually show the variables plotted on logarithmic axes because probability and cost usually vary by orders of magnitude. Lines of equal risk quotient are frequently drawn on risk maps and are very useful for comparing risk presented by highly diverse risk events. In addition, risk maps clearly differentiate between risk events that pose similar risk, but differ substantially in their component likelihoods or consequences.

Figure 6.6 is a risk map that shows an insurance example of the risk relationships for the home and car described in Chapter 2. The risk map also shows plots of the commercial third-party liability and tailings dam examples discussed in Chapter 15.

Chapter 7 describes, in the discussion of formulation of risk management strategy, the ways in which the types of risk profile are interpreted and used in risk analysis.

CALCULATE RISK COST: THRESHOLD METHOD

Risk cost is a reasonable estimate of the combined cost that will be incurred over a specified future time period due to the occurrence of risk events. For most businesses, risk cost is an important component of future expenditure and should be allowed for during business planning.

Uncertainty associated with forecasting the magnitude of future costs is well recognized. Forecasts of risk costs contain the additional uncertainty of whether specific risk events will occur in the future. It is clearly not possible to predict

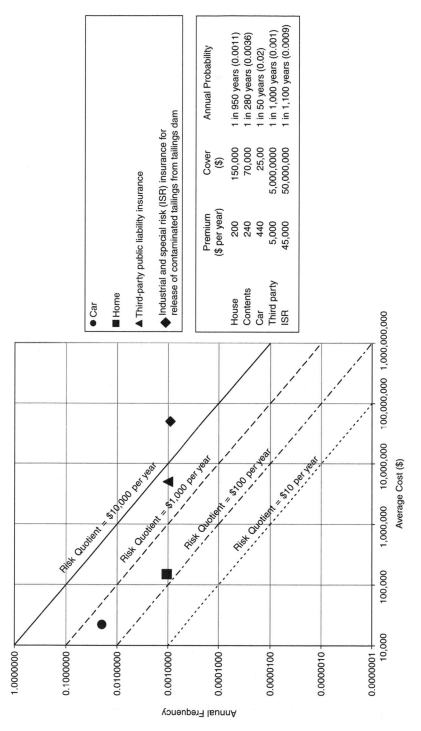

Figure 6.6 Example risk map showing the relationship between risk quotient, likelihood, and cost using a household insurance illustration.

Legend:

● Car
■ Home
▲ Third-party public liability insurance
◆ Industrial and special risk (ISR) insurance for release of contaminated tailings from tailings dam

	Premium ($ per year)	Cover ($)	Annual Probability
House	200	150,000	1 in 950 years (0.0011)
Contents	240	70,000	1 in 280 years (0.0036)
Car	440	25,00	1 in 50 years (0.02)
Third party	5,000	5,000,0000	1 in 1,000 years (0.001)
ISR	45,000	50,000,000	1 in 1,100 years (0.0009)

Chart axes:
- Y-axis: Annual Frequency (1.0000000, 0.1000000, 0.0100000, 0.0010000, 0.0001000, 0.0000100, 0.0000010, 0.0000001)
- X-axis: Average Cost ($) (10,000, 100,000, 1,000,000, 10,000,000, 100,000,000, 1,000,000,000)

Diagonal lines:
- Risk Quotient = $10,000 per year
- Risk Quotient = $1,000 per year
- Risk Quotient = $100 per year
- Risk Quotient = $10 per year

which events will actually occur in the future; for this reason, an estimate of risk cost is a best estimate of the future cost of risk events.

For any business or activity, there is a possibility that no risk events will occur over a given future period. At the other end of the scale, there is also a possibility that all of the identified risk events will occur in the future. It is usually reasonable to assume that some, but not all, of the risk events will occur in the future. In order to derive an estimate of risk cost, it is necessary, therefore, to assume that certain risk events will occur over the specified future time interval and that the risk cost is the total cost of occurrence of those events.

The assumption of whether a risk event occurs, and is therefore included in the risk cost calculation, can be made according to two methods: (1) the threshold method and (2) the chance method.

The threshold method differentiates between occurrence of risk events on the basis of risk, that is, the risk quotient, and assumes that the most risky events occur. This method is appropriate for all estimates of risk cost. It is used by the RISQUE method mainly where selection of the risk events that are assumed to occur is based on the risk presented by the events, as represented by risk profiles derived during the risk analysis process.

Risk cost is calculated by the threshold method as the cost of consequences for the riskiest events and is expressed as a cost distribution. The threshold that separates the riskiest events from the remainder can be selected on the basis of two measures: (1) the quantum of risk quotient or (2) the contribution to overall risk. In practice, both measures usually are considered prior to selection of a specific measure to represent the threshold that defines the riskiest events.

Threshold Based on Risk Quotient

Quantified estimates of risk quotient usually do not directly relate to business costs, and a quantum of risk quotient has limited meaning in a business sense. For this reason, selection of risk thresholds on the basis of risk quotient is more difficult.

Most ranked risk profiles show that there is a substantial difference in the quantum of risk quotient posed by each of a small proportion of relatively high-risk events and the risk posed by each of the remaining events. A common method of selecting the threshold is to evaluate the ranked risk profile in order to identify those events that are clearly the riskiest and then select the risk threshold to include those events.

For example, the mining example ranked risk profile of Figure 2.1 shows that the risk posed by each of the five most risky events (which all exceed a risk quotient of $100 per year) is substantially higher than the risk posed by the other 15 events. In this case the risk analysts could select $100 per year as the risk threshold and calculate the risk cost as the combined occurrence cost of the five riskiest events. However, risk analysts could have justifiably selected the threshold to include the eight most risky events, because the remaining 13 events pose risk at an order of magnitude less than the other four events.

An alternative method, based on experience and judgment, can be used to select (or verify) a risk threshold. In this case, project managers, with assistance from risk analysts, review the ranked risk profile in order to link quantitative estimates of risk quotient with perceived risk. During this process, project managers evaluate the low-risk events and progressively scan upward along the risk profile.

When scanning a ranked risk profile, risk managers usually can identify some specific risk events that, on the basis of experience or intuition, do not pose substantial risk and that project managers would feel comfortable about excluding from the estimate of risk cost at that time. Project managers then are able to attach a maximum risk quotient to those specific events. The risk quotient (which becomes the risk threshold) also indicates that events posing similar or lower risk should be excluded from the risk cost calculation.

Threshold Based on Contribution to Overall Risk

Proportional risk profiles also are used (usually concurrently with ranked risk profiles) to identify appropriate risk thresholds. Using this approach, project managers (assisted by risk analysts) select the risk threshold on the basis of proportional risk. Project managers select a risk quotient threshold that includes all risk events that together contribute to more than a given percentage of the total risk.

The risk threshold, which is dependent on the shape and slope of the cumulative risk curve, usually includes events that together contribute between 80 and 95 percent of total risk. Risk managers often feel that thresholds that include less than 80 percent of the total risk are likely to exclude exposure to important events from the risk cost estimate. On the other hand, the proportional risk profile frequently indicates that a threshold that incorporates more than 95 percent of the contribution to overall risk is very conservative and that the estimated risk cost would be excessively high.

For example, the mining example proportional risk profile of Figure 6.5 shows that the five most risky events together contribute to approximately 92 percent of the total risk. The risk threshold could, therefore, be set to include the occurrence cost of only the five most risky events in the estimate of risk cost. However, project managers may consider that the estimate of risk cost needs to be more conservative and include the cost of events that contribute to a higher proportion of the total risk.

Examination of Figure 6.5 shows that the eight most risky events contribute to almost 98 percent of the total risk. The risk manager may consider that the more conservative threshold is appropriate and include the cost of the events that together contribute to 95 percent or less of total risk in the estimate of risk cost.

Sensitivity to Threshold

Both of the approaches to selection of the threshold are defensible because they are based on clear interpretation of relative risk. However, the decision of which approach to use can be arbitrary. The risk analyst should perform sensitivity calculations to evaluate the impact of threshold selection on the ultimate estimate of risk cost. Where the risk cost estimate is sensitive to the threshold selected, risk analysts should report this sensitivity together with the risk cost.

Threshold Selection across Options

When risk assessment aims at comparing the risk posed by several options, a single risk threshold must be applied across all of the alternatives under consideration. When a substantial difference exists between the risk posed by some options, the number of events included in calculation of risk quotient cost can vary widely between options. The experience approach to threshold selection is highly applicable to selection of a consistent risk threshold across different options. Project managers should evaluate the risk profiles for all options to ensure that risk events that could, in reality, pose substantial risk are not excluded from estimates of risk cost.

Risk Cost

Using the threshold method, the occurrence costs of the events that lie above the selected risk threshold are expressed as probability distributions; therefore, the combined cost of consequences for the riskiest events is also expressed as a cost distribution. Risk cost is calculated using Monte Carlo simulation. The risk cost usually is reported at three levels of confidence.

Project managers usually consider the 50 percent confidence level to represent an optimistic calculation of cost. At the other end of the scale, they usually feel the 90 to 99 percent range of confidence levels to represent pessimistic estimates of risk cost. Project managers often consider conservative but reasonable estimates of cost to lie within the 70 to 85 percent range of confidence levels.

CALCULATE RISK COST: CHANCE METHOD

The chance method is an alternative method of calculating risk cost. This method assumes that a risk event occurs according to its probability of occurrence. For example, the cost of a risk event with an 80 percent chance of occurring will be included in the risk cost calculation in 80 percent of trial simulations. Where most risk event frequencies are relatively low, the chance method inevitably returns a lower risk cost than the threshold method at any given level of confidence. The risk cost calculated using the threshold method always includes the cost of high-risk events, regardless of whether they have a low likelihood of occurring. The chance method, on the other hand, effectively excludes the cost of all risk events that have a lower chance of occurring than the lowest confidence level selected to represent the risk cost.

A risk event that has a relatively low probability of occurrence but a very high cost compared with the other risk events serves as a simple example that demonstrates the difference between the threshold method and the chance method. In this example the event has the highest risk quotient of all risk events but a probability of occurrence of 1 in 100.

Using the threshold method, the very high cost associated with the riskiest event would be included in the estimate of risk cost in all trials and would be a contributor to the risk cost at all levels of confidence, notwithstanding its relatively low chance of occurrence. In this case, financial exposure is determined by risk, that is, the true combination of likelihood and cost.

Using the chance method, the risk event will occur only once in every 100 trials of the model. The model returns a zero consequence for each of the other 99 trials. In this case, the major cost item would be excluded from the estimate of risk cost at all levels of confidence lower than 99 percent. For an event with a 0.1 percent likelihood (which is typical of many residual risk events), the event would occur once every 1,000 trials and returns a zero consequence for the other 999 trials. In this case, financial exposure is effectively determined by likelihood alone, and the estimate of risk cost therefore does not truly incorporate the concept of risk.

Despite the acknowledged limitation, the chance method is mathematically correct. It derives true estimates of the probability distribution of risk cost and can be used to derive estimates of risk cost that can be predicted for any desired confidence limit. Risk cost calculated by the chance method is appropriate where the likelihoods of all of the risk events are substantially greater than the probability of exceeding the upper (pessimistic) confidence level selected to describe risk cost.

The chance method is appropriate for risk events with high likelihoods of occurrence, but it quickly becomes limiting where a relatively low likelihood of occurrence exists. The RISQUE method uses the chance method when all risk events have a relatively high likelihood of occurrence (usually greater than a 10 percent chance).

Application of the Chance Method: Example

In this example, the chance method was used to assist the negotiation process with respect to the sale of contaminated land. The land had previously been used for industrial purposes, and site investigations demonstrated that some areas of the site were contaminated. In addition, while other areas of the site were not proven to be contaminated, the environmental specialist identified them as having some likelihood of contamination.

Both the vendor and the intended purchaser agreed that the price should be discounted to some extent to provide for the cost of environmental remediation. The parties therefore needed to reach agreement on a fair and justifiable estimate of remediation cost. At the commencement of the negotiation process, each party

Table 6.2   Cost Estimate for Environmental Impairment

		Estimated Cost ($ × 1,000)	
Event	Likelihood	Mean (50% CL)	High (95% CL)
Existing oil spill—soil clean-up	100%	500	1,200
Undiscovered oil spill—soil clean-up	80%	350	650
Existing USTs—removal	100%	120	200
Undiscovered USTs—removal	70%	120	200
Groundwater contamination—interception	60%	1,200	2,000
PCB-contaminated soil—removal	40%	200	600

derived initial estimates of remediation costs. However, the estimated remediation costs were strongly divergent, due to inherent uncertainty of the extent, cost, and severity of contamination, and possibly also due to differing perspectives on the sale and levels of conservatism.

The chance method was used to estimate remediation costs. Table 6.2 shows a list of the contamination issues on site, their probabilities of occurrence within the next three years, the estimated mean cost, and the estimated high cost at the 95 percent confidence level. Two of the issues (cleanup of an existing oil spill and removal of several underground storage tanks) were known to require remediation; the likelihood of occurrence of the remaining four issues ranged from 40 to 80 percent.

The costs were entered into the spreadsheet model as probability distributions, not as single-point values, and a log-normal distribution was applied to the costs. The model was run using Monte Carlo simulation and the answer was calculated 2,000 times. The estimated cost was a forecast distribution that showed the likelihood of incurring specific costs. Figure 6.7 shows a plot of the forecast distribution and the estimated remediation cost at 10 percent confidence-level intervals. It shows that the range of cost derived by the simulation was $250,000 to $5.1 million.

Together, the parties reviewed the inputs to the model and agreed that the derived costs were representative of site conditions. The parties discussed the estimated rehabilitation cost distribution and agreed that a cost of $2.6 million (the 80 percent confidence level) was a reasonable cost estimate of the potential rehabilitation cost, which should be discounted from the sale price.

APPLICATION OF RISK MODELING RESULTS

Output from the risk modeling is used to derive an understanding (on the basis of risk) of whether the exposure to risk is acceptable. If the exposure is unacceptable,

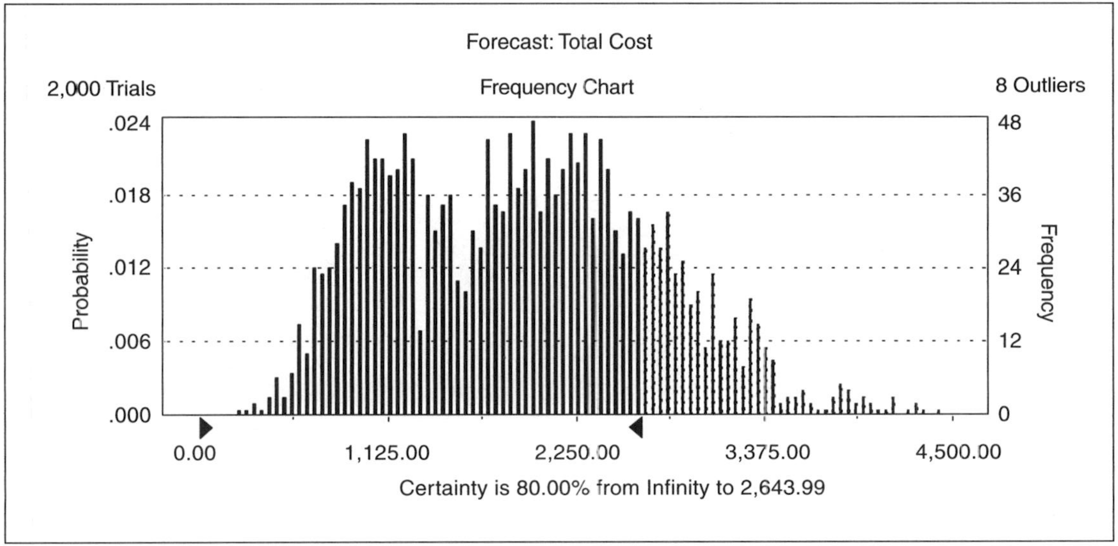

Forecast: Total Cost	
Percentile	Value
0%	248.93
10%	917.23
20%	1,139.53
30%	1,389.61
40%	1,705.39
50%	1,938.85
60%	2,166.70
70%	2,384.45
80%	2,643.99
90%	2,987.41
100%	5,110.04

Figure 6.7 Typical forecast distribution and estimated remediation costs including the forecast cost at selected confidence levels.

and project managers are responsible for the risk (or may be deciding whether to become responsible), then ways of reducing the risk need to be developed.

Identification of risk treatment options is carried out concurrently with assessment of the potential benefits and costs of reducing the exposure to risk to acceptable levels. These actions are important steps in the process of formulating a risk treatment strategy, which is discussed in Chapter 7.

WATER UTILITY EXAMPLE

The following water utility example demonstrates application of the steps in the risk analysis stage.

The event tree of Figure 6.8 shows that the annual frequency of a sunny-day failure caused by earthquake-induced cracking of the embankment is estimated to be 9×10^{-8} per year (or around 1 in 11 million years). The estimated frequency of a sunny-day failure caused by earthquake-induced slippage of the embankment is estimated to be 9×10^{-7} per year (or around 1 in 1.1 million years).

The total likelihood of an earthquake triggering a sunny-day failure was estimated, by summing the above frequencies, to be 9.9×10^{-7} per year (or around 1 in 1 million years). The event tree shows that earthquake-induced slippage of the embankment is the predominant contributor to the total likelihood of earthquake-induced sunny-day failure.

Figure 6.8 indicates that the likelihood of sunny-day failure of the embankment due to all trigger events is estimated to be 1.01×10^{-4} per year (or almost 1 in 10,000 years). The likelihood of embankment instability during full storage conditions (9.08×10^{-5} per year) is by far the greatest contributor to the overall likelihood of sunny-day failure.

Figure 6.9 indicates the forecast distribution chart of consequential cost assuming that a sunny-day failure occurs. It also includes a table of forecast cost for increasing confidence level intervals of 5 percent. The chart shows that the estimated cost distribution is highly skewed toward the high cost end. A central estimate for the consequential cost of a sunny-day failure would be approximately $350 million. The table shows that the lowest cost estimate computed during the 2,000 trials was around $120 million; the highest calculated cost derived in the trials was approximately $5 billion.

The Utility decided that for the assessment, a conservative yet reasonable cost that could be used for planning purposes would be defined as the 80 percent confidence-level cost. The Utility selected the 50 percent confidence-level cost as representing an optimistic position and the 95 percent confidence-level cost as pessimistic. In the sunny-day failure example, the estimated optimistic cost, planning cost, and pessimistic cost values were approximately $340 million, $560 million, and $1 billion, respectively.

Table 6.3 shows the calculated risk quotient, using the conservative estimate of consequence cost, for each dam failure type. It also shows the total risk (the sum of the risk quotients of all failure types) posed by the dam.

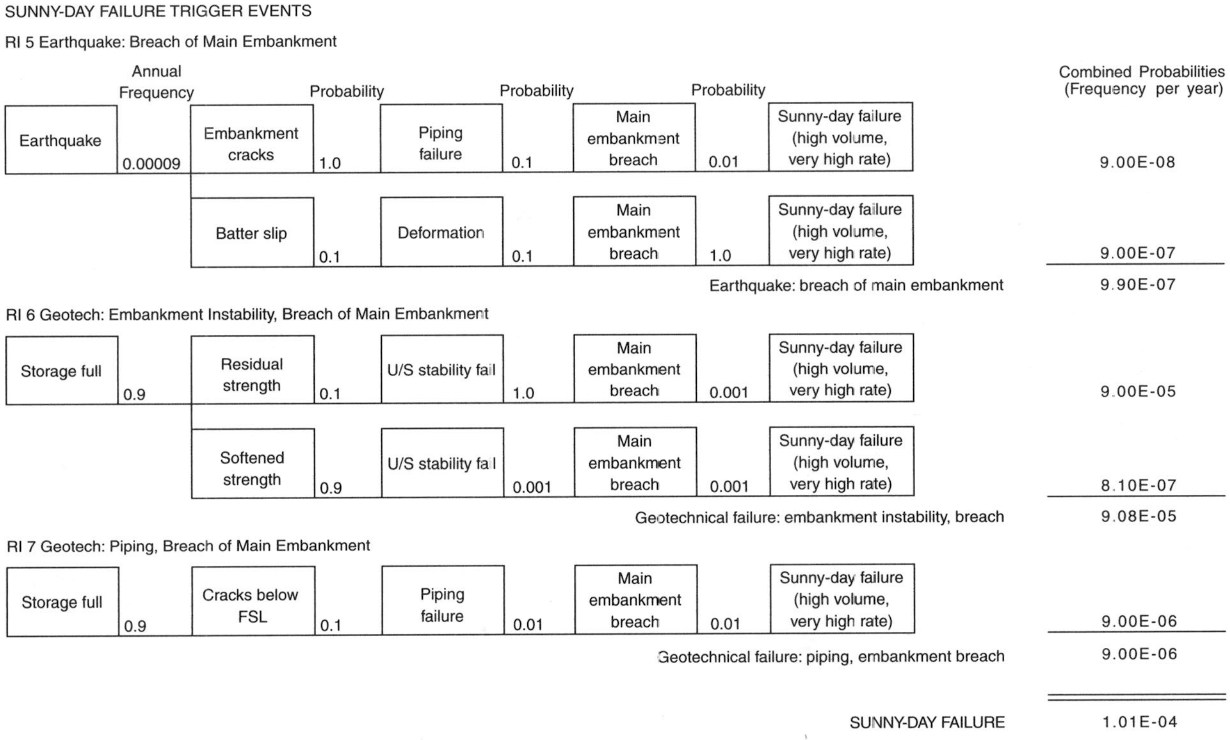

SUNNY-DAY FAILURE TRIGGER EVENTS

RI 5 Earthquake: Breach of Main Embankment

	Annual Frequency		Probability		Probability		Probability		Combined Probabilities (Frequency per year)
Earthquake	0.00009	Embankment cracks	1.0	Piping failure	0.1	Main embankment breach	0.01	Sunny-day failure (high volume, very high rate)	9.00E-08
		Batter slip	0.1	Deformation	0.1	Main embankment breach	1.0	Sunny-day failure (high volume, very high rate)	9.00E-07

Earthquake: breach of main embankment   9.90E-07

RI 6 Geotech: Embankment Instability, Breach of Main Embankment

Storage full	0.9	Residual strength	0.1	U/S stability fail	1.0	Main embankment breach	0.001	Sunny-day failure (high volume, very high rate)	9.00E-05
		Softened strength	0.9	U/S stability fail	0.001	Main embankment breach	0.001	Sunny-day failure (high volume, very high rate)	8.10E-07

Geotechnical failure: embankment instability, breach   9.08E-05

RI 7 Geotech: Piping, Breach of Main Embankment

Storage full	0.9	Cracks below FSL	0.1	Piping failure	0.01	Main embankment breach	0.01	Sunny-day failure (high volume, very high rate)	9.00E-06

Geotechnical failure: piping, embankment breach   9.00E-06

SUNNY-DAY FAILURE   1.01E-04

Figure 6.8   Sunny-day failure event tree showing the combined probabilities of events that could lead to a sunny-day failure.

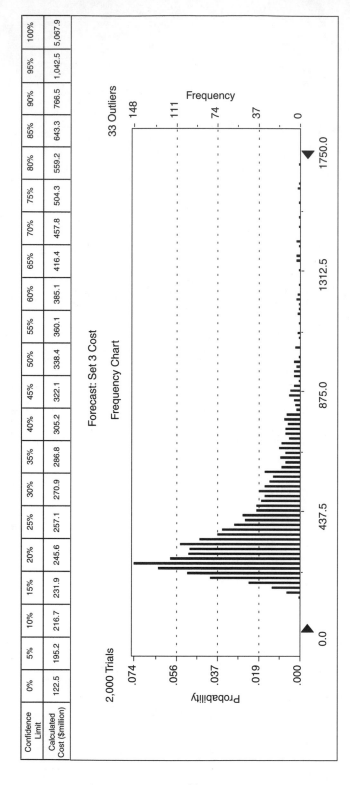

Confidence Limit	0%	5%	10%	15%	20%	25%	30%	35%	40%	45%	50%	55%	60%	65%	70%	75%	80%	85%	90%	95%	100%
Calculated Cost ($million)	122.5	195.2	216.7	231.9	245.6	257.1	270.9	286.8	305.2	322.1	338.4	360.1	385.1	416.4	457.8	504.3	559.2	643.3	766.5	1,042.5	5,067.9

Forecast: Set 3 Cost

Frequency Chart

2,000 Trials

33 Outliers

Figure 6.9   Sunny-day failure forecast distribution of consequential cost and tabulated forecast values at 5 percentile confidence levels.

86

Table 6.3   Calculated Risk Quotients

Failure Type	Financial Risk Quotient ($ × million per year)
F1 Flood & Main Embankment Breach	6.08E–05
F2 Flood & Secondary Embankment Breach	6.07E–05
F3 Sunny-Day Failure	2.96E–02
F4 Outlet Works—short-term outage	3.37E–03
F5 Outlet Works—long-term outage	1.21E–02
F6 Vehicle-Accident	1.71E–02
Total Dam Financial Risk Quotient	6.23E–02

Figure 6.10 shows a ranked risk profile of the failure types applicable to the dam. The risk profile is a bar chart and shows that the riskiest failure type (sunny-day failure with a calculated risk quotient of $30,000 per year) is approximately twice as risky as the second riskiest failure type (vehicle accident, $17,000 per year). In turn, the second riskiest event presents approximately 1.5 times more risk

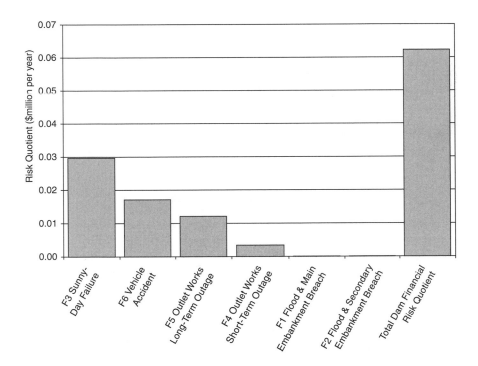

Figure 6.10   Financial risk profile showing a comparison of the risk of each failure and the total risk presented by all failure types.

than the third most risky event (outlet works failure and long-term outage, $12,000 per year).

The risk profile is quite typical, in that it shows that a relative handful of events accounts for the vast majority of the total risk amount. Total risk is the sum of the calculated risk quotients for all relevant risk events, shown in Figure 6.10 as the total dam financial risk quotient bar.

Figure 6.11 shows an example of a proportional risk profile. It shows the events ranked in order of decreasing risk quotient. The height of each bar indicates the proportion (percentage) contribution of each event to total risk. The bar chart indicates, for example, that the riskiest event, sunny-day failure, contributes to around 48 percent of the total risk and that the second most risky event (vehicle accident) is responsible for around 28 percent of the total risk.

The line plot of Figure 6.11 shows an alternative way of expressing the contribution of each additional risk event to total risk. The line plot shows the progressive contribution to total risk, from the most risky event to the least risky event. The line plot shows that proceeding on from the riskiest event, the two most risky

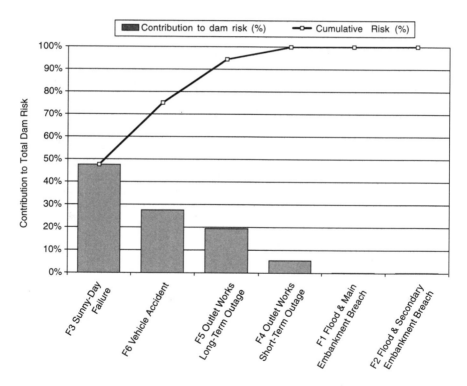

Figure 6.11 Contribution of failure types to total dam risk showing the cumulative increase in risk for failure types ranked in order of decreasing risk quotient.

events contribute to approximately 75 percent of the total risk and the three most risky events contribute to around 95 percent of the total risk. The plot also clearly indicates that the two least risky events (both events related to flooding) provide a negligible contribution to total risk.

Figure 6.12 shows the exposure profile for the example water storage. The risk events are ranked in order of decreasing risk quotient, as shown by the line graph of "financial risk." Exposure profiles reflect the exposure to residual risk resultant from ongoing business risk management. Consequently, exposure profiles ideally show that the least risky events present the greatest exposure. The exposure profile of Figure 6.12 is unusual (and undesirable) because the riskiest event (sunny-day failure) presents the greatest financial exposure of all the identified risk events.

Figure 6.12 shows that a conservative estimate (at the 80 percent confidence level) of the potential cost if a sunny-day failure were to occur would be approximately $560 million. An optimistic estimate of the exposure would be approximately $340 million; a pessimistic estimate would be over $1 billion. In contrast,

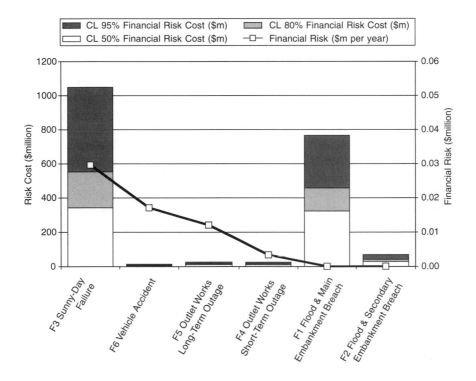

Figure 6.12 **Financial risk and exposure profile showing the estimated costs if the failure types occur, with failure types ranked in order of decreasing risk.**

the combined pessimistic cost of the remaining three events that contribute to most of the total risk would be approximately $65 million.

Figure 6.12 also allows comparison of uncertainty associated with the cost estimates. The large range of optimistic and pessimistic cost estimates ($340 million to $1.05 billion) for sunny-day failure clearly shows that there is considerable uncertainty in the estimate of cost of that event. Compared with sunny-day failure, the second lowest risk event (flooding leading to a breach of the main embankment) presents a similar optimistic estimate of exposure ($320 million). However, the cost range (uncertainty) is substantially less than sunny-day failure, as shown by the pessimistic cost estimate of approximately $770 million for the flooding event.

Figure 6.13 shows a risk map of the potential dam failure modes. For comparison, the map shows plots of the house and car risk parameters from the household insurance example discussed earlier and illustrated in Figure 6.6.

Using the lines of equal risk in Figure 6.13 as a guide, sunny-day failure is clearly the riskiest event, with a relatively low likelihood (approximately one in 10,000 years) but a very high cost if it occurs (average around $300 million). In comparison, the vehicle accident event poses almost as much risk as sunny-day

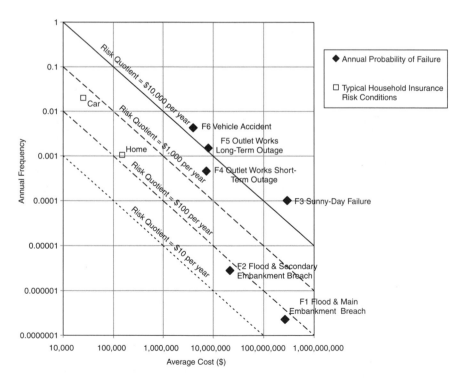

Figure 6.13   Risk map of dam failure modes showing the risk relationship of each failure type and a comparison with the household insurance example.

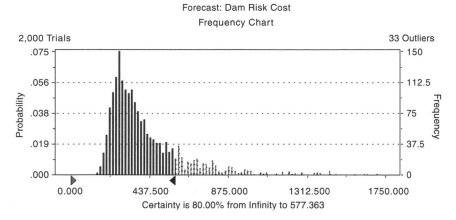

Figure 6.14   Forecast risk cost distribution of sunny-day dam failure.

failure, which is achieved because the accident has a relatively high chance of occurring (around one in 250 years) but has a relatively low financial consequence
($4 million).

In contrast to sunny-day failure, the lowest risk event shown on Figure 6.13 is
a major flood leading to failure of the main embankment. This event has the same
consequences as sunny-day failure but has almost three orders of magnitude less
likelihood of occurring (likelihood is approximately one in 4.5 million years).

The project manager and the risk analyst evaluated the ranked financial risk
profile (Figure 6.10) and the proportional risk profile (Figure 6.11) and selected
the risk threshold for calculation of the risk cost at $10,000 per year. Thus, the
combined occurrence cost of the three riskiest events (which contributed to almost
95 percent of the total risk) was included in the risk cost calculation.

Figure 6.14 shows the forecast risk cost distribution for the example dam. The
risk cost distribution consists of the combined cost of sunny-day failure, vehicle
accident, and outlet works damage leading to long-term outage. The distribution
is dominated by the largest cost component (sunny-day failure) and is heavily
skewed toward the high cost end of the distribution. The Utility project manager
selected the 50 , 80, and 95 percent confidence levels to represent optimistic, planning, and pessimistic estimates of risk cost. The estimated optimistic, planning,
and pessimistic risk costs are $360 million, $580 million, and $1.06 billion,
respectively.

The calculated risk cost at the optimistic, planning, and pessimistic confidence
levels is shown graphically in Figure 6.15. The bar chart confirms that there is
considerable uncertainty in the estimate of dam risk cost, as indicated by the wide
range of cost between the estimated 50 and 95 percent confidence levels.

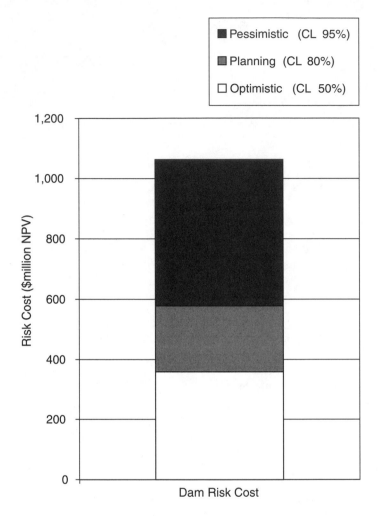

Figure 6.15   Calculated dam risk cost at the optimistic, planning, and pessimistic confidence levels, the range of which provides an indication of the uncertainty associated with the cost estimate.

7

STAGE 4: FORMULATE A RISK
TREATMENT STRATEGY

The objective of risk treatment is to identify and implement appropriate management actions to address targeted risks, with the objective of reducing their likelihood of occurrence and/or the severity of the consequences. Development of a risk treatment strategy involves selection of one or more risk treatment options, which collectively will reduce the overall risk exposure to the project or business to an acceptable level. The options that are selected depend on the degree of control that the organization has over the risk and the relative benefits and costs of treating the identified risks. The greater the level of control, the more likely the risks will be able to be treated using proactive measures.

The aim of a risk treatment strategy is to progressively reduce risk in a timely and cost-effective manner. This aim recognizes the constraint that most businesses cannot implement all actions that may be required to reduce risk to acceptable levels. Some actions may be more costly to perform compared with the consequential reduction in exposure to risk. In addition, most businesses have a limited annual budget allocation for risk reduction actions. Due to these limitations, businesses usually need to establish interim risk reduction goals.

In order to develop a risk treatment strategy that satisfies the above aims, it is necessary to develop an appreciation of the:

- Level of risk that would be acceptable, in both the short and the long term
- Events that should be addressed first
- Actions that should be taken to reduce the risk
- Projected effectiveness of any actions
- Cost of actions
- Available budget to perform required actions
- Financial benefits of risk treatment actions

Risk analysts and project managers, often in consultation with other stakeholder representatives, develop the risk treatment strategy.

Formulation of risk reduction strategy utilizes the results of the risk assessment process. Figure 7.1 shows a flow chart of the process required to develop a risk reduction strategy. Each step of the flow chart is described below.

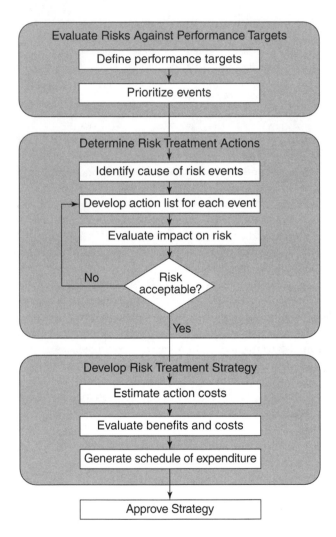

Figure 7.1   Procedure for risk strategy development.

EVALUATE RISKS AGAINST PERFORMANCE TARGETS

Define Performance Targets

Criteria need to be established that indicate target levels of risk quotient that would be acceptable, in both the short and the long term. For example, a short-term target might be to substantially reduce the risk posed by a specific event within the coming year, but the long-term target might be to further reduce the risk posed by the event to "best available technology." In the meantime, the organization's resources are applied to achieving substantial risk reductions across a wide range of events.

Short-term and long-term risk targets need to be established. The targets indicate levels of risk quotient that would be considered acceptable for the indicated period. In situations other than compliance breaches, often short-term criteria cannot be set realistically until project managers have gained a clear understanding of risk events through a risk assessment process. Long-term performance objectives and evaluation criteria, however, can be set in advance, at the commencement of the risk assessment process.

Short-term criteria are applied specifically during development of risk treatment strategies to determine whether a proposed action (or set of actions) will achieve an adequate reduction in risk quotient. The following discussion focuses on development of risk treatment strategies that are designed to meet predominantly short-term criteria.

Development of a risk treatment strategy is therefore an iterative process. In most cases, it is appropriate that the initial target risk quotient is set at the risk threshold value which was selected to calculate the risk cost. The threshold is appropriate because the aim of the risk reduction process is to reduce the risk quotients to levels where the estimated risk cost would be negligible. However, it may not be possible in the short term to perform all of the necessary actions to achieve the threshold target, and the criterion may need to be revised.

Prioritize Events

At this stage of the process, project managers and risk analysts need to re-enlist the assistance of the expert panel. The risk events that should be addressed first need to be identified in order to limit development of risk reduction actions to events that will be effective in reducing overall risk. The panel therefore needs to differentiate between those events that need prompt attention and those that can be entered onto a "watch list" and monitored in the interim.

The ranked risk profiles are used to confirm the events that should receive priority consideration. All events for which the calculated risk quotients are greater than the target need to be identified and listed in order of priority.

DETERMINE RISK TREATMENT ACTIONS

Identify Cause of Risk Events

During this process the panel needs to refer to the original event trees that were produced for risk analysis. The appropriate panel experts review the branches of the event tree leading to the end consequence of the risk event under evaluation. The experts evaluate the contributing likelihoods and consequences to identify the key elements in the pathway that primarily contribute to the current magnitude of risk quotient. The panel members use the event-tree input information to develop a list of actions that will progressively reduce the risk quotient to the ultimate target value.

Develop Action List for Each Event

The panel members need to consider each risk event in turn, until a series of actions that can potentially reduce the risk has been identified. The actions need to be considered for all substantial risk events (usually those that contribute to risk cost exposure).

In many cases a risk event has a low likelihood of occurring but is high risk because the consequences are very high. In these cases, insurance may be an appropriate instrument to reduce the exposure to acceptable levels.

If a risk event has a high likelihood of occurring, then appropriate action might be to replace the risk cost of an event occurring with a known, planned expenditure. In this case risk managers need to reduce the likelihood of the event occurring to negligible levels. For example, installation of backup pumps would effectively prevent release of sewage to the environment. Other examples are strengthening a water supply dam embankment to prevent catastrophic failure and installing complex monitoring systems to allow rapid response to potential failures.

In the case of risk events with large consequences, risk managers would seek ways of reducing the consequences. For example, exposure might be limited by constructing lined bunds around oil tanks to prevent any spills due to tank failure from leaving the immediate area or by storing mine explosives underground to prevent injury by fly-rock to residents in the vicinity of the mine site.

In cases where the risk event is considered relatively low cost, risk managers may decide either to plan for the expenditure in the project budget or to take the risk that the event occurs and to pay for the consequences from the operational budget.

The output of this process should be an itemized list of actions that can be carried out for each risk event, the current risk presented by each event, and the expected future risk posed by the risk event, after implementation of the risk reduction actions.

Evaluate Impact on Risk

The creation of a preliminary version of the risk model by risk analysts greatly aids in the process of developing a progressive list of actions and assessing their potential impact on risk. The interactive model should readily incorporate the impact of risk treatment actions and generate visual comparisons with the existing risk conditions. Using the model, panel members can instantly assess the reduction in the risk quotient that the action should generate and decide whether additional action is required to reduce the event risk to the target level.

DEVELOP A RISK TREATMENT STRATEGY

The aim of the RISQUE method is to create a sufficient understanding of the nature and extent of risk facing an organization that will lead to generation of an appropriate strategy to reduce the risk. The tables, risk profiles, and risk maps generated by application of the RISQUE method are designed specifically for direct use when planning the most appropriate sequence of risk reduction activities.

Risk treatment activity over a given period is usually constrained to some extent by practical (budgetary) and logistical factors. It is usually not possible to implement immediately all of the potential risk reduction actions that have been identified during the previous process. It is therefore necessary to develop a schedule of actions that is designed to progressively reduce exposure to risk events.

A well-conceived risk treatment strategy usually aims initially to maximize the reduction in total risk that can be gained within the available budget. In addition, project managers often face a decision of whether to concentrate or spread risk reduction dollars. In order to obtain the best risk reduction value for money, project managers need to compare the benefits and costs of such competing strategic options.

Estimate Action Costs

The expert panel provides estimates of the cost of risk reduction actions for the higher-priority risk events. The panel should adopt the same procedure for costing the risk reduction actions as was followed when costing the consequences of the risk events. The costs should be provided at the 50 and the 95 percent confidence level so that the uncertainty in the cost estimates can be included in the analysis.

Evaluate Benefits and Costs

The panel identifies the reduction in risk quotient of each action at the time the actions were selected. The benefit of each action can be measured as a reduction in the individual event risk quotient, the total risk quotient, the reduction in exposure to the risk event, or the reduction in risk cost.

Outputs that are generated to assist development of strategy are typically some combination of:

- A prevention profile, which compares the estimated risk reduction costs with the exposure costs for the ranked risk events; prevention profiles are useful in evaluating value for money with respect to risk management implementation scenarios
- Cumulative plots of risk reduction action cost vs. exposure reduction
- Cumulative plots of risk reduction action cost vs. percentage of total risk quotient reduction
- Graphical plots of base cost vs. risk cost for options
- Graphical plots of base cost vs. total risk quotient for options
- Graphical plots of benefit-cost relationships for various options

Generate Schedule of Expenditure

A simple schedule of expenditure that reduces the risk quotient of progressively less risky events is usually more easy to derive and defend than a schedule based on more sophisticated analysis.

In many cases, the actions that are required to reduce the risk quotients of the riskiest events to target levels also reduce the risk quotients of lower-priority risk events. Thus, the actions that address the riskiest issues frequently represent very good risk reduction value. Under these circumstances, the risk treatment strategy that offers the best risk reduction value for the money is to perform the identified risk treatment actions that progressively work down the prioritized list of risk events until the accumulated costs meet budget.

In other cases, however, it may be more prudent initially to spread the reduction in risk over a larger number of issues rather than to fully address a relatively small number of the riskiest issues. For example, expenditure of the entire first-year budget may be required to reduce the risk quotient of the three riskiest issues to target levels. However, for a much lower expenditure, it may be possible to reduce the risk quotient of the three riskiest issues substantially, but not to target levels. Then the remainder of the budget could be used to gain substantial reductions in risk quotient for the next 10 priority risk events. Spreading the expenditure in this way can result in achieving greater initial reduction in overall risk. Depending on the nature of the modified risk profile, expenditure in subsequent years can be allocated to progressively reduce the risk quotients of all risk events to target levels.

APPROVE STRATEGY FOR IMPLEMENTATION

Gaining organizational approval to implement the risk treatment strategy is a critical milestone. This is often the point at which project managers must convince senior management, including the board of directors, that a risk treatment expenditure program is warranted.

Approval by senior management is more likely to be gained if the decision-makers:

- Generally understand and support the process followed
- Have been informed of key findings (and associated scope changes) during the process
- Have confidence in the expertise of the expert panel
- Are presented with a concise, to the point, synopsis of the results, together with one or two simple yet meaningful illustrations
- Are aware that the synopsis of the study (e.g., briefing paper for the board of directors) is backed by a large amount of supporting information and analysis
- Consider that the process is transparent and defensible to third-party stakeholders

Clearly, this stage is the culmination of a carefully planned and executed process that starts at the context definition stage and secures the commitment of the decision-makers at the beginning of the process.

WATER UTILITY EXAMPLE

The following water utility example demonstrates application of the steps in the risk strategy formulation stage.

The project manager decided that the target risk quotient for each event would be equal to the threshold value ($20,000 per year) used to calculate risk cost. However, it was also decided that at this stage a target would not be set for the overall risk posed by the dam.

The panel confirmed that the risk derived from the three riskiest events (sunny-day failure, vehicle accident, and outlet works long-term outage) needed to be reduced to the target level. The panel members dealt with the three riskiest events in turn.

They considered that the consequences of sunny-day failure would be very large, irrespective of some measures that could be taken to reduce the impact of a major, uncontrolled release of water into the wider downstream environment. The panel, therefore, decided to concentrate on reducing the likelihood of a sunny-day failure occurring.

The panel members referred to the event trees that lead to sunny-day failure and which were constructed during the risk assessment process (Figure 6.8). The sunny-day failure event tree of Figure 6.8 shows that the annual frequency of a sunny-day failure was estimated to be 1.01×10^{-4} per year. Perusal of the event trees showed that the event that contributed most to the relatively high likelihood was geotechnical instability of the embankment. The panel members previously estimated the likelihood of this event occurring to be 9.0×10^{-5} per year, which is approximately 90 percent of the total likelihood of a sunny-day failure.

Under high storage conditions in the reservoir behind the dam, low residual strength of the embankment could lead to embankment failure and consequent breach of the main embankment. The panel members considered that the most appropriate action to reduce the likelihood of embankment failure was to increase the embankment residual strength by performance of stability defense and piping defense.

The proposed stability defense consisted of placement of a rock-fill buttress on the upstream and downstream batters of the embankment. The piping defense consisted of placing new filter zones on the upstream batter of the embankment.

The panel considered that the impact of the embankment stability works and piping defense would be to reduce the likelihood of failure of the embankment under full storage conditions by 1,000 times. Furthermore, the works would reduce the potential for embankment failure due to low residual strength by a factor of 10 times. The combined effect of the proposed actions would be to reduce the likelihood of the critical geotechnical pathway (embankment stability) from 9.08×10^{-5} per year to 1.7×10^{-7} per year. The ultimate impact of reducing the likelihood of this pathway would be to reduce the overall likelihood of sunny-day failure from 1.01×10^{-4} per year to 1.02×10^{-5} per year. This reduction of approximately one order of magnitude would reduce the overall risk quotient of sunny-day failure by an order of magnitude, to $\$3 \times 10^{-3}$ million per year, which achieves the target risk quotient for sunny-day failure.

The panel members also recognized that the proposed stability and piping defense would reduce the likelihoods of other elements within the sunny-day failure event trees. Figure 7.2 shows the sunny-day failure event trees with the estimated likelihoods after performance of the stability and piping defenses. The revised event tree indicates that the combined annual probability of sunny-day failure after performance of the proposed risk reduction actions would be approximately 2.6×10^{-7} per year. The estimated risk quotient would reduce to less that $\$1 \times 10^{-4}$ million per year, which is two orders of magnitude less that the target risk quotient for sunny-day failure.

The panel members pointed out that the proposed embankment stabilization actions also would reduce the likelihood of occurrence of the second most risky event, an earthquake event leading to embankment failure and a vehicle accident. The estimated likelihood would be reduced by almost three orders of magnitude, which would have the effect of reducing the event risk quotient to approximately $\$2 \times 10^{-5}$ million per year, which is considerably lower than the target risk quotient.

Graphical illustrations show the impact of the proposed risk reduction actions. Figure 7.3 shows the risk profile prior to implementation of the risk reduction ac-

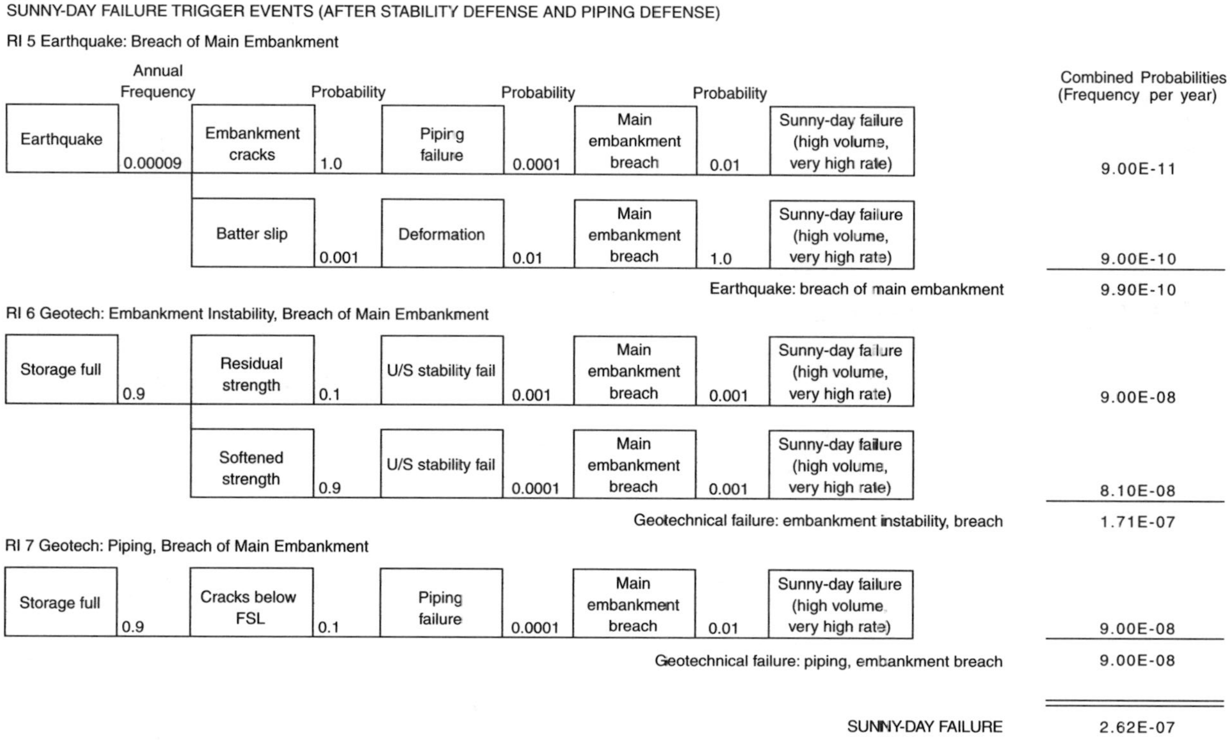

SUNNY-DAY FAILURE TRIGGER EVENTS (AFTER STABILITY DEFENSE AND PIPING DEFENSE)

RI 5 Earthquake: Breach of Main Embankment

	Annual Frequency		Probability		Probability		Probability		Combined Probabilities (Frequency per year)
Earthquake	0.00009	Embankment cracks	1.0	Piping failure	0.0001	Main embankment breach	0.01	Sunny-day failure (high volume, very high rate)	9.00E-11
		Batter slip	0.001	Deformation	0.01	Main embankment breach	1.0	Sunny-day failure (high volume, very high rate)	9.00E-10

Earthquake: breach of main embankment   9.90E-10

RI 6 Geotech: Embankment Instability, Breach of Main Embankment

Storage full	0.9	Residual strength	0.1	U/S stability fail	0.001	Main embankment breach	0.001	Sunny-day failure (high volume, very high rate)	9.00E-08
		Softened strength	0.9	U/S stability fail	0.0001	Main embankment breach	0.001	Sunny-day failure (high volume, very high rate)	8.10E-08

Geotechnical failure: embankment instability, breach   1.71E-07

RI 7 Geotech: Piping, Breach of Main Embankment

Storage full	0.9	Cracks below FSL	0.1	Piping failure	0.0001	Main embankment breach	0.01	Sunny-day failure (high volume very high rate)	9.00E-08

Geotechnical failure: piping, embankment breach   9.00E-08

SUNNY-DAY FAILURE   2.62E-07

Figure 7.2   Sunny-day failure event tree and probabilities for example case.

101

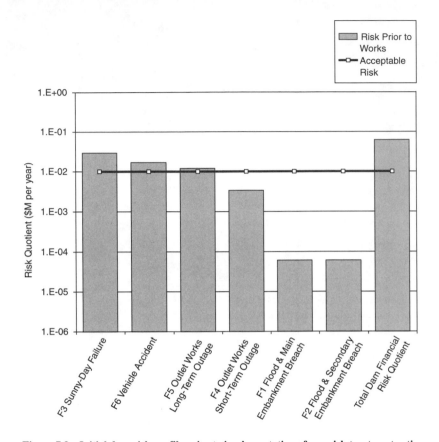

Figure 7.3 Initial dam risk profile prior to implementation of any risk treatment actions.

tions and shows that the three riskiest events lie above the target level that had been set by the panel members. Figure 7.4 shows the predicted dam risk profile after implementation of the embankment stabilization works and also shows the change from the initial risk profile. This figure indicates that only one event, the third riskiest event, remains above the target risk quotient.

The panel members reviewed the event trees leading to long-term uncontrolled release via the outlet tower. The main pathway for this risk event was a faulty butterfly valve that had a high likelihood of failure to close. The action recommended by the panel members was replacement of the faulty butterfly valve, which also would reduce the likelihood that there would be long-term release of water in the event of an earthquake and consequent collapse of the outlet tower.

The combined effect of butterfly valve replacement was to reduce the likelihood (and hence the risk) of both outlet works events by two orders of magnitude. The revised risk quotient associated with the outlet works falls considerably

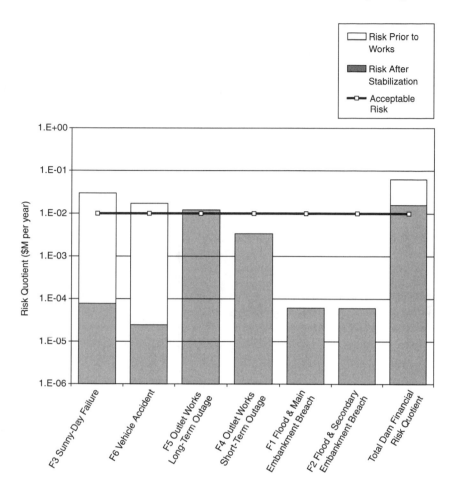

Figure 7.4 Dam risk profile after implementation of stabilization works.

within the target set by the panel members. The risk profile of Figure 7.5 shows the additional effect of butterfly valve replacement.

The following treatment actions were costed and recommended. The primary risk reduction action is to carry out embankment stabilization works at a cost of $9 million. This action will reduce the two-highest priority issues (sunny-day failure of the main embankment and vehicle accident) to well below the target level. The second risk reduction action is to replace the butterfly valve and strengthen the outlet tower at a combined cost of $1.75 million. These actions will reduce the risk of the third and fourth highest-risk issues (both involving the outlet works) to well below the target level.

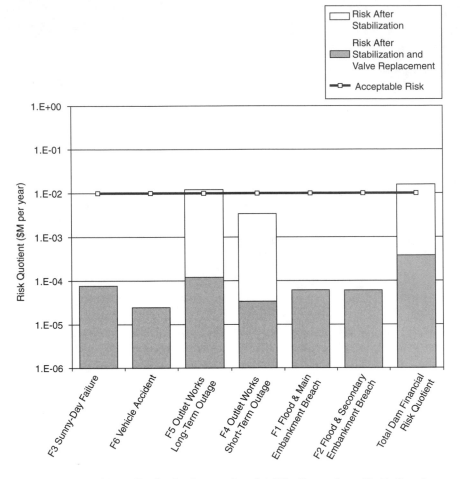

Figure 7.5   Dam risk profile after implementation of stabilization works and butterfly valve replacement.

The third potential risk reduction action is to install a fuse plug and parapet wall on the secondary embankment for a cost of approximately $2 million. These actions would address the remaining two issues, which relate to overtopping of the main embankment during very major flood events. The risk posed by these events is already well below the target level.

Benefit-cost analysis was performed. Figure 7.6 shows plots of the cumulative risk reduction cost and the concomitant reduction in exposure to risk events. The figure shows that embankment stabilization works will reduce risk substantially but will not achieve the target. Also, the embankment works represent good value for money; $9 million must be spent, but the benefit will be to reduce around $350 million of potential exposure.

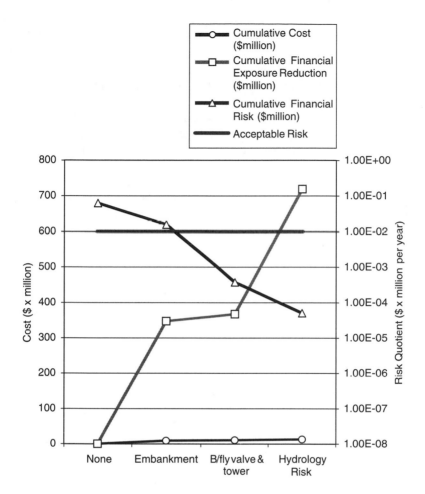

Figure 7.6 Benefit-cost relationship of risk treatment works showing the progressive cost to implement the works, and the progressive reduction in risk and exposure to financial consequences.

The additional work of replacement of the butterfly valve and tower strengthening would reduce the total risk quotient to below the target. The Utility decided to perform embankment stabilization and to replace the butterfly valve and strengthen the outlet tower. These actions should reduce the total risk quotient for the dam to approximately 3×10^{-4} million per year, which is considerably less than the target of $0.2 million per year.

Inspection of Figure 7.6 shows that if work was carried out to address the hydrology (flood) risk, there would be approximately $350 million of exposure reduction, for an expenditure of $2 million. This represents good value for money.

Figure 7.7 shows the percentage of risk reduction. It shows that the embankment stabilization works will derive good risk reduction value. The first action, embankment stabilization, reduces the total dam risk quotient by 75 percent. The additional action (valve and tower) sees a combined reduction in risk quotient of around 99 percent. The additional $2 million cost to carry out the hydrology work would not significantly reduce the risk.

The Utility decided to perform embankment stabilization and to replace the butterfly valve and strengthen the outlet tower. The decision was made because these actions would achieve all of the targets required and could be done in the first year.

The Utility decided not to address the flood risk because the risk was very low already and the action would not significantly reduce the total dam risk quotient. In addition, the Utility decided that the $2 million could be better spent, this year, to reduce risk at another facility.

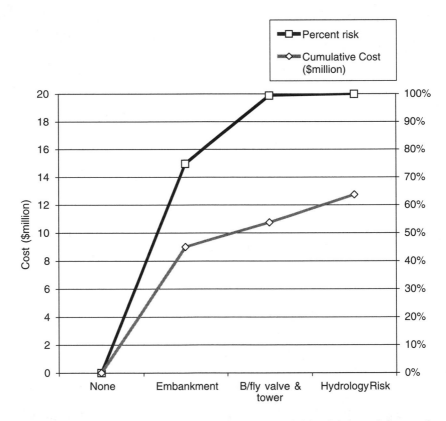

Figure 7.7   Relationship between the proportion of the total risk reduction and the cost of treatment actions.

8

STAGE 5: IMPLEMENT THE RISK TREATMENT STRATEGY

A risk treatment strategy forms the basis for developing action plans that, when implemented, will reduce the overall exposure of a business to risk events. The actions are designed to reduce the likelihood that the risk events will occur and/or the magnitude of the consequences if the event does occur.

RISK TREATMENT ACTIONS

Risk treatment actions can be separated into the following categories:

- Risk transfer or sharing with other parties
- Risk reduction (i.e., reduction of the likelihood of occurrence and/or reduction of the severity of the consequences)
- Risk acceptance (i.e., the organization prepares to take on full responsibility for the consequences of event if and when it occurs)

Treatment strategies may include doing nothing (i.e., accepting the risk as an unavoidable fact of life) or a combination of proactive measures to reduce the likelihood of occurrence or the consequences and reactive measures to limit or repair damage if it occurs. Examples of risk treatment options and their application are described in the following sections.

RISK SHARING AND RISK TRANSFER

Contra-Positioning or Hedging

Hedging is a risk sharing technique involving the creation of a cash flow to offset an existing cash flow. For example, gold commodity prices are inherently volatile, so gold mining companies commonly negotiate a fixed price per unit of production with a buyer and enter into a hedge contract to forward sell some or all of their future production up to their current reserves. However, hedging as a treatment measure introduces its own risks, which need to be evaluated on a benefit-cost basis. While hedges reduce potential losses, they also tend to reduce potential profits. For example, in a rising gold market, a highly hedged gold producing company may not fully benefit from the higher gold price and therefore may not perform as well as an unhedged gold producer.

Contracts and Indemnity Agreements with Other Parties

Contractual arrangements may be used to partially transfer or share risks. The principal party may choose to exercise extensive control over the contractor or, alternatively, just set broad policy, activity outlines, and budgets, and leave detailed implementation to the discretion of the contractor. The latter approach is seen most often at the conceptualizing stage of a project. Once the project moves to the development stage and the scope of risks and financial expenditure significantly expands, the principal may insist that the company has the right to exercise a high degree of supervision over the activities of its contractor. In high-risk situations, the contractor may be very closely supervised by a principal's representative or technical committee.

Where risks cannot be removed by contractual controls, it is usual for the contracting parties to share financial risks through indemnification. For example, a principal may require a contractor to indemnify the principal for loss incurred by the contractor's gross negligence or willful misconduct. There may also be a contractual requirement for the chain of indemnity to be maintained through to subcontractors, to ensure that the interests of the principal are protected.

Insurance Coverage

In many cases a risk event has a low likelihood of occurring but has a high risk quotient because the potential financial consequences are substantial. In these cases, insurance may be an appropriate instrument to reduce the exposure to a level that is acceptable to the business. Insurance acts to transfer or shift risk from one entity to a group, so that losses are shared on an equitable basis by all members of the group.

Many types of insurance product are available in the market. Examples of insurance options include:

- *Industrial and special risk (ISR) insurance:* Typically covers first-party repair to damage and third-party property and environmental damage due to sudden events.
- *Environmental impairment liability (EIL) insurance:* Typically covers the cost of remediation of environmental impairment from gradual events.

- *Finite risk insurance:* Essentially a self-funding mechanism whereby the planned premiums paid over a specified time frame effectively cover the cost of an expected future event. The underwriter covers the cost if the event occurs earlier than anticipated.
- *Cap insurance:* Additional insurance layer that covers the cost of an event in excess of the primary insurance layer. Cover is provided by cap insurance to a specified maximum cost per event.

Divestment

Companies need to evaluate the businesses they own on the basis of the risks they pose, relative to the benefits that are derived from their ongoing operation. In some cases, the best risk treatment option for the company may be to divest a high-risk, low-return business, in order to protect the company's other assets from exposure to debt or other liabilities associated with the poorly performing business unit.

In the case of premises located on contaminated sites, the divestment process may first involve an environmental site contamination investigation to assist in defining the scope and magnitude of the liability, followed by remediation work to treat or remove some of the contamination. This option may reduce the residual risk associated with the site and increase its market value, but the reduction in liability and added value needs to be balanced with the up-front capital expenditure to prepare the site for sale.

RISK REDUCTION

Further Studies and Investigations

In some cases the risk quotients that are calculated for risk events are high because of the high degree of uncertainty about the likelihood of occurrence or the financial consequences. Panels may tend to take a conservative approach in assigning these values because they believe that they do not have good understanding of the risk event characteristics. In these situations, further investigations or studies may be warranted to develop a better understanding of the risk events, such as engineering failure modes, to enable the risk quotient to be refined and possibly reduced, or to identify the appropriate risk treatment measures to implement in order to reduce the likelihood of occurrence or the severity of the consequences.

Staff and Contractor Training

It is widely known that many risk events arise from human error, such as inadequate understanding of the hazards being worked with or inappropriate behavior. Provision of risk awareness and management training to staff and contractors can assist in overcoming these deficiencies and instill a workforce culture of greater accountability and responsibility, with the effect of reducing the likelihood of risk events and the severity of the consequences.

Engineering Modifications and Monitoring Systems

If a risk event has a high likelihood of occurring, then the appropriate risk treatment action might be to replace the risk cost of an event occurring with a known, planned capital expenditure to reduce the likelihood of occurrence and/or the severity of the consequences. For example, in a sewage pumping station, installation of backup pumps can effectively prevent release of sewage to the environment. Structural strengthening of a water supply dam embankment can prevent catastrophic failure, and the installation of sophisticated monitoring systems can provide early warning of potential failures. Construction of lined bunds around oil tanks can prevent spills arising from tank failure from leaving the immediate area. Storage of mine explosives underground can prevent injury by fly-rock to residents in the vicinity of the mine site.

Asset Maintenance Programs

Financial commitment to scheduled asset preventive maintenance programs can reduce the likelihood of occurrence of risk events and the severity of their consequences. Timely replacement of parts, in accordance with manufacturers' recommendations, will reduce the likelihood of catastrophic failures. Regular servicing of equipment and inspection of facilities can also provide an opportunity for early detection and rectification of potential problems, such as slow leaks from chemical or fuel storage containers.

Acquiring Competitors or Suppliers

Competition and continuity of supply are threats to business that are operating in highly competitive markets. Removal of a competitor through acquisition can increase market share and increase the organization's resource base, while acquisition of a supplier can ensure supply of critical raw or processed materials or services to the business. However, the strategic decision to adopt this approach needs to be fully cognizant of the operational capital and cultural risks associated with mergers. There is a recognized tendency for merging organizations to become internally focused for a period of time; therefore, they may lose sight of what is happening in their external operating environment.

Lobbying to Offset Political Threats

One of the implicit financial threats associated with the occurrence of catastrophic risk events may be political intervention in response to community upset, particularly in marginal or vociferous electorates. The consequences of this intervention may be pressure on the responsible company to pay higher-than-anticipated compensation to affected parties in the local community, or pressure from regulators to install an overdesigned engineering solution to minimize the likelihood of recurrence of the risk event. Development of an informed and cooperative working relationship with the media, local political representatives, and the regulatory agencies responsible for the industry sector to which the business belongs can assist with ensuring that these parties are fully aware of the inherent risks associated with business operations. Equipped with this understanding, they are less likely to react in an emotionally charged manner if a foreseen risk event occurs.

Community Consultation and Risk Communication

Development of both internal and external stakeholder appreciation of the characteristics of these risks and the reasons underlying the company's risk management strategy can go a long way toward mitigating the consequences if a risk event occurs. Stakeholders make judgments about the acceptability of a risk based on their perception of that risk. If they perceive that information is being withheld from them or that their concerns are not being considered, their level of outrage when an event occurs will be greater than if they have involved in assessments of the risks and development of the risk strategies through informed two-way consultation. Examples of this approach include establishment of community representation on consultative management committees for industrial estates and major industrial facilities as is provided for in the International Council of Chemical Associations' Responsible Care Program adopted by the chemical manufacturing industry.

RISK ACCEPTANCE

Rarely is it financially viable to remove all risk through risk reduction measures; and therefore, some element of residual risk may remain. An organization's acceptance of risk is an individual matter, being dependent on the:

* Financial capacity of the business to absorb the consequences of risk
* Level of conservatism of the decision-makers
* Amount of risk inherent in the business activities normally undertaken by the business
* Diversity of the business
* Extent to which risk can be transferred or treated (laid off)

Self-Insurance

Commercial insurance coverage can be an expensive option for treating risks that are well understood and of relatively low-cost consequences, as insurance providers calculate the premiums to exceed average losses in the long run. Therefore, in these situations, a more financially viable option for a business may be to retain the risk and self-insure.

Self-insurance can be achieved by establishment of a captive insurance company to take advantage of reinsurance funding benefits and, in many cases, taxation benefits. The need to invest substantial up-front capital restricts this option to larger organizations.

Financial Assurances, Bonds, and Bank Guarantees

Financial assurances (or bonds) are mostly required by government regulatory agencies to be placed to cover the cost of occurrence of future risk events. Financial assurances are commonly required in the mining and waste management industries. In the United States, for example, financial assurances for landfills are required to cover premature closure, contingent environmental liability, and postclosure care.

Financial assurance strategies can be developed using one or a combination of several mechanisms. The mechanisms can include:

- Establishment of a trust fund
- Placement of a surety bond guaranteeing payment or performance
- Provision of a letter of credit
- Insurance
- Conformance with a corporate or local government financial test
- Corporate or local government guarantees

Contingency and Crisis Management Plans

Companies also should provide for the eventuality of risk events by developing contingency and crisis management plans, such as oil spill contingency plans, emergency response plans, and bomb threat and fire evacuation plans. These plans should be:

- Actions executed before a crisis event occurs to reduce its likelihood of occurrence, such as staff training, safety procedures, audits and inspections, desktop and field drill of the response plans
- Actions taken in the event of a crisis, including the roles and responsibilities of key individuals; notification, media communication, and reporting protocols; and sources of response resources, such as oil spill clean-up equipment

Staff familiarity with these plans is essential to ensure that they are effective tools when called on in a risk event. Implementation of the plans therefore requires training of the key response personnel and regular testing and updating of the plans to maintain their currency.

Rapid Response Systems

Rapid response systems may complement emergency response plans to enable organizations to respond promptly and effectively when a risk event occurs. Such systems may include automated systems, such as smoke detectors and sprinklers in buildings, and automated emergency service calls.

Other approaches may include prearranged response actions. For example, offshore oil exploration and production operators sometimes can negotiate conditional preapprovals with environmental regulatory authorities to allow the operators to promptly apply chemical dispersants in the event of an oil spill. The preapproval avoids delays associated with bureaucratic communication protocols, thereby enabling operators to optimize an opportunity to disperse an oil slick before it spreads too widely and causes harm to sensitive marine resources.

IMPLEMENTATION

Risk treatment strategies may comprise one or more of the treatment options just described, depending on the characteristics of the targeted risks. Risk management should begin at the strategic planning stage of a proposed project or business activity and continue throughout its life. The risk management strategy should reflect the current analysis and thinking about risk in the project or business activity; therefore, it invariably needs to change as the project or business activities progress and the risks change, are resolved, or change their urgency status.

To ensure that the strategy is implemented and performs as intended, a structured approach is recommended, involving the use of risk action plans, risk registers, and monitoring and reporting tools.

Documentation of the Risk Management Strategy

Resources need to be assigned to implement and monitor the risk management strategy and the risk action plans. Implementation should address the following six steps:

1. Set performance objectives
2. Specify responsibilities
3. Allocate and control resources
4. Specify schedules and milestones
5. Monitor progress and achievements
6. Assist in the resolution of problems

For most projects or activities, the documented risk management strategy should be an integral part of the project execution plan. For significant projects or new business initiatives, the risk management plan should be included in the capital submission or the business plan.

The typical contents of the risk treatment strategy document may include:

- A description of the context, including the project or activity description, scope, issues, stakeholders and objectives, criteria, and critical success factors
- Risk assessment results, including a description of the risk events, their likelihoods of occurrence, consequences, and risk quotients, and a prioritized list of the risks
- Risk reduction options, their advantages and disadvantages and benefits and costs
- Recommended risk reduction action, including statements of its benefits (why) and constraints (residual risk)
- Details of the risk action plan, including proposed actions (what), responsibilities (who), resource requirements (how), timing (when), reporting (outcome), ongoing review and monitoring (is the treatment measure effective and efficient)

Risk Action Plans

Risk action plans address details of the implementation of the risk treatment strategy. Such plans should be developed for each risk that is selected for treatment. The form of the risk action plans may range from a single sheet, such as a tabular checklist, to a more comprehensive management plan, depending on the complexity of the risk treatment measure and its relationship to other project or business activities. The plans for each risk should consider the preparedness of the staff for occurrence of the risk event. Roles and responsibilities at the time of the crisis and potential consequence strategies for financial, operational, and human impact of the risk must be considered. Risk communication with internal and external stakeholders is also an important component of the plan.

Risk Register

The individual risks should be registered to facilitate tracking of their status and to provide an indication of the residual risk. A risk register is a tool for managing and monitoring risk on a continuing basis. The details of individual risks may be entered into a risk register database that records the following information:

- An identifying number
- A brief description of the risk event
- An outline of the controls in place
- An analysis of the likelihood and potential consequences of the risk, given the controls

- An evaluation of its importance to the organization, expressed as an agreed priority
- The inherent level of risk if the controls did not work as intended
- The team leader or manager with overall responsibility for the risk
- A summary of the risk treatment actions proposed or undertaken
- The current status of the actions
- Date of entry of the risk
- Latest revision date
- Reasons for the revision
- Name of revision initiator

At each level of management in the organization, staff should be assigned to maintain the risk registers that contain a list of the risks relevant to the area for which they are responsible.

Monitoring, Auditing, and Review

Effective implementation of the risk action plans requires regular monitoring and progress reviews to determine whether the desired level of risk treatment has been achieved, whether further corrective action is required, and when the risk can be removed from the database. New risks may be identified in the process of continuing project review and new risk action plans developed and added to the risk register.

Monitoring techniques include the following initiatives:

- Risk management should be a regular agenda item at project review workshops; a watch list of all the major risks should be reviewed and, if necessary, updated.
- Regular surveys of risks and responses should be used in projects of long duration to revise lists of major, moderate, and minor risks; to generate new risk action plans; and to revise the watch list; the responsibility for conducting surveys, and their frequency, should be specified in the risk treatment strategy.
- Regular and ongoing risk audits provide an opportunity for those responsible for risk issues in the business to determine whether the detailed implementation of the project or activity continues to meet the defined performance requirements.

Reporting Outcomes

Reporting processes should be defined to keep management informed of the progress of risk management activities. There are many reasons for recording the outcomes of risk management:

- Accountability and auditability, so that managers are accountable for their decisions.
- Information source for future projects/activities.
- Record for postcompletion project evaluation. An evaluation of the effectiveness of the risk assessment and risk management processes should be incorporated into the postcompletion reviews for all projects. It is through this mechanism that the company can monitor its performance with regard to risk management and build on the collective experiences to improve overall performance.
- Communication within the risk management team and tracking the decision-making processes.
- Communication with internal stakeholders. It is important that the end users, or "owners" understand the risks and the trade-offs that have been made in strategy formulation process.
- Communication with external stakeholders, such as providers of finance and insurance coverage. Often, they will want to understand the residual risks that remain after all reasonable management actions have been taken and the "worst-case" outcomes, after prudent risk treatment action plans have been implemented.
- Capital expenditure authorizations that provide rational justification for spending money now or taking a particular course of action. Requests should contain an explicit analysis of risks as well as sensitivity analyses of key variables. Business cases should move away from single "point" estimates toward forms of risk analysis that highlight the expected ranges of outcomes and describe how the business will manage the inherent risks associated with these variations.
- Due diligence defense in the event of a future problem. A due diligence defense requires proof that risks were identified and addressed. What action was taken, how, why, by whom, when, what was the outcome; and what follow-up action, monitoring, and review were undertaken?

A risk report also can be used to help generate monthly, quarterly, and annual reports for use by other sections of the organization.

RISK MANAGEMENT SYSTEMS

The preceding sections outline the process and tools that should be developed and implemented to ensure adequate management of risks. Some organizations may choose to take this process further and develop a formalized risk management system. The aim of a risk management system is to provide a framework within which business risks are systematically and proactively identified, assessed, managed, and monitored across the full spectrum of the organization.

Such a system offers a tool to assist company directors and managers demonstrate due diligence in the execution of their responsibilities. The essence of a due diligence defense is the establishment and implementation of procedures designed to ensure that managers, employees, agents, and third-party contractors comply with the applicable laws, license conditions, and industry standards and prevent the occurrence of adverse impacts.

Identifiable structures and recording systems must make up the due diligence system. For this reason, management systems (i.e., environmental management systems, quality management systems, and integrated risk management systems) have become popular organizational management tools. The scope and structure of the due diligence system may vary according to the area of operations and organizational characteristics of the business, but typically, the key elements include:

- Procedures are in place to facilitate upward information transfer from the lower levels of the company to the company's controllers.
- The controllers of the company exercise, in relation to the subject matter of the due diligence system, reasoned and consistent judgments on the basis of all relevant information and material.
- Judgments made by company controllers at all levels of management of the company's affairs are effectively implemented.
- The system is effectively monitored and improved, where appropriate.

The core components of a risk management system are defined as:

- *Policy and objectives:* What are the business's performance objectives? What level of risk is acceptable to the organization?
- *Strategy:* What are the options for achieving the business's risk management policy and objectives? What is the preferred risk management strategy (organization, resources, and processes)?
- *System elements:* What are the key elements of the risk management system?
- *Procedures:* What existing system procedures can be used/augmented? What specific risk management instruments are to be used?

The conceptual framework for a risk management system is presented in Figure 8.1.

The underlying philosophy of this model is that the corporate vision and mission define the organization's risk management ethos and that the risk management policy states the organization's commitments to managing risks.

The risk management system defines the risk management policy, performance objectives, and checks and balances to ensure that the organization's corporate vision and mission, and external corporate governance obligations are satisfied. A structured, integrated management approach offers a mechanism for integrating risk management with related business activities, reduces the risk that important factors will be omitted inadvertently, and ensures that unnecessary duplication or overlap of effort can be avoided.

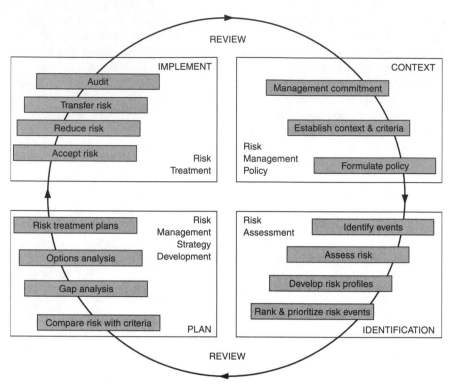

Figure 8.1   Risk management system conceptual framework showing the continuously cyclic nature of risk management.

Business risk management overlaps with many other management processes that may already form part of normal operational procedures within the organization, through its existing quality management system, health and safety management system, and/or an environmental management system. Areas of commonality may include the risk identification, audit, monitoring, corrective action, and management review functions. If well-established management systems are in place, the additional requirements of a business risk management system may be implemented through existing systems and by building and strengthening the links between those systems to capture the necessary planning, assessment, implementation, reporting, checking, corrective action, and continuous improvement processes.

Specific guidance for risk assessment and risk management may be introduced through technical guidance documents and procedures that are designed to work in conjunction with activity-specific guides or procedures that may exist at some of the organization's operations, or such documents may need to be developed as part of the system.

SUMMARY

Risk management is directed toward continuous improvement and achievement of realistic long-term performance targets. The risk treatment strategy for a project or business activity and its associated action plans serve several purposes. They provide a transparent and defensible trail that summarizes the results of the risk assessment process and describe the detailed risk management measures to be implemented to treat and monitor risks.

Risk strategy implementation and monitoring are critical steps in the risk management process, and this process should be recognized as a dynamic, continuous management responsibility. As projects and activities change with time, so risks can change, be resolved, or become more urgent. Responsible managers therefore need to ensure that the risk treatment strategy is reviewed regularly to reflect this dynamic situation.

To ensure business continuity, it is imperative that senior managers endorse a risk-based management approach for the organization. It is also desirable that they support integration of risk management practices with existing business operations and programs, to ensure a consistent and coordinated examination of risks from both a strategic and operational perspective. In this regard, an organization-wide risk management system may be warranted to ensure that a structure is in place to identify and manage risk using an appropriate risk management process, such as the RISQUE method. The best risk management systems are specifically designed to fit comfortably within the business structure, activities, and ethos—through this approach, risk management will be inherent in all decision-making, implementation, reporting, and auditing processes.

9

BENEFITS OF THE RISQUE METHOD

Business managers deal with risk as an integral part of strategic planning and operations and usually are familiar with the traditional financial bottom-line aspects of their business. The potential to expand the scope of their management practices to address the triple bottom line lies in developing a better understanding of the environmental and social aspects of their business risk profile.

RISK MANAGEMENT AND THE RISQUE METHOD

In Parts One and Two we have described risk management as a process, supported by tools and administrative structures, that is directed toward the effective management of potential opportunities and adverse effects associated with risk events. The RISQUE method has been developed as a practical tool to address the information-gathering, processing, and decision-making needs of the risk management process. We believe that the process is a sound business management tool that has broad application from strategic planning through to detailed operational planning and management.

The RISQUE method is particularly well suited to assist business managers to integrate triple bottom line considerations into their planning processes. The method places emphasis on defining the business context, including performance objectives, the organization's stakeholders and their interests, and the "bigger picture" relationship between the proposed project or activity and other decision-making processes.

The method also actively encourages teamwork and participation in the interests of fostering information sharing, informed decision making, and development of a broader appreciation of the multifaceted nature of all projects and business activities.

Finally, the RISQUE method presents information in a consistent form using financial measures, which ensures that financial, social, and environmental aspects are considered collectively, and not artificially separated (and dismissed) because they could not be measured in the same units on a balance sheet. The RISQUE method specifically incorporates issues that have in the past been treated as "non-quantifiable," such as loss of amenity, community outcry, business reputation, legal culpability, and environmental impacts. Until now, such risk events have rarely been successfully included in financial assessments of the risks (both positive and negative) posed by business activities.

All in all, we believe that the RISQUE method offers many benefits for responsible triple bottom line risk management, some of which are:

- Provision of a clear understanding of corporate risk—use of risk profiles to compare the relative risk between risk events and estimation of risk cost.
- Development of a sound basis for formulation of risk management strategies, mainly through identification of risk event priorities and cost-effective actions.
- Feedback to design of project financial structure and infrastructure based on minimization of risk.
- Direct comparison and rational assessment of both similar and dissimilar options.
- Translation of complex elements of risk into financial terms that are readily understood and used by most project managers.
- Clear identification of current and future liabilities to provide a sound basis for negotiation (e.g., the asset bid process and setting of realistic performance bonds).
- Application of a robust, logical, systematic, transparent, auditable process that uses best available experience. Decisions made on the basis of results are defensible and clearly demonstrate due diligence.
- Application of the process to a wide range of industry sectors and activities.

All aspects of the triple bottom line management (financial, social, and environmental performance) can be improved through application of the RISQUE method. Reduction of business risk through sound management practice leads directly to increased profit, improved environmental performance, and enhanced community benefits. The following sections present specific examples that demonstrate these benefits. These examples are presented as detailed case studies in Part Three.

FINANCIAL ACCOUNTABILITY

Benefit-Cost Analysis

Attention to financial profit is demonstrated when business decisions incorporate benefit-cost analysis. In most cases, benefit-cost analysis involves a comparison of future income vs. capital, operating, and maintenance expenditure, sometimes with an arbitrary contingency included to account for risk. Benefit-cost analyses rarely include a reasoned estimate of the potential cost of future risk events. Using the RISQUE method, benefit-cost analysis includes a reasonable estimate of future financial cost associated with the occurrence of risk events.

A typical profit-focused benefit-cost application is shown in Chapter 16 ("Corporate Reporting and Insurance"), where the company compared the implementation costs of risk treatment measures with the expected reduction in exposure to risk cost. In the example, using an insurance strategy, the company could reduce approximately $185 million of financial exposure by investment of $5.7 million per annum.

An innovative form of benefit-cost analysis is demonstrated in Chapter 10 ("Project Selection"), where the organization compared the additional cost of construction and operation for each risk treatment option with the benefit gained by reducing the financial risk compared with the current condition.

Risk Cost

Consideration of risk events as costs has a direct impact on the financial bottom line. In many cases the potential costs associated with future risk events are not considered in a systematic manner. Therefore, frequently financial adjustments to account for risk are based on broad-scale overview and "gut feel" rather than a rational assessment of the likely cost. In these circumstances the estimate usually represents an extremely conservative position, which in most cases is a competitive disadvantage and can ultimately lead to lost financial opportunity. In contrast, the RISQUE method uses a rational approach to derive a realistic estimate of risk cost.

Chapter 11 ("Acquisitions") presents an example of using risk cost to value an asset for a potential acquisition. During the initial valuation of the project, the bidder estimated that a realistic estimate of risk cost would be approximately $115 million. The bidder felt that, in order to be competitive, the project risk cost would need to be reduced by restructuring the project to incorporate risk reduction measures. The costs of achieving the risk reduction were input separately into the financial model, and the estimated risk cost of the restructured project was reduced to approximately $40 million, resulting in a marked net reduction in estimated project cost.

Return on Investment

Cost savings and targeted expenditure are common methods of improving profit. Often, it is difficult to identify areas where cost savings can be achieved. In addition, often costs are incurred to deal with risk events that are perceived (but not demonstrated) to be priority issues. Using the RISQUE method, decisions can be made that consider return (as measured by reduction in risk cost) on investment.

The case study in Chapter 17 ("Asset Management") presents an example of how an organization could demonstrate that by spending $1.2 million, it could lay off approximately $9 million of risk cost. Expenditure of a relatively small additional cost ($300,000) could reduce the risk lost by an additional $12 million.

Corporate Reporting

Corporate reporting of contingent financial liability is mandatory for U.S.-listed public companies and will become more common elsewhere. The impact on the bottom line reported in the financial statement can be very marked if a company has not considered all of the potential liabilities and developed a strategy to gain recoveries on the other side of the balance sheet.

The case study in Chapter 16 ("Corporate Reporting and Insurance") shows how the RISQUE method was applied to consider all material issues, to calculate the contingent financial liability, and to develop an action plan to progressively reduce the financial bottom-line impact. In the initial report the company would book $675 million but would recover $185 million through insurance and include $5.7 million for risk transfer costs. Over the next three years, through a process of progressive implementation of risk reduction works, the company could plan to reduce the reserve to $15.7 million by booking only $195 million.

Financial Assurances

Financial assurances can be expensive to establish; therefore, the amount placed should reflect realistic exposure to the indicated risk events. In cases where there is some uncertainty or extreme regulatory conservatism, there is a tendency to seek excessive financial assurances. The RISQUE method is useful in deriving, defending, and negotiating appropriate financial assurances.[1]

Placement of a reasonable quantum of financial assurance is demonstrated in Chapter 14 ("Financial Assurances"). In that case study the RISQUE method is used to derive estimates of the sums that should be set aside to cover premature closure, environmental impairment, and postclosure management of a landfill site. The landfill owner was able to demonstrate to the regulator that the total financial assurance should be around $3 million. (Previously, the regulatory authority had sought $20.1 million for a landfill of similar character.)

Chapter 15 ("Indemnity in Perpetuity") describes how the RISQUE method was used to determine an appropriate bond amount to cater for postclosure management of a mine that was scheduled for closure eight years in the future. The rationally derived bond of approximately $5 million was successfully defended in court against an opponent's claim that over $100 million should be placed.

ENVIRONMENTAL RESPONSIBILITY

Prioritization

Improved environmental performance is achieved by rationally prioritizing expenditure on risk events that pose the most risk to the environment. In many cases the relative risk of events with environmental consequences is not well understood, and resources are allocated to address risk events that are relatively unimportant. In the meantime the environment remains exposed to degradation associated with higher-risk events.

The RISQUE method has been applied in the case study of Chapter 17 ("Asset Management") to identify which assets pose the greatest risk to the marine environment and to develop a risk action plan to reduce environmental risk.

Least-Risk Options

The RISQUE method also can be used in operational planning to assist in the selection of an option that will pose least environmental risk. The case study of Chapter 10 ("Project Selection") shows the extent to which reduction in environmental risk was a key factor in determining the most appropriate mine waste management option. In this case, each mine waste management option was assessed with regard to risk posed to a comprehensive range of receptors (environmental and community receptors). In the final analysis, environmental impact was considered a major factor in selection of the most appropriate option.

Focused Technical Studies

Often, substantial investment in environmental studies is made available to evaluate the impacts of an existing or proposed business activity. Many studies of potential environmental impacts of business activity involve specialist investigations. In many instances the environmental specialists performing the studies determine the scope and methodology of the studies without reference to other concurrent investigations. Frequently, the studies are well advanced before the results are brought together to assess the overall impacts and risk. In some cases the scope of the study turns out to be much more detailed than ultimately required, while others are found to be inadequate considering the importance of the issues they address.

Prior to the risk assessment described in Chapter 10 ("Project Selection"), a comprehensive range of world-class environmental research had been carried out. Very little work had been done on the social impacts of each option. As a result, the first pass of the risk assessment using the RISQUE method indicated that while environmental risk events were very important, it was likely that the consequences of social and community impacts would be similar to or greater than the environmental impacts. Subsequently, social impact studies were carried out, and the results included in the overall revised risk assessment.

SOCIAL RESPONSIBILITY

Community Benefits

During the initiation stage of many projects, it is clear to proponents that, in addition to the demonstrable commercial benefits, the project will provide substantial benefit to the wider community. However, it is not possible to demonstrate community benefits in similar financial terms due to the perceived difficulty in placing a financial value on such benefits. In too many cases, the inability to demonstrate the true worth of a project has led to its termination, and the wider community has suffered from the effects of lost opportunity.

The land development example in Chapter 12 ("Quantifying Intangibles") shows how substantial financial opportunities can be generated if so-called non-quantifiable consequences, such as community diversity, amenity, and image, are valued in dollar terms and used to make decisions. In addition, as a result of the study, the state-owned developers were able to justify their decision to enhance community benefit by performing otherwise marginally economic capital works.

Public Safety

Many business activities involve situations where the consequences of risk events predominantly involve potential to cause death or serious injury to people. In these cases, often social concerns cannot differentiate between the value of human life and measurement of the consequences of loss of life. In such cases it is often inappropriate to use financial terms to measure consequences of risk events. Often, there is intense social pressure to retain a qualitative view of life loss, and attempts at quantitative risk assessment have stalled, resulting in decisions based more on emotion rather than on sound reasoning.

In Chapter 13 ("Community Safety"), a quantitative assessment of community safety was carried out for a tourism operator. The assessment evaluated the safety risk of underground tours using human life as the measure of consequence applied by the RISQUE method rather than a financial measure. This approach assumed no judgment on the value of life but still used loss of life as the sole discriminant with respect to risk. The results of the risk assessment were used to formulate a strategy that markedly reduced risk to the public.

Stakeholder Welfare

In the past many business decisions have been only based on consideration of economic and, more recently, environmental factors. Community representatives have criticized subsequent activities of the businesses for not having taken community impacts into account. The multifaceted RISQUE method effectively requires risk analysts to consider community impacts as part of normal decision-making process. Chapter 17 ("Asset Management") shows how community concerns and impacts were formally considered in the commercial decision-making process. The example also indicates how the process encouraged greater community involvement by incorporating community action into some solutions. As the community was better informed and involved in risk prevention, there was improved likelihood of community understanding, as opposed to outrage, in response to the occurrence of any future risk events.

Note

1. A. R. Bowden, "A Systematic Method for Determining Appropriate Financial Assurances for Waste Management Facilities," *Proceedings of the 4th National Hazardous and Solid Waste Convention*, Brisbane, Australia, April 1998.

Part Three

SELECTED CASE STUDIES

The following synopses present the nature and key aspects of the detailed case studies discussed in Chapters 10 through 17. The synopses are executive summaries that are provided to enable readers to quickly gain a good understanding of the overall content of each of the detailed case studies. The synopses should allow readers to judge the relevance of the case studies to their current or future needs and whether to study the specifics of selected case studies.

"Project Selection" (Chapter 10)

A very large copper and gold mine is located in the highland headwaters of one of the world's large rivers. Extremely high rainfall, high seismicity, weak geology, and highly complex natural and social environments characterize this tropical environment.

Shortly after mining started in 1984, a landslide destroyed the proposed tailings dam site, causing it to be abandoned, and since the late 1980s the tailings and waste rock have been discharged to the river system.

During the mid-1990s it became apparent that the discharge of waste and tailings into the catchment was creating an adverse environmental effect. In 1996 the mine operator commenced its Mine Waste Management Project (MWMP), which aimed at selecting the best of five mitigation options for the remaining life of the mine. Quantitative risk assessment was an integral component of the MWMP.

The risk assessment study objectives for each option were to:

- Identify and quantify the significant engineering, environmental, and social risk events
- Combine the engineering risks with the environmental/social risks to derive a total risk
- Quantify the operator's highest realistic financial exposure

- Present the base cost and the total risk cost in a way that enabled comparison of the options

The assessment included numerous workshops and interviews with highly skilled, world-recognized specialists. The principal risk assessment outputs consisted of a few easily understood graphs showing the relationships of base cost to risk cost and benefit-cost for each option.

In 1997, on the basis of the risk assessment results, the board decided on an 18-month dredging trial and commissioned numerous environmental and community-related studies.

In 1999 the assessment structure was modified to reflect the significant improvements in knowledge afforded by the studies conducted during the preceding two years. The conclusions from the 1999 assessment were that:

- The understanding of the complicated inter-relationships between the mine, the river system, and the people of the catchment had improved considerably.
- There was no quantifiable difference between the mitigation options in terms of overall ecological benefits.
- Social risk events provided greater differentiation between the options than did the ecological risk events.
- There remained considerable uncertainty about the ecological and social risk event that would impact on the overall cost of the mitigation options.

An important benefit of the rigorous approach imposed by the RISQUE method was an increased understanding of the issues and intricacies of this particularly complex project. One of the natural outcomes of this process was the progressive refinement of the risk profile associated with each mitigation option as high risks were identified and solutions designed to reduce those risks. The eventual outcome was that the difference in overall risk between the options was relatively small.

"Acquisitions" (Chapter 11)

A large power utility was engaged in acquisition of power generation assets. During the tender process, the utility's senior management required that environmental and regulatory risk be properly considered in the financial assessment.

The process included identification by an expert panel of key risk events and estimation of their likelihoods and consequential costs. Risk modeling derived risk profiles and estimates of risk cost. Potential risk reduction options were developed, and their impacts on the restructured project were assessed. A plan of risk management actions was devised and incorporated into the bid.

The assessment derived an initial estimated planning risk cost for contingent environmental and regulatory events that was clearly material and should be reduced. In addition, the utility considered that the uncertainty of risk cost also should be reduced.

Four risk events (generation performance standards, global warming, mercury emissions, and wastewater discharge) posed the greatest risk, accounting for over 99 percent of the total risk. The first three events presented substantial exposure to financial liability.

Risk treatment actions were developed for each risk event, and assessment of the financial benefit of implementing the proposed actions was carried out. After implementation, the estimated risk cost was substantially less than the initial estimate. In addition, the uncertainty of risk cost magnitude was reduced markedly. The costs of achieving the risk benefits were separately input to the financial model as project base costs.

A schedule of risk costs was derived to account for timing and magnitude of future expenditure and directly input to the financial model.

Overall, the risk profile information was used to adjust the quantum of the tender and to assist with structuring the bid. On the basis of the risk assessment results, the utility was comfortable that risk had been adequately considered and that the bid should proceed.

"Quantifying Intangibles" (Chapter 12)

The government recognized an undeveloped coastal area of high potential community value as having high potential for future urban development. In preparation, the government water authority purchased the large area of coastal land for wastewater and groundwater infrastructure development.

A consortium of developers for the area believed that there would be substantial advantages in relocating the proposed wastewater and groundwater treatment plants to release higher-value coastal land for greater residential and other community uses.

One of the major difficulties was considered to be translation of "intangibles" such as community values into dollar terms, which then could be used to support and justify business decisions that demonstrably enhanced community benefit.

The developers and the authority undertook a total community benefit-cost analysis to assess whether any additional costs incurred by relocation of the wastewater and groundwater treatment plants would be adequately compensated by additional community benefits. The benefit-cost analysis needed to consider a broad range of events and views and take a holistic view of the impacts (both positive and negative) on the community. The analysis used the RISQUE method to compare the two options for siting the wastewater treatment facilities.

The panel derived methods of estimating the financial costs and benefits associated with issues that are normally considered to be nonquantifiable, such as community diversity, beach access, odor, public reputation, and accessibility.

Results of the benefit-cost analysis clearly indicated that the financial benefits far outweighed the additional costs to relocate the facility.

Having demonstrated the benefit of relocation, the authority and the developers evaluated the potential options to how to distribute the costs to the stakeholders in some proportion to the benefits accrued.

"Community Safety" (Chapter 13)

An underground power station is located in a popular tourist region with considerable scenic attraction. One of the many tour options offered in the region includes a tour of the power station. The overall aim of this study was to evaluate and ensure the safety of members of the public from unacceptably high exposure to hazards and incidents that could potentially cause serious injury or death during a tour.

For this study, consequence was defined as a serious injury or fatality. While placing a financial estimate for the loss of human life or serious injury is accepted and used in certain areas, publicly it remains a controversial practice. By using personal injury as the measure of consequence, this project avoided the controversy while still ensuring robust and valid outcomes from the risk assessment process.

Where loss of life is concerned, risk was considered using two differing measures: individual risk and societal risk. Acceptability guidelines exist for both individual and societal measures of risk. The development of these guidelines is based largely on statistical data relating to fatalities associated with common activities such as smoking, driving, and flying. The study used several individual and societal risk acceptance guidelines.

For individual risk, the calculated risk quotient indicated that a tour through the power station presented a risk approximately equivalent to that of flying. This low level of risk was considered acceptable.

The societal risk for all events evaluated was within the tolerable limit of the most conservative acceptability criterion adopted for this study, and all but two events fell below the objective criterion of that standard. The risk quotient of the two highest risk events indicated that while posing an acceptable level of risk, some risk treatment should be carried out if cost-effective reduction measures could be identified. This finding was confirmed by sensitivity analysis.

The operator accepted the recommendations of the assessment and has introduced a number of initiatives to reduce the risk posed by the two most risky events.

"Financial Assurances" (Chapter 14)

The owner operates both a basalt quarry and a sanitary landfill. Landfill operations involve six progressive stages that will take place over a 30-year period.

The regulator required the owner to place a financial assurance for the landfill. The value of the financial assurance was to be determined by the owner, but at that time no guidelines had been developed by the regulator. The aim of the financial assurances assessment was to identify the specific components that should be covered by the financial assurance and suggest fund component amounts that reflect realistic operational and management costs and environmental risk.

The U.S. Environmental Protection Agency financial assurance criteria for municipal solid waste landfills were used as a guide, and all costs were estimated using a probabilistic approach.

The estimated cost of premature closure would have to cover the costs of management and administration, landfill capping, revegetation of the landfill surface, trimming of waste and earthworks around the landfill, gas management, rehabilitation of roads and hard stand areas, and removal of site facilities and services. A realistic but conservative estimate of the closure financial assurance was selected as the 80 percent confidence-level cost.

The costs of postclosure management activities were derived for a 30-year period and included costs for management and administration; landfill fire; leachate management; groundwater monitoring; gas management; rehabilitation of the landfill surface; and drainage control. The 50 percent confidence-level cost estimate was considered to represent an appropriate postclosure financial assurance.

The cost of corrective action was related to the potential occurrence of risk events, such as leachate discharge to the surface and to the groundwater, fire, earthquake-induced slope failure, washout, rehabilitation failure, out-of-specification waste, flora damage, fauna damage, and landfill gas explosion. A conservative yet reasonable financial reserve for potential corrective action costs was estimated to be the 80 percent confidence-level estimate of risk cost, calculated using the RISQUE method.

The regulator broadly agreed with the owner that the estimates were reasonable. A structured financial assurance was successfully negotiated based on the recommended categories and cost estimates.

"Indemnity in Perpetuity" (Chapter 15)

Mining involves excavation and placement of a large quantity of soil and rock, a portion of which typically contains elevated concentrations of metals such as gold, silver, copper, zinc, iron, and manganese. If released into the environment, many of these metals could potentially cause significant environmental damage over a considerable period of time.

The mine operator adopted best-practice mining and rehabilitation methods throughout the mine's operating period, and as a result there was a high expectation that the site would pose an acceptably low level of long term risk to the environment once mining ceased and the site was rehabilitated. However, some residual risk to the environment would still remain, which, if realized, could impose a significant cost to the taxpayer to mitigate or remedy contamination.

The government required establishment of postclosure bonds or equivalent financial instruments for all mine operations to indemnify the community against the potentially large costs of preventing or remediating future adverse environmental effects originating from a closed mine after the mining company departed. The postclosure securities were to exist in perpetuity.

The operator was the first mining company in the country (and possibly in the world) faced with the need to establish a perpetual postclosure bond. While the proposal was accepted in principle, neither the operator nor the regulators could adequately define:

- The meaning of "perpetuity" and hence the term to be covered by the security
- A rational method of assessing the events to be covered by the security
- A means of determining an appropriate quantum that was both realistic and adequate

The RISQUE method was used to define and quantify the insurable events and to determine a reserve capable of funding uninsurable events that might occur in the future. Third-party insurance, which a specifically established trust would need to maintain, and the administration and management costs incurred by the trust, were derived using traditional cost-estimating techniques.

An agreed definition of "perpetuity" was crucial to the development of a successful assurance strategy. Using the concept of the time value of money, the risk analyst demonstrated that perpetuity could be defined in financial terms.

The regulators adopted the strategy and the proposed quantum. The regulators supported the operator's proposal, without change, in a court appeal. In his decision, the judge generally agreed with the quantum, and the operator posted a capitalization bond of this quantum.

"Corporate Reporting and Insurance" (Chapter 16)

The company had 10 operating companies engaged in manufacturing, mining, and mineral processing at over 30 sites located throughout the world. The company needed to restructure its environmental and third-party liability insurance strategy and to comply with corporate reporting requirements.

The RISQUE method was applied to facilitate development of the insurance strategy and identification of contingent liabilities.

Quantitative risk profiles were generated that considered third-party and environmental impairment from sudden events, insurable gradual events, and uninsurable gradual events.

Development of a targeted risk reduction strategy was achieved by risk transfer through insurance or otherwise through planned actions to reduce either the likelihood of occurrence of risk events or the financial exposure to the events.

Transfer of risk via purchased insurance could be achieved using a range of instrument types and opportunities, such as finite risk, industrial and special risk (ISR), and environmental impairment liability (EIL) insurance.

The company was able to use the risk profiles to develop a plan that adequately addressed risk in the financial reports and that represented the company's realistic exposure to contingent liability.

For the current year financial statement, the company could plan to book a specified sum but would recover a substantial proportion through insurance. Substantial benefits would be gained over the first three years, where, through planned expenditure, the contingent liability could be reduced to a quarter of its initial value.

Application of the RISQUE method assisted with compliance with corporate reporting regulations and guidelines, balance sheet recovery of contingent liability, and development of an appropriate, targeted insurance strategy.

"Asset Management" (Chapter 17)

A water utility owns and operates 102 wastewater pumping stations within a metropolitan region. Many of the stations are located close to environmentally sensitive areas, such as coastal waterways and aquifers. The utility required a strategy of appropriate risk management actions.

The objectives of the study were to identify and quantify the main risk contributors at each of the pumping stations, rank the pumping stations in order of risk, and develop a staged risk management strategy. The RISQUE method was applied to achieve the required outcomes.

The risk analysis showed that less than one-quarter of the pumping stations presented substantially more risk than the remaining stations. In addition, the nine riskiest pumping stations were responsible for 43 percent of the total risk posed by all the pumping stations combined.

Pumping station risk treatment options that were available to the utility were aimed either to reduce the likelihood of a sewage release or to reduce the consequences of a spill.

Engineering solutions included increasing pumping station storage capacity, improving monitoring, installing audible alarms, upgrading pumps, and installing protective bollards. Community solutions included public involvement in response to alarms and educational public relations programs.

Analysis of the benefits of the proposed risk reduction actions showed that the actions would comprehensively achieve an initial risk acceptability criterion. In most cases, the actions would reduce the risk posed by the riskiest pumping stations to less than one-half of the acceptability criterion.

Benefit-cost analysis of the risk management actions demonstrated that expenditure of a relatively small sum would effectively eliminate around 75 percent of the risk and reduce risk exposure by around 10 times more than the cost of prevention.

In this evaluation, the use of risk profiles clearly indicated which pumping stations presented the greatest risk. Actions were formulated that targeted the highest-risk pumping stations and demonstrably reduced the overall risk to the harbor waterways.

10

PROJECT SELECTION: MINING, PAPUA NEW GUINEA

This case study will look at the:

- Iterative nature of the risk management process and its benefits
- Application of the RISQUE method to a large, very complex project
- Selection of the expert panel
- Use of differing modeling techniques
- Project selection on the basis of total cost including risk cost
- Project selection on the basis of benefit-cost ratio including risk cost
- Significant advantages in addition to the modeled outcomes provided by the RISQUE method

BACKGROUND

This case study examines the risk assessments performed for the Ok Tedi copper-gold mine, which is located in the Star Mountains in the Western Province of Papua New Guinea (PNG) and is operated by Ok Tedi Mining Limited (OTML).

Environment

The Star Mountains region is one of the wettest places on earth, receiving around 40 feet (ft) (12 m) of rain annually. The open-pit operation is located at an elevation of approximately 5,000 ft (1,500 m) in the headwaters of the Ok Tedi (Ok means river in the local language), a tributary of the Fly River.

For most of its 105-mile (170-km) length, the Ok Tedi is typified as a steep, braided river. Approximately 30 miles (50 km) upstream of its confluence with the Fly River, the riverbed gradient reduces dramatically, the bed sediments change from predominantly gravel to sand, and the form of the river changes to an incised, meandering single channel within a large floodplain. From the confluence, the Fly River meanders a further 500 miles (800 km) before disgorging into the Gulf of Papua.

With an average water discharge of approximately 210,000 cubic feet per second (ft^3/s) (6,000 m^3/sec), the Fly River is one of the world's largest rivers, comparable to the Yukon and Columbia rivers in North America (250,000 ft^3/s and 235,000 ft^3/s, respectively) and the Danube in Europe (230,000 ft^3/s). It also carries a considerable natural sediment load, discharging in excess of 90 million tons (84 Mtonnes) per year.

The vegetation along the banks of the Ok Tedi is highland rain forest. Below the confluence with the Fly River lies an extensive floodplain that consists of oxbow lakes, drowned river valleys, tie-channels, lagoons, swamp, and wetland forest. Passing downstream, the floodplain vegetation changes from lowland rain forest to swamp grass; the change to swamp grass is associated with longer duration of flooding.

Regional Geology

The central mountainous spine of PNG, of which the Star Mountains region is a part, delineates the Pacific-Australian tectonic plate boundary. Upthrust marine sediments including limestone dominate the geology.

The project area has a record of seismic activity that is similar to California Zone 4, which includes the San Andreas Fault. The geotechnically weak marine rocks make the area very prone to landslides. Detailed structural mapping of the area around the mine showed that 25 to 30 percent of the 45 square miles (120 km^2) consists of landslides and associated features. The largest landslide, referred to as the Hindenburg Rock Avalanche, measured approximately 1.7 cubic miles (7 km^3). Seventeen landslides of about 200 million tons (180 Mt) have been identified over a 230-square-mile (600-km^2) area around the mine. Within this area, landslides of a similar magnitude have a probability of occurrence of 64 percent (i.e., a slightly better than even chance of occurrence) every 30 years.

The seismicity and geology raise issues relating to long-term integrity for any permanent man-made structures in the catchment and need to be, and have been, accounted for in the designs of the waste retaining structures considered here.

The Mine

The mining operation is regulated by the state under the Mining (Ok Tedi Agreement) Act 1976 (the Act) as amended and supplemented. It comprises an open-cut mine, a mill, a 97-mile (156-km) slurry pipeline and access road, a port, a hydroelectric power station, a township, and related support infrastructure. Copper concentrate, also containing gold and silver, produced at the mill is pumped down the pipeline to the port of Kiunga, which is on the Fly River upstream of the Ok Tedi confluence. Specially designed barges transport the copper concentrate from Kiunga down the Fly River to a floating silo vessel moored at the mouth of the delta from where it is transported in oceangoing vessels to worldwide copper smelter destinations.

Mining of the ore body commenced in June 1984. As originally envisaged, the project was to include stable and unstable waste rock dumps adjacent to the open pit and a conventional valley-fill tailings dam in an adjacent river valley. However, in 1984, whilst under construction, a slow-moving landslide entered the abutment key of the tailings dam, forcing abandonment of this site. In 1989 a major landslide, the Vancouver Ridge Landslide, of approximately 180 million tons (160 Mt) occurred immediately to the north of the open pit, undermining the toe of the northern waste dump.

Following the landslide at the tailings dam site, the Interim Tailings System of waste disposal was approved by the state. This provided for retention of part of the tailings, the finer material being discharged to the river system. The Interim Tailings Dam was a short-term measure, the dam being filled by 1988. Since then all tailings have been discharged directly from the mill into the Ok Mani, a headwater tributary of the Ok Tedi.

As of March 1997, mine production was approximately 33 million tons (30 Mt) of ore and 50 million tons (44 Mt) of mined waste rock annually. Ore production is expected to continue at the same rate until closure, whereas waste rock production is expected to increase to approximately 60 million tons (55 Mt) per year to be followed by a gradual decline from 2002 to 2009. The mine is scheduled to close in 2009.

MINE WASTE MANAGEMENT PROJECT

In addition to the tailings and waste rock that are discharged from the mine to the river system, a significant volume of sediment originates from valley wall erosion caused by the movement of mined waste rock from the edge of the open pit and down various creeks.

The Vancouver Ridge Landslide was a sudden impact event that also contributed sediment to the river system, which resulted in an immediate increase in the riverbed level of the Ok Tedi.

The annual quantities of mined waste rock, tailings, landslide material, and valley wall erosion that have entered the river system since the commencement of mining in 1984 have been considerably greater than the recorded premine natural sediment loads. During the mid-1990s it became apparent that the discharge of waste and tailings into the catchment was creating an adverse environmental effect. In particular, there was a rise in riverbed level (caused by the deposition and storage of mine-derived sand in the river channel) and a resultant increase in the annual frequency of flooding of the lower Ok Tedi. The increased flooding in turn led to die-back of forest along the banks of the Ok Tedi. The increased river and sediment levels also led to loss of gardens and agricultural land, loss of some amenities, and declining fish populations. Environmental monitoring has shown increased effects on the river system over time. Adverse effects along the Ok Tedi were factors in the widely publicized litigation action initiated against the mine owners in April 1994 by PNG landowners.

Risk Assessment History

In 1995 OTML began a review of all work previously conducted on alternative waste management methods to seek an acceptable method of managing the mine impacts. The detailed study was called the Mine Waste Management Project (MWMP). The aim of the study was the selection of the best mitigation option for the remaining life of mine. Quantitative risk assessment was an integral and critical component of the study and in the selection of the preferred option.

Of the numerous waste management options that OTML had investigated over the preceding decade, four mitigation options were selected for the MWMP and for comparison with the "null" option (i.e., continuation of the current operation). The options were:

- *Lukwi option:* A conventional tailings dam sited at Lukwi
- *LOT-N:* Sand dredging and a tailings dam at a northern site in the Lower Ok Tedi area
- *LOT-S:* Sand dredging and a tailings dam at a southern site in the Lower Ok Tedi area
- *Dredge option:* Dredging and storage of sand from the Lower Ok Tedi

The risk assessment was carried out during 1996, the findings being reported in 1997. One outcome of this exercise was a commitment by OTML to continue the MWMP. The extended scope comprised a significant volume of environmental, social, and engineering investigation of three of the mitigation options and the null option.

The options for the subsequent 1999 risk assessment were:

- *Dredge option:* Continuation of the trial dredging scheme at a nominal rate of 22 million tons (20 Mt) per annum until the end of mine life in 2009.
- *Tailings option:* Continuation of the dredging scheme to the end of 2001 to build an embankment in which to store tailings, and the piping and storing of tailings until the end of mine life in 2009.
- *Early closure option:* Closure of the mine in 2000, this would be the earliest practicable time for an orderly conclusion to the project.
- *No-dredge option:* A revised null option, which involved demobilizing the dredge at the end of the trial period in 1999 and reverting to disposal of waste rock and tailings into the river system.

The aim of the work was to refine the uncertainties identified in the 1997 report. The findings were reported in 1999. The risk assessment was again revisited in

2000, this time to assess the changes arising from the improvements in knowledge from the previous 12 months of study. Some of the studies continued past 2000.

INITIAL RISK ASSESSMENT (1996–1997)

Organizational Commitment

OTML demonstrated clear commitment to the project. Originally, the MWMP was initiated in response to the litigation that OTML faced in 1994. The OTML board approved the study. When in 1996 the parties reached a settlement, continuation of the study and of the risk assessment was one of the agreement conditions.

OTML made staff at all levels of the organization (including board level) freely available to the project, and the individuals themselves were committed and gave their time willingly. OTML's commitment was also evident in the selection of acknowledged world specialists to perform the studies it commissioned and to contribute to the risk management process as members of the expert panel.

Stakeholders

The stakeholders in the project were defined through discussion with OTML. The stakeholders were:

OTML board/shareholders	Local government	Local community
OTML manager	Provincial community	Provincial government
OTML employees	PNG public	National government
OTML contractors	International public	Environmental groups/NGOs

Risk Management Aims

OTML defined the overall objective of the MWMP as providing a Life of Mine and Aftercare Mine Waste Management Plan, taking into account business costs, socioeconomic benefits, and environmental benefits of the available options.

The risk assessment study objectives against which OTML would compare its MWMP options were to:

- Identify the significant engineering, environmental, and social risk events associated with the approvals, construction, operation, and aftercare phases for each of the mitigation options.
- Quantify the risk events associated with each phase of each option, that is, quantify the frequency of occurrence and the financial consequences of the

identified engineering, environmental, and social risk events that could occur during the life of the project.

- Combine the engineering risks with the environmental/social risks to provide a total scheme risk for each phase of each option and for the overall option risk.
- Quantify OTML's highest realistic financial exposure associated with each option.
- Present the base cost and the total risk cost of each option in a way that enabled comparison of the options.

Target Audience

The ultimate decision-maker for OTML, and hence the target audience for the study outputs, was its board. On a number of occasions during the project, presentations were given to the board and shareholder organizations. The presentations explained the process and the proposed form of the study outputs. Buy-in to the risk management process and its results was first required from those people responsible for promoting the findings to the board (i.e., by senior technical and executive management level staff).

Acceptance throughout the hierarchy of OTML was enhanced by the commitment given to the project by the individuals at all levels. This was achieved through personal contact with the study team and by attendance at, and contribution to, the workshops and data gathering meetings.

Keeping in mind that the risk assessment report would be part of a large volume of reports and other material on which the board would draw in making its decision, the assessment outputs were structured in a concise format that clearly showed the study results. After six months of study, the 1997 report and appendixes contained more than 500 pages of figures and text. The board's executive summary comprised two figures and three pages of text that carried the full meaning of the report (although clearly not the detail).

Risk Assessment Structure

Everything about the Ok Tedi project was large and complex, from its setting in a remote, tropical area of dense rain forest, the adjacent river system, to the mine itself. The environmental systems were poorly understood, and in spite of more than a decade of extensive environmental monitoring, the cause-and-effect relationships between the mine activities and the measured environmental responses were also poorly understood and often unknown. It took most people a significant time (a matter of weeks) to gain even a rudimentary understanding of the operation and the natural and social environment in which it was situated.

The full complexity of the project could clearly not be modeled, and the structure of the assessment (and the risk model) therefore required simplification in a way that retained integrity of the critical components.

DURATION OF RELEASE ⟶

RATE OF RELEASE

Short Duration Low Rate	Nonissue	Med Duration Low Rate	Nonissue	Long Duration Low Rate	Nonissue
Short Duration Moderate Rate	Nonissue	Med Duration Moderate Rate	Nonissue	Long Duration Moderate Rate 3 Mtpa	**Objective** Lower Ok Tedi Dredged Sand Storage
Short Duration High Rate	Nonissue	Med Duration High Rate 30 Mtpa	**Repairable failure** Lukwi Tailings Dam LOT - South LOT- North	Long Duration High Rate 30 Mtpa	**Irrepairable failure/Null Case** Lukwi Tailings Dam LOT - South LOT- North Null Case
Short Duration Very High Rate >100 Mtpa	**Catastrophic failure** Lukwi Tailings Dam LOT - South LOT- North	Med Duration Very High Rate	Not Applicable	Long Duration Very High Rate	Not Applicable

Figure 10.1   Tailings release mode matrix based on rate and duration of tailings release.

Simplification, with respect to environmental risk events, was achieved, for example, in the 1996–1997 assessment through the development of the concept of release modes. Each uncontrolled release mode from a tailings storage was considered to represent a magnitude of environmental impact. Each release mode was defined by a specific range of rate and duration of release of mine waste into the river system. The basis of this approach came from the concept that neither the environment nor the people living in affected areas downstream of the mine would be concerned with differentiating the type of event that initiated an uncontrolled release. That is, it would be immaterial to a damaged fishery or to a villager whose land becomes flooded, whether the long-duration, moderate rate of release of mine waste that caused the damage occurred through the adoption of the null option or through a failure of a tailings dam. In structuring the assessment, 12 release modes were identified (as shown in Figure 10.1), although ultimately only four of them (shaded release modes in the figure) were used to describe the various environmental impacts.

Scope of Additional Works

The MWMP involved numerous workshops at which the direction of the ongoing studies was examined and confirmed. Following the final workshop in 1996, the remaining outstanding data were collected from direct contact with the relevant specialists.

Timing

In setting the original time frame for the MWMP risk assessment in 1996, OTML recognized the complexity of the project and allocated a reasonable schedule of five months. Its aim was to report to its board at the end of the third quarter of 1996. The results of the risk assessment were available for reporting to the board within six months from starting (although the final report was not completed until the first quarter of 1997).

Establishing Initial Criteria

No formal risk assessment criteria were established prior to starting the 1996–1997 assessment because the process was new to OTML, and there was no prior experience of what the risk assessment process would produce in the way of outcomes.

Several different measures of risk and risk cost were assessed and reported in the 1997 study developed during the process in consultation with OTML's peer reviewer. The different expressions of risk were used to provide a measure of uncertainty. The various measures were:

- Expected value
- Risk cost defined as the total occurrence cost for those risk events that contribute 95 percent of the total risk
- Risk cost defined as the total occurrence cost for those risk events that have a likelihood of greater than 10 percent over the project term

Selection of the Expert Panel

From the outset, OTML recognized the complexity of the project and its capacity to attract international attention. The project therefore required the scientific and other technical work that supported the MWMP to be of the highest quality.

In selecting its advisers for the MWMP studies, OTML sought out specialists who were recognized as world leaders in their field. These specialists were supported, in turn, by OTML staff with significant on-site experience and who were often also recognized specialists.

OTML also required its advisers to become familiar with the mine and the natural and social environment in which it was situated. It provided guided tours of the Ok Tedi and Fly River catchments and access to its staff for introductory briefings to new specialists on the project. Throughout the project, numerous, routine workshops were held at which the various advisers, both staff and consultants, reported progress on their studies, received feedback from peer reviewers and specialists in related areas, and developed the future stages of the studies in consultation with others on the project team. Knowledge held by staff and consultants involved in the project encompassed recent and long-standing experience on the site.

By adopting these practices, OTML ensured that knowledge of the project was maintained or enhanced, that contributors' understanding of the project went beyond their field of expertise, and that the important interrelationships between the various specialties were recognized early and incorporated into the ongoing work. The risk workshops tapped the combined broad, in-depth knowledge of the Ok Tedi operation that was married to the specialist knowledge provided by each panel member.

Identifying and Quantifying Risk Events

The process for identifying risk events used the expert panel in a facilitated workshop forum. The required size of the panel and number of workshops mark this case study. In the workshops held in 1996, expert panel numbers varied from around five people up to 30 or more. In all, a total of 10 major workshops plus numerous meetings and reviews and extensive correspondence between experts were used to define the risks associated with each of the proposed mitigation options.

The process necessitated a focused and in-depth review of all reasonably identifiable aspects of the existing situation at Ok Tedi, and the changes anticipated to result from the adoption of any of the proposed mitigation options. An important and inevitable benefit of the rigorous approach imposed by the RISQUE method was an increased understanding of the issues and intricacies of this particularly complex project. One of the natural outcomes of this process was the progressive refinement of the risk profile associated with each mitigation option as high, sometimes unacceptably high, risks were identified and solutions designed to reduce those risks. The eventual outcome was that the difference in overall risk between the options was relatively small. On this basis, the design standard applied to each of the options is comparable, which was one of the initial objectives of the project.

Risk Analysis

The threshold method of risk modeling was used to generate the 1997 risk assessment results.

Modeling Results

The results presented in the 1997 report are best summarized in Figures 10.2 and 10.3. The dollar values presented to the board in the original two figures have been omitted for reason of commercial sensitivity.

Figure 10.2 shows the base cost-risk cost relationships for each of the mitigation options. The net present value of the operations and management costs and the base costs were given on the horizontal axis, with the risk cost appearing on the vertical axis. The various symbols for each option represent a different measure of risk cost. For each option, the spread between the various measures indicates the uncertainty associated with risk cost estimation.

This figure shows that the null option had the lowest base cost and the highest risk cost. The dredge option had the next highest base cost but showed a significant

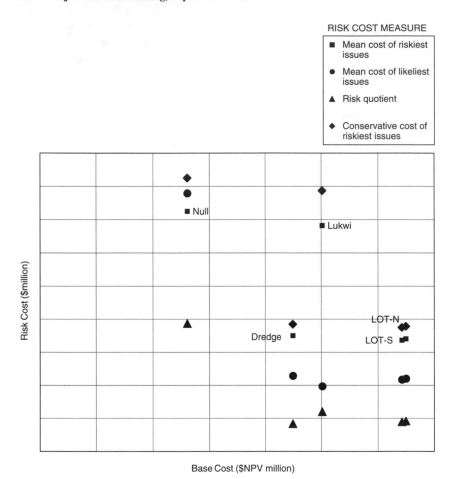

Figure 10.2   Base cost-risk cost relationship for tailings management options; 1997.

reduction in risk cost and uncertainty. The Lukwi option had considerable uncertainty, and its risk cost ranged from a value equivalent to the dredge option value to a value that was almost equivalent to that of the null option. The two LOT options were similar, having the highest base cost and a risk cost approximately equivalent to the Dredge option.

Figure 10.3 shows how the same data were reconfigured to produce a benefit-cost graph. The null option is plotted at the origin of the graph. The horizontal axis shows the difference between the null option base cost and the base cost of each of the other options. The vertical axis shows the reduction in null option risk cost (benefit) achievable by adopting the other options. The diagonal lines show various benefit-cost ratios. The upper line is equivalent to a risk cost reduction of $4 for every $1 spent. It is clear from this graph that the dredge option provided the greatest benefit-cost ratio.

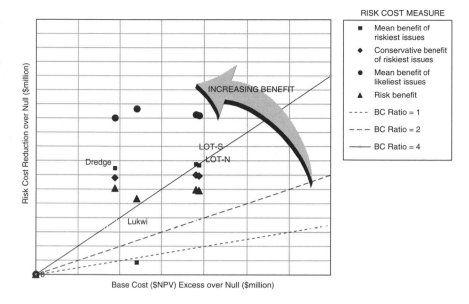

Figure 10.3   Benefit-cost relationships for the tailings management options; 1997.

Strategy

While the dredge option provided the greatest benefit-cost ratio, and was therefore the best overall option in economic terms, the risk assessment identified that there was considerable uncertainty in the results. This was particularly true for the environmental data, due to the lack of understanding about the cause-effect relationship between the mine activities and the corresponding effects in the river system.

On the basis of the risk assessment results, rather than adopt the dredge option for the remaining life of mine, the board decided on an 18-month dredging trial. The trial required government approval under the act, and this was duly obtained and the dredging project started.

OTML also commissioned a large number of environmental and community-related studies targeting those areas of high uncertainty. The purpose of these studies was to expand the available knowledge of the river system and its people during the 18 months of the dredging trial. The objective of this additional work was to enable a decision to be made on the preferred permanent mitigation option by the end of the dredging trial.

FIRST REVIEW RISK ASSESSMENT (1999)

The first review of the risk assessment in 1999 followed the same basic methodology that was developed for the 1997 assessment. Again the aim was to determine the preferred, permanent tailings mitigation scheme incorporating the additional study findings and dredge trial results.

Scope of Additional Works

As already discussed, one of the outcomes of the 1997 assessment was the commissioning of a diverse range of scientific and engineering studies. The purpose of this work was to provide supporting information for the MWMP risk assessment to reduce the uncertainties associated with the environmental consequences and, to a lesser degree, with the community consequences identified during the 1997 assessment. The outcome of these additional studies was a quantum leap forward in knowledge.

Figure 10.4 shows the main studies and their relationship to the risk assessment review and the MWMP as a whole.

Expert Panel

As with the 1997 risk assessment, OTML used world-recognized specialists to conduct the additional studies and form the expert panel. Many of these experts were the same as those who contributed to the 1997 assessment, but the panel also included additional people, especially where new areas of science were added to the MWMP.

As with the 1997 assessment, the expert panel for the MWMP risk assessment was very large and was composed of a number of experts with the same or very similar technical backgrounds. In this case, duplication of several technical fields was appropriate because the experts were breaking new scientific ground or were using state-of-the-art techniques, and levels of understanding were sometimes in their infancy. The expert panel members therefore felt it was necessary to be able to discuss, formulate, and agree on conclusions with their peers, based on the maturity of knowledge at the time.

In the 1999 assessment, a significant effort was made to validate the integrity of the supporting scientific studies and of the risk assessment. For this purpose, OTML appointed a peer review group of leading experts to guide the studies and assess the validity of the study methodologies and outcomes.

Modified Approach

The overall process involved in the 1999 assessment is shown in Figure 10.5. The complexity of the project (which, of course, had not diminished since 1997) required simplification. In the 1997 assessment, the consequences of risk events encompassed engineering, environmental, and social outcomes. However, the improvement in knowledge gained during the intervening years through the ongoing studies indicated that the approach needed to be modified. It was recog-

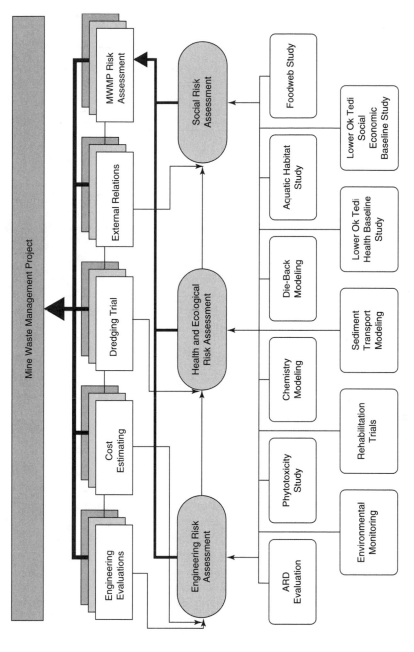

Figure 10.4 Mine waste management project structure developed for the risk assessment.

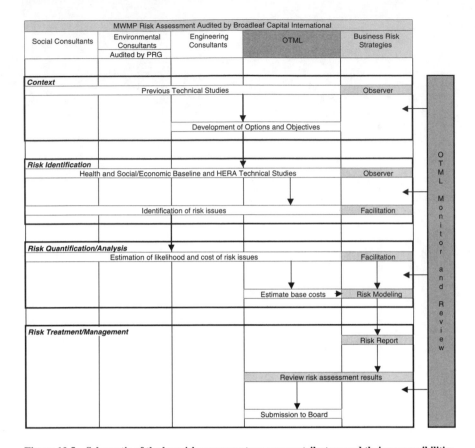

Figure 10.5 Schematic of the key risk assessment process contributors and their responsibilities.

nized that the relationship between engineering and the natural and social environments was different from that originally visualized. The engineering works proposed by OTML for each of the options had different consequential environmental impacts, which in turn had different social impacts. Ultimately, the social outcomes of the identified risk events presented the most severe consequences.

At this stage, the engineering options were well defined, and OTML had structured the assessment of the environmental impacts on selected geographic entities. The areas consisted of six different reaches of the Ok Tedi/Fly River system, plus the Fly River estuary and the Gulf of Papua. Each area comprised a different type of environment on the expectation that the impacts would be different. The selected areas are shown on Figure 10.6 and were:

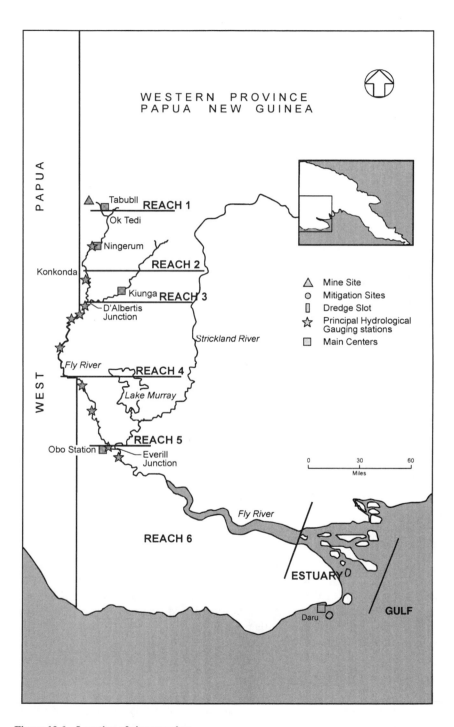

Figure 10.6   Location of river reaches.

Reach	Location	Description
1	Ok Mani	Mine waste deposition site
2	Upper Ok Tedi	Steep braided gravel section, highland rain forest
3	Lower Ok Tedi	Meandering channel, confined floodplain, lowland rain forest
4	Upper Middle Fly	Meandering channel, extensive floodplain, off-river water bodies, lowland rain forest
5	Lower Middle Fly	Meandering channel, extensive floodplain, off-river water bodies, swamp grass
6	Lower Fly	Meandering channel, extensive floodplain, Strickland River contribution to flow/ sediment, swamp grass
Estuary	Fly Estuary	Freshwater/saltwater interface, mudbanks, high turbidity
Gulf	Gulf of Papua	Marine environment

In preparing the structure for the risk workshops, the key drivers of community risk were identified. At the workshops the expert panel was asked to quantify the environmental impact for each option and each reach and then to quantify the community consequences for each of the key drivers. Figure 10.7 shows a schematic structure for the 1999 risk assessment and the key drivers of community risk.

In addition to identifying risks and providing numerical inputs to the risk assessment process, each specialist was specifically requested to identify potential fatal flaws for each option. This exercise assisted with the identification and quantification of several major environmental issues (e.g., acid rock drainage). Again, the rigor of the approach assisted with improving the understanding of the issues and in their quantification in absolute terms.

Timing

The end of the dredging trial period, which was May 1999, set the timing of the first risk assessment review. This meant a period in excess of two years was available for performance of additional investigations and studies. A number of studies commenced during the intervening period that had a significantly shorter time frame, and many of those studies were completed or brought to a conclusion. Some of the studies that were initiated, however, were of an ongoing nature and extended beyond 2000.

Establishing Initial Criteria

For the 1999 assessment, the initial expectation was to adopt the likelihood and consequence threshold criteria that had been developed during the 1997 assess-

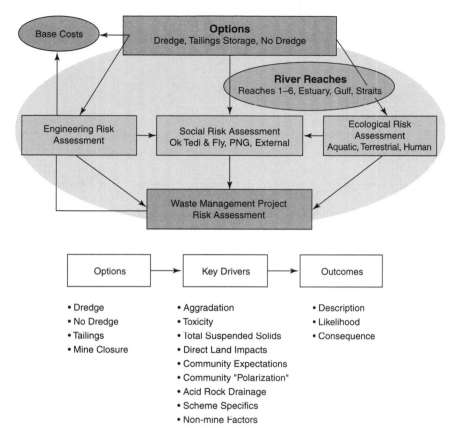

Figure 10.7   Risk assessment structure and the relationship between the technical assessments and key drivers.

ment. However, through the process OTML was better able to define a set of criteria that established the significance of the risk quotient. These criteria are shown in Figure 10.8. It was also decided that the criteria would form the initial criteria for any future risk assessment, with little expectation that the criteria would change substantially.

Identifying and Quantifying Risk Events

In the 1999 MWMP Risk Assessment, each of the supporting studies (Engineering Risk Assessment, Health and Ecological Risk Assessment, and Social Risk Assessment) shown in Figure 10.4 involved numerous meetings and workshops. The Health and Ecological Risk Assessment and its supporting studies involved about 10 major workshops between May 1998 and March 1999. One major engineering workshop and two major social risk workshops also were held during

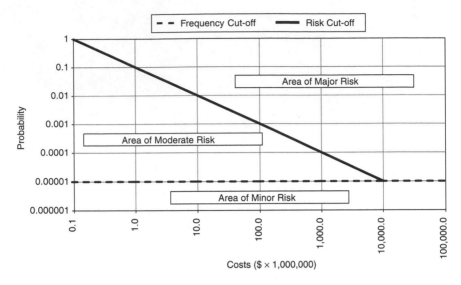

Figure 10.8   Risk thresholds and events ranking.

1998. The workshops culminated in a four-day combined risk workshop in March 1999. As was the case in 1996, the number of advisers on the expert panel for the final workshop exceeded 30.

All previously included risk events were reviewed. The risk events that were retained for analysis in the 1999 study are summarized in Table 10.1.

Risk Analysis

The threshold method for risk modeling was the predominant method used to produce the 1999 risk assessment results. The risk modeling differed from the initial risk assessment because an additional modeling technique (the chance method) was developed and used to address issues raised by OTML's peer reviewer. The results of both methods were reported, providing a measure of risk cost uncertainty.

The chance method was different from the threshold method because it did not assume occurrence of each of the risk events. The chance method predictably returned lower estimates of risk cost than the threshold method at any given level of confidence. In order that the risk cost calculated using this method was appropriately conservative, it was necessary to increase the upper (pessimistic) confidence level from 95 percent (which was selected for the threshold method) to 99.9 percent for the chance method.

Table 10.1 Risk Comparison Matrix

Risk Event	Consequence	Early Closure	Tailings	No Dredge	Dredge
Additional compensation in Lower Ok Tedi	Compensation	Minor	MAJOR	MAJOR	MAJOR
Additional compensation in Upper Middle Fly	Compensation	Minor	MAJOR	MAJOR	MAJOR
Compensation in Lower Middle Fly	Compensation	na	MAJOR	MAJOR	MAJOR
Compensation in Lower Fly	Compensation	na	Moderate	Moderate	Moderate
International reaction incites road closure	Additional compensation	na	Moderate	Moderate	MAJOR
International reaction requires legal defense	Legal costs	na	Minor	MAJOR	Moderate
International reaction incites Kiunga closure	Production loss	na	Moderate	Minor	Moderate
International reaction incites sabotage	Production loss	na	Moderate	MAJOR	Moderate
International reaction causes market losses	Embargo on products	na	Moderate	MAJOR	Moderate
International reaction requires remediation	Dredge or equivalent	MAJOR	na	na	na
Compensation paid to Irian Jaya	Compensation	na	MAJOR	MAJOR	MAJOR
Community reaction leads to civil unrest	Production loss	na	Moderate	Moderate	Moderate
Relocation of villages due to flooding	Relocation costs	na	MAJOR	MAJOR	MAJOR
Access difficulties lead to relocation	Relocation costs	na	MAJOR	MAJOR	MAJOR
River avulsion leads to increased compensation	Compensation	na	Moderate	Moderate	Moderate
Aggradation compromises Fly River navigation	Operations costs	na	MAJOR	MAJOR	MAJOR
Tie channel blockage	Unsustainable fishery	na	Moderate	Moderate	Moderate
Floodplain Cu toxicity & TSS reduces fish catch	Compensation	Moderate	MAJOR	MAJOR	MAJOR
Floodplain Cu toxicity & TSS damages fishery	Unsustainable fishery	Moderate	MAJOR	MAJOR	MAJOR

(Continues)

Table 10.1 *(Continued)*

Risk Event	Consequence	Early Closure	Tailings	No Dredge	Dredge
Pb toxicity damages human health—healthcare	Additional healthcare	Minor	Minor	Minor	Minor
Pb toxicity damages human health—mine closure	Mine closure	na	Minor	Minor	Minor
Pb toxicity damages human health—litigation	Litigation	Minor	Minor	Minor	Minor
Current lease compensation package inadequate	Increased lease	na	MAJOR	na	MAJOR
Enforced displacement of Kwiapae and others, civil unrest	Mine closure	na	Moderate	na	na
Population increases—pressure on food sources	Increased compensation	na	MAJOR	MAJOR	MAJOR
Population increases—mine staff safety	Increased security	na	MAJOR	MAJOR	MAJOR
Population increases—civil unrest	Temporary mine closure	na	Moderate	MAJOR	Moderate
OTML payment of job redundancies	Redundancy payments	MAJOR	na	na	na
Outrage leading to mine asset loss	Loss of asset sale income	MAJOR	na	na	na
Community outrage leading to mine staff injury/loss of life	Damages claims	Moderate	na	na	na
Community outrage requires remediation action	Dredge or equivalent	MAJOR	na	na	na
ARD occurs	Ecosystem damage	Moderate	Moderate	Moderate	Moderate
Engineering failure causes 100 million m^3 dredge sand release	Repair and remediation	na	Moderate	na	Moderate
Engineering failure causes 30 million m^3 dredge sand release	Repair and remediation	na	Moderate	na	Minor
Tailings ARD prevention costs	Additional costs	na	MAJOR	na	na
Pipeline failure causes road and property damage	Repair, remediation, & compensation	na	MAJOR	na	na
Rehabilitation failure on tailings storage	Recovering and replanting cost	na	MAJOR	na	na

Modeling Results

The main outputs from the 1999 report are shown in Figures 10.9, 10.10, and 10.11 (again the dollar values that were provided to the OTML board have been omitted for commercial reasons). Figure 10.9 shows the risk profiles for the four mitigation options. The vertical scale is the same on each of the four graphs, providing a comparison of the risk quotient posed by each of the risk events and overall option risk.

It can be seen from Figure 10.9 that for the dredge option, the event risk quotients were less than those of the no-dredge option and were similar to those of the tailings option. The early closure option had fewer risk events, but the magnitude of the risk quotients was markedly higher compared with the other options.

Figure 10.10 shows the estimated risk cost (calculated by the threshold method) for each of the options. It can be seen that the risk cost was similar for the dredge and tailings options, which were each less than the risk cost for the early closure option. The no-dredge option had the greatest risk cost.

Figure 10.11 shows the comparison between the risk cost and base cost for each option calculated by both the threshold and chance methods and expressed at various levels of confidence. The conclusions drawn from Figure 10.11 are:

- The tailings and early closure options appeared to be unattractive alternatives.
- Either the dredge option or the no-dredge option provided a workable solution for the remaining mine life.
- The total cost (base cost plus planning risk cost) of the no-dredge option was close to the base cost of the dredge option.
- As the least-cost option, the no-dredge option may have provided the better overall alternative but carried greater uncertainty than the dredge option.
- These conclusions were considered to be robust as they held true under the different measures or methods used for calculating risk cost.

The 1999 report also identified a number of option-specific conclusions. In addition to the modeled risk quotient and risk cost estimates, the study also identified the following important findings:

- The understanding of the complicated relationships between the mine, the river system, and the people of the catchment had improved considerably since 1996, when the first mine waste project risk assessment was undertaken.
- The improved understanding of the systems significantly improved the inputs to the 1999 risk assessment and resulted in more robust and defensible outcomes.
- There was no quantifiable difference between the mitigation options in terms of overall ecological benefits. Even immediate mine closure would not prevent the spread of die-back and other mine-related effects in the upper middle Fly River over the next decade or so.

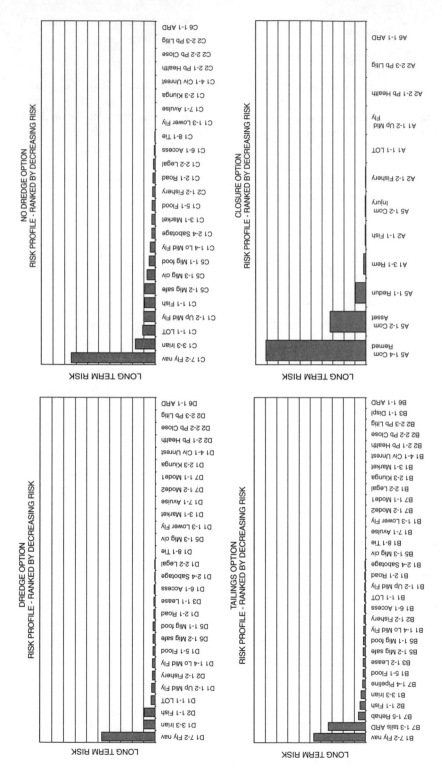

Figure 10.9   Risk profiles for the tailings management options; 1999.

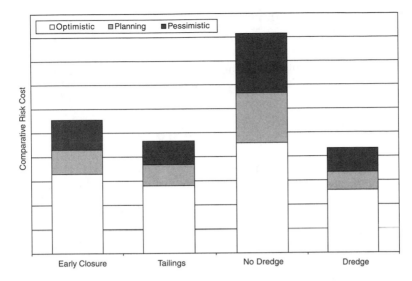

Figure 10.10 Risk cost at selected confidence levels for the tailings management options; 1999.

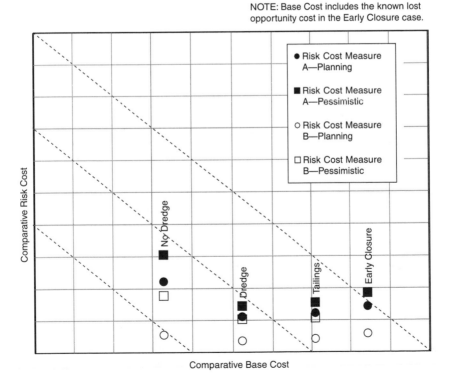

Figure 10.11 Comparison of risk cost and base cost for the tailings management options; 1999.

- Social risk events provided greater differentiation between the options than did the ecological risk events.
- Notwithstanding the advances and advantages associated with the assessment, there remained considerable uncertainty about the ecological and social risk events that would impact the overall cost of the mitigation options.

SECOND REVIEW RISK ASSESSMENT (2000)

The aim of the second review risk assessment was essentially an updating process designed to evaluate any advances that had been made in the 12 months following the 1999 risk assessment and, if appropriate, to incorporate those advances into a new risk assessment.

The risk assessment update was undertaken in 2000, and the new information was gathered from specialist staff and advisers through one-on-one interviews. The information update indicated that a significant improvement in understanding in some areas had been achieved. However, the added knowledge had not been translated into hard data that, at the time, warranted remodeling of the risk and a full risk assessment review.

In 2000 it was expected that some investigations could continue for some time into the future. OTML clearly indicated a desire to revisit the risk assessment in the future, possibly when major studies end or meaningful advances are made in scientific knowledge.

SUMMARY

The risk assessments performed in both 1996–1997 and 1999 provided valuable insights into the future operation of the mine and the mitigation options under consideration. In both cases the rigorous investigation process:

- Improved the understanding of the issues facing OTML
- Identified several matters that, left unattended, would pose unacceptably high risks to the project
- Prompted design and operating changes to prevent or reduce the risk to a level acceptable for the continued mine operation
- Prompted refinement of the options so that within each study, the options ended with broadly comparable levels of risk

The result was several risk reduction strategies and studies were identified and implemented during the course of the studies, and work on these started ahead of completion of the reports.

Into the future, OTML is looking to implement a feasible and viable tailings mitigation scheme that will enable mining to continue until the planned end of mine life in 2009. The management of risk is a critical component for determining the best option.

A key concern was the level of environmental benefit provided by the available mitigation options. Significant, measurable, environmental benefit is a critical success criterion for any selected option because OTML would have to invest several hundreds of millions of dollars over the remaining 12 years of mine life. The 1996–1997 risk assessment results clearly showed the dredge option to be the most cost effective of the options under consideration. However, the results also showed that there was significant uncertainty associated with all the options, particularly with respect to the environmental benefits that each provided. The amount of uncertainty was one of the contributing factors to the OTML board's decision to adopt an 18-month dredging trial rather than commit to this scheme for the remainder of the mine life.

The trial period ended in 1999, but OTML continued dredging. This was one of the outcomes of the 1999 study, along with the continuation of several technical and community studies. The thrust of these studies is to determine how best to close the mine (either in 2009, as planned, or earlier) in a way that best provides for all of the stakeholders. Until these studies are completed, it is expected that dredging will continue, at which time OTML's options will be to close the mine, adopt another mitigation scheme, or dredge until the end of mine life.

11

ACQUISITIONS: POWER, UNITED STATES

This case study examines:

- Including risk in asset valuations
- Including risk in setting a bid price
- Restructuring bids to account for risk

BACKGROUND

The client is a large U.S.-based independent power producer. At the time of the case study, the client was engaged in a phase of aggressive acquisition of power generation assets, both within the United States and globally. As a matter of fiduciary responsibility, the client's senior management maintained a policy of risk sensitivity (particularly environmental and regulatory risk) in relation to acquisitions. Until a year or so before this case study, accumulation of the client's power generation assets had traditionally been concentrated on "green field" sites or demonstrably "clean" sites.

However, as opportunities for "clean" assets diminished, the client needed to consider acquisition of older, operating sites in order to maintain planned growth. Along with these facilities came the potential of inheriting environmental and regulatory liabilities from past and, potentially, future activities. Through application of the RISQUE method, the client felt more able to bid for these older power generation assets and adopted the method of risk profiling during the due diligence process as the key determinant of potential environmental and regulatory liability. The client also considered that use of the method allowed the company to gain some competitive advantage in the marketplace.

SETTING

The client was engaged in a bid (that was ultimately successful) for the purchase of a large, 2,000 megawatt, coal-fired power generation facility located in the eastern half of the United States. The bid process was performed under conditions of strict confidentiality.

Due to past and/or present activities, the client considered that there was some potential for environmental liability at the site. Under draft contract conditions, the purchaser was required to indemnify the vendor against claims due to environmental impairment. The client needed to understand the potential liability that it could assume in order to:

- Structure the bid to minimize exposure to risk events
- Adjust the bid price as appropriate to reflect the extent of exposure to liability

In addition, the client needed to understand the cost implications of future environmental regulatory changes as they might affect plant operations. These changes, too, could impact the bid price.

Project Objectives

The purpose of the risk profiling was to identify and quantify the potential financial liability from environmental and regulatory risk events. In the event that the bid was successful, the risk profiling findings would provide a useful basis for later development of an environmental risk management strategy.

The specific objectives of the risk assessment were to:

- Identify the significant environmental and regulatory risk events associated with the past, ongoing, and future operation and management of the generation facilities.
- Quantify the frequency of occurrence and the financial consequences of the identified issues that may occur during the life of the project.
- Identify the riskiest issues and the cost (risk cost) if these issues were to occur over the life of the project.
- Provide schedules of potential risk expenditure that could be directly incorporated into the comprehensive financial model.
- Present the results in an easy-to-understand, graphical format.

Risk Assessment Structure

The approach used in the risk assessment was to consider the following two types of cost that could reasonably be incurred over the life of the project: (1) base cost and (2) risk cost.

The base cost for the project was the cost of purchase, operation, and management plus any associated costs to which the client would be committed (e.g., planned plant upgrades, taxes). The risk cost for the project was considered to be the cost of the consequences of those risk events that may occur over the life of the scheme (e.g., the cost of soil remediation due to past spills at a site). For the purposes of this assessment, the project life was set at 15 years.

By the end of the 15-year project life, the project's cost would be equal to the base cost of the project plus the consequential costs of the risk events that actually occurred. The base cost is relatively easy to determine in advance using conventional financial modeling. However, the cost component associated with risk events (risk cost) is very difficult to predict due to uncertainty.

The risk assessment method involved determination of the two key financial measures of risk: (1) risk quotient and (2) risk cost (described above).

The risk quotient is the product of probability and cost and is widely referred to elsewhere in the literature as "expected cost." The risk quotient was used to rank the identified risk events according to this measure of risk and then determine the riskiest issues.

The client employed the RISQUE method because it was a systematic, defensible, and transparent methodology. The following summary steps explain the risk assessment procedure that was followed during the due diligence process to achieve the risk assessment objectives.

Step 1: Identification of Risk Events. This step entails identification, by a diverse panel of selected experts, of the significant environmental, regulatory, engineering, and other risk events that potentially could occur over the project life.

The panel judged costs associated with the occurrence of some environmental and regulatory events initially identified as risk events to be base costs rather than risk costs. The client decided, as part of the bid structure, to implement actions that addressed events that were considered to be almost certain to occur (probability of occurrence was close to 100 percent). Events assigned to the base cost were indicated in the risk register. Base costs were not included in the risk model but, instead, were transferred into the comprehensive, in-house financial model.

Step 2: Quantification of Risk Events. In this step the expert panel quantified the frequency of occurrence of potential risk events and the consequences (as costs) of relevant risk events.

Step 3: Modeling of Risk Costs. Here the risk analyst determined the risk quotient for each risk event, determined the riskiest issues, and quantified a reasonable estimate of the liability (risk cost) associated with the riskiest issues for the power plant.

Step 4: Development of Risk Management Strategies. In this step the client identified risk reduction options and the risk analyst assessed impacts on model results and the restructured project.

Step 5: Selection of Bid Structure. In the final step the client selected the ultimate risk management actions and incorporated the calculated risk cost into the bid.

RISK IDENTIFICATION

Expert Panel

Identification and quantification of the risk events associated with the plant site was performed by a qualified expert panel composed of representatives from environmental and regulatory consultants and senior client staff with expertise in operations, finance, legal, regulatory, and environmental fields.

Nature of Risk Events

The process of risk event identification and quantification was begun at a team strategy meeting. During the meeting, environmental and regulatory issues were discussed in terms of air- and water-related issues and contamination issues for each facility.

Following this meeting, the environmental consultant prepared issue sheets for each facility. These sheets formed the basis for the formal risk register. The purpose of creating the risk register was to:

- Enable those involved in the risk identification process to review the issues raised to ensure that the list was complete
- Specify reasons for excluding particular risk events in the model
- Document and justify the risk events

The frequency and cost of each risk event was based on the consensus of expert panels and historical data (if available).

Frequency was expressed as chance of occurring over the next 15 years of the project life. Probability was expressed as the likelihood of a consequence occurring, assuming the initiating issue has occurred. Due to uncertainty of magnitude of costs, all costs were provided by the experts in current dollars, to represent "the likely cost if the issue occurs," or estimated mean cost and "the cost unlikely to be exceeded more than 5 percent of times," or 95 percent confidence limit.

For each event, the above cost pairs were assumed to represent the respective control points on a log normal distribution, unless otherwise stated. The spread between the mean and 95 percent values provided a relative comparison of uncertainty. The larger the spread of values, the larger the uncertainty contained in those estimates.

Net present value (NPV) costs of risk events were more difficult to estimate because assumptions of timing of risk event occurrence needed to be made. Although it was not possible to predict when a risk event would occur, the panel was able to estimate the earliest year in which each risk event could most likely occur. Assuming that the costs were incurred at the earliest time enabled calculation of a conservative estimate of NPV risk cost for each issue.

Several sets of risk calculation were performed throughout the risk assessment process, and input costs and frequencies of occurrence were adjusted as the level of understanding of events increased or management plans were modified (sometimes in order to mitigate unacceptable risk events). The values that were presented in the risk register were those finally agreed on and adopted for the risk model.

Panel Conclusions

Table 11.1 lists all of the environmental risk events identified by the expert panel in relation to the plant. It includes a site code, which was derived from the evaluation sheets, and a brief description of each event. The category refers to whether the event was classified as a base cost (included directly in the comprehensive, in-house financial model) or a risk event for inclusion in the risk model. The right-hand column shows whether the issue was included in the risk model. Some issues were excluded either due to low potential liability or because the risk was covered elsewhere in the financial assessment.

RISK ANALYSIS

Risk Modeling

The risk modeling process consisted of the following steps:

Step 1. *Input.* Issues and consequences were input in event-tree format. Values input into the model were event frequencies and a schedule of potential event costs over time.

Step 2. *Calculations.* Calculation of cost (NPV) assuming each risk event occurs and the risk quotient for each risk event.

Step 3. *Determine riskiest issues.* The riskiest issues were defined as those issues that contributed to 95 percent of the total project risk. The 95 percent mark was selected because at around this point, additional issues did not add significantly to the total project risk.

Step 4. *Run the risk model.* Perform Monte Carlo simulation for 2,000 trials.

Step 5. *Generate output.* Produce graphical risk profiles and risk relationships.

Table 11.1 Potential Risk Events Associated with Power Plant

Site Code	Risk Event	Description	Category	Risk Analysis
1-1	Phase II Acid Rain sulfur dioxide	Phase II of Title IV of the CAA will apply starting in the year 2000. Emissions of sulfur dioxide will be limited to .7 lb/MMBtu. The plant has a sulfur dioxide shortfall of 90,000 tons in 1997. Options: low-sulfur coal, cleaning, FGD, allowances.	Base Cost	Included
1-2	Phase II nitrogen oxides	The plant is subject to Phase II and has an allowance deficit of 2,521 tons in 1997. Assume $2,000/ton for allowances in 1999–2002.	Base Cost	Included
1-3	Phase III nitrogen oxides	More stringent nitrogen oxides emission restrictions take effect in the year 2003 and continue through 2009. Will add SCR in 2003.	Base Cost	Included
1-4	Global Warming carbon dioxide	The plant's carbon dioxide emissions were 20% higher in 1997 than 1990, so a 27% reduction will be required. Assume $3/ton allowance. Need to reduce carbon dioxide by 3,500,000 tons/yr.	Risk	Included
1-5	Mercury Emissions	U.S. EPA has identified coal-fired power plants as the largest source of mercury emissions. It is possible that new regulations limiting mercury will be promulgated by the year 2009. The plant will need to reduce mercury emissions by 619 lb. Assume $25,000–$47,500/lb control cost.	Risk	Included
1-6	Generation Performance Standards	Congress is considering regulations called Generation Performance Standards, which would regulate emissions of oxides of nitrogen and sulfur from each power plant. The plant may need SCR to achieve the emission limits. Assume nitrogen oxide controls in 2007 and sulfur dioxide controls in 2009.	Risk	Included (Excluded in Final Run)
2-1	Wastewater Treatment Arsenic	New limits may be imposed on NPDES based on a study of discharges at plant. Arsenic control is key and would require reverse osmosis system in 2000.	Risk	Included
2-2	Pond Breach	Dam breach at the pond could cost $400,000 in 1999.	Base Cost	Included
3-1	Subsurface Contamination– Mining Activities	Studies and possible remediation may be required for groundwater contamination from various mining activities in 2005.	Risk	Included
3-2	Surface Impoundment	Studies will be required in connection with impoundment liners. Assume $750,000 per year for three years beginning in 1999.	Base Cost	Included
3-3	Nursery Groundwater	The third-party nursery site may require groundwater remediation in 2008.	Risk	Included
3-4	Mine Bond	The bond posted for the mine may not be adequate to cover potential liability associated with this issue. Year is 1999.	Risk	Included
3-5	Mine AMD	The mine is an abandoned mine on the plant site. An acid mine drainage problem may need remediation in 2005.	Risk	Included
3-6	Coal Pile Liner	A coal pile liner may be needed in 2007.	Risk	Included

168

Model Results

The primary aim of the first run of the risk model was to assess whether the environmental and regulatory risk cost of the project, as perceived at the time, was material to the bid. If so, the model results were to form the basis of development of the most cost-effective strategy to reduce the risk cost to the lowest reasonable amount. After several iterations to progressively reduce the risk cost, the client would be in a position to judge whether the exposure was material and, if necessary, incorporate the risk cost and risk reduction measures into the bid.

Initial Risk Cost. Table 11.2 shows the identified risk events tabulated in order of decreasing risk quotient for Run 1. The risk quotient was estimated at three levels of confidence selected by the client to represent optimistic, planning, and pessimistic cost estimates. The selected confidence levels were 50, 75, and 95 percent, respectively.

Preliminary inspection of the results of Table 11.2 was carried out to determine the riskiest events, that is, the risk events for which the costs of occurrence should be included in the calculation of risk cost. The client considered that the costs associated with the three lowest-risk events were not material; therefore, neither was the risk. The cost of the fourth lowest-risk event (Mine bond) was around $6 million (planning confidence level) and was considered by the client to be material. However, the client considered that the risk quotient of $0.05 million per year was low (due to a low likelihood of occurrence) and that the risk was probably acceptable. It was decided that the occurrence cost of all risk events with a calculated risk quotient of greater than $0.05 million would be included in the risk cost. Those events excluded from contributing to risk cost are shaded in Table 11.2.

Figure 11.1 shows a bar chart of the initial estimated risk cost. The estimated risk cost at the planning level of confidence for contingent environmental and regulatory events was $115 million NPV. The client decided that the risk cost was

Table 11.2 Modeling Results

Abbreviated Event Name	Risk Quotient	Cost ($ × million)			Cumulative percent of risk
		Optimistic (CL 50%)	Planning (CL 75%)	Pessimistic (CL 95%)	
R1 1-6 GPS	18.83	25.61	30.53	40.32	39.72%
R1 1-4 Global	18.28	20.35	22.81	26.87	78.29%
R1 1-5 Mercury	7.72	38.89	59.85	110.95	94.57%
R1 2-1 WTP	2.30	4.67	5.13	5.90	99.43%
R1 3-6 Coal pile	0.09	1.86	2.10	2.50	99.63%
R1 3-1a Mine stud	0.07	0.14	0.17	0.21	99.77%
R1 3-4 Bond	0.05	4.96	5.73	6.93	99.88%
R1 3-3 Nursery	0.04	0.71	0.80	0.96	99.95%
R1 3-1b Mine rem	0.02	0.39	0.44	0.53	99.99%
R1 3-5 AMD	0.00	0.36	0.41	0.50	100.00%

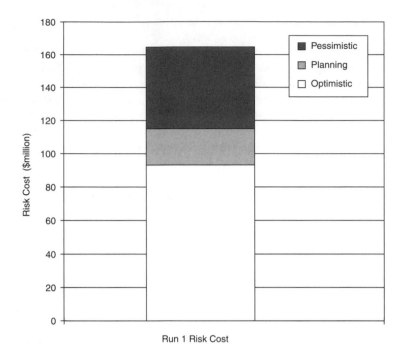

Figure 11.1   Estimated risk cost of power station acquisition: Run 1 results.

clearly material and that the estimated risk component of the project was too high. Therefore, that the client required the risk cost be reduced, if possible.

The client also evaluated the inherent uncertainty contained within the estimate of risk cost. Uncertainty of cost is independent of uncertainty of occurrence. In this case, the uncertainty of cost was defined as the cost range between the optimistic and pessimistic cost estimates. The client considered that the cost range ($75 million) between the optimistic estimate of risk cost ($90 million) and the pessimistic estimate ($165 million) was very large, particularly as a proportion of the estimated planning cost, and should also be reduced if possible.

Initial Risk and Exposure Profile.   Figure 11.2 shows a combined risk and exposure profile, ranked from highest- to lowest-risk quotient. The line graph showing the risk quotient for each risk event indicates that the four most risky events (generation performance standards, global warming, mercury emissions, and wastewater discharge) posed the greatest risk. These four risk events accounted for over 99 percent of the total risk (as shown in Table 11.2). The bar graphs of the occurrence costs of the risk events clearly show that the three highest-risk events each presented substantial exposure to financial liability.

The third ranked risk event (mercury emissions) presented by far the greatest exposure. The planning cost estimate of the mercury emission risk event was $60

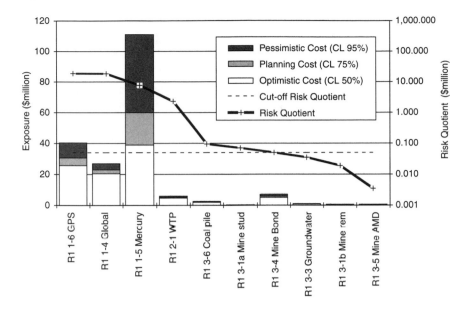

Figure 11.2   Exposure profile for power station acquisition: Run 1 results.

million NPV, which was almost three times the estimated planning cost of the two higher-risk events. The uncertainty of mercury emission cost was also much greater than for the other risk events.

The exposure profile of Figure 11.2 indicates that the estimated cost of each of the remaining three risk events that contribute to the risk cost are either marginally material (arsenic concentrations in wastewater discharge) or clearly not material (coal pile liner and mining contamination of groundwater studies).

Interpretation of Figure 11.2 led the client to conclude that any strategy developed to reduce the risk cost of the project should concentrate on reducing the risk posed by the top four risk events.

BID STRUCTURE

The ultimate structure of the client's bid depended on many factors. While mitigation of environmental and regulatory risks was only one component that contributed to the final structure, risk reduction was a key input to restructuring the final bid.

Risk Reduction Options

Several options, which could be drawn together in various combinations to reduce risk, were available to the client. The general options that could be adopted to address each substantial risk event were to:

- Virtually eliminate exposure to a risk event by budgeting a known expenditure to carry out actions that will erase the source of the problem.
- Commit a predetermined expenditure on activities to effectively prevent occurrence of the event.
- Carry out actions that reduce the risk, either by reducing the likelihood of the event occurring or by reducing the magnitude of financial exposure to a risk event, assuming it does occur.
- Transfer risk through insurance or other financial instruments.
- Accept the risk.

Risk Reduction Plan

Risk reduction actions were developed for each risk event, in progression along the risk profile from the highest- to the lowest-risk event that contributed to the risk cost. Mitigation actions were considered for the six highest-risk events at the plant. The proposed actions that were finally selected are shown in Table 11.3.

Computer modeling was progressively carried out in order to assess the financial benefit of implementing the proposed risk reduction plan. The risk model was run for the sixth time using the final information and assuming that the above risk reduction plan had been implemented.

Benefits of Action Plan

Figure 11.3 shows a bar chart of the calculated risk cost for Run 6 assuming that the risk reduction measures would be carried out. This figure shows that the esti-

Table 11.3   Proposed Risk Mitigation Actions

Risk Event	Proposed Action
Generation Performance Standards	Install selective catalytic reduction (SCR) to eliminate exposure to future nitrogen oxides and sulfur oxides emission limits. Install within three years.
Global Warming	Engineering solutions to carbon dioxide emissions from coal-fired power stations are unavailable. The costs of purchasing carbon dioxide allowances would most likely be passed on to the consumer. There remains some risk (likelihood reduced by 15 times) that the costs will not be passed on.
Mercury Emissions	Install emission controls (scrubber) to reduce the volume of emissions and also reduce the likelihood of nonacceptable emissions by five times.
Wastewater Treatment Plant	Install reverse osmosis system to remove arsenic from wastewater and reduce the likelihood of the risk event occurring by 25 times.
Coal Pile	There is no cost-effective way to reduce the risk. Propose to accept the risk and plan to install a coal pile liner in seven years.
Mine Groundwater Remediation	Financial exposure is not material. Plan to perform studies prior to action. Accept the risk.

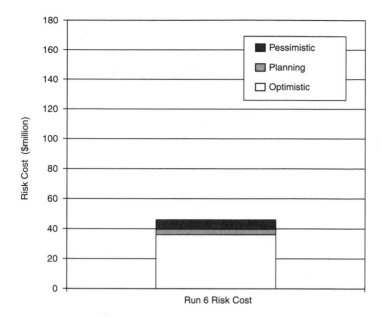

Figure 11.3   Estimated risk cost of power station acquisition after project restructuring to reduce risk: Run 6 results.

mated risk cost of $40 million would be substantially less than the initial estimate of $115 million, which represents a very substantial benefit to the project. The costs of achieving the risk benefits were input separately to the financial model as project base costs.

Figure 11.3 also shows that the uncertainty associated with the risk cost would reduce markedly as a result of implementation of the proposed risk reduction actions. The range of uncertainty between the optimistic cost estimate of $36 million and the pessimistic estimate of $46 million is approximately $10 million, compared with the $75 million range of the initial estimate of risk cost.

Figure 11.4 shows the combined risk and exposure profile for Run 6 assuming that the risk reduction measures have been implemented. The risk events are presented in the same order (decreasing initial risk) as Run 1 and shown in Figure 11.2, so that direct comparison of the profiles can be made. Comparison of Run 6 with the initial risk and exposure profile of Run 1 shows that the overall risk and financial exposure have been substantially reduced.

Exposure to the initially most risky event (generation performance standards) would be eliminated, and exposure to the third most risky event (mercury emissions) would be greatly reduced, from $60 million to $9 million. The profiles show that financial exposure to the global warming issue would remain the same, but that the risk would reduce by more than one order of magnitude.

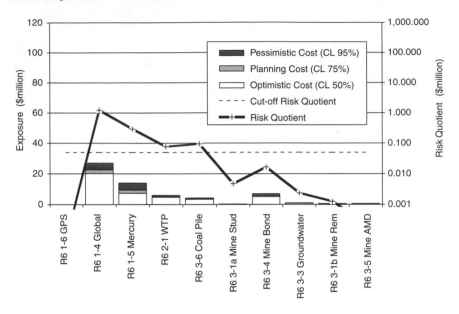

Figure 11.4   Exposure profile for power station acquisition after project restructuring to reduce risk with events ranked by Run 1 risk quotient: Run 6 results.

Inputs to Financial Model

Figure 11.5 shows a bar chart of the schedule of risk costs that should be budgeted and directly input to the financial model. The graph represents costs that could be reasonably expected to arise due to the occurrence of risk events. The schedule of risk expenditure is in current dollars and represents the estimated costs at the planning confidence level.

The client requested the schedule of risk costs because the company needed to account for timing and magnitude of future expenditure. The client was aware that the schedule was, at best, a reasonable estimate of how much (and when) expenditure might be incurred due to the occurrence of risk events and that the schedule does not represent a prediction of the occurrence of future risk events.

The figure indicates that around $10 million should be budgeted to cover the occurrence of risk events during the first two years of operation of the plant. Approximately $14 million should be budgeted within the first four years. Approximately $15 million (current dollar value) should be budgeted each year after year 2009 to cater for purchase of carbon dioxide allowances due to the global warming issue.

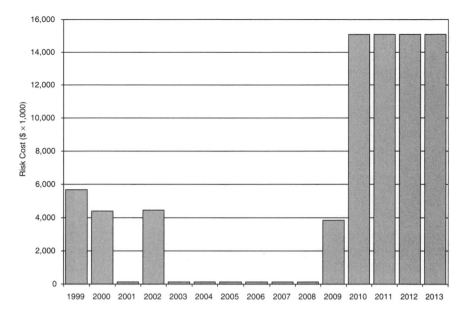

Figure 11.5   Schedule of risk expenditure.

SUMMARY

Using the RISQUE method during the bid process provided several benefits. The principal benefits were:

- An increased understanding of the nature and severity of risk events associated with the acquisition
- Identification of events with initial risk that was unacceptable and reduction of that risk to acceptable levels by planned changes to the project structure
- Clear separation of events that should be assigned either as base costs or as risk costs
- A schedule of expenditure that could be input to the financial model

12

QUANTIFYING INTANGIBLES: LAND DEVELOPMENT, AUSTRALIA

This case study examines:

- Quantification of events formerly considered intangible or nonquantifiable
- Translating community values into dollar terms
- Using quantified community values to enhance community benefit

BACKGROUND

Alkimos, an undeveloped coastal area located north of Western Australia's capital city, Perth, was an area recognized by the state government as having high potential for future urban development. Planning for the new development had advanced over a period of time to the point where there was a broad zoning framework for the area. The Water Corporation of Western Australia (Water Corporation) had purchased an area of coastal land of around 395 acres (160 ha) that had been zoned for a wastewater treatment plant (WTP), including a surrounding buffer zone, and a groundwater treatment plant (GTP) to service the development. This purchase made the Water Corporation a major landowner in the area.

In the decade following the Water Corporation's purchase of the land, Alkimos had been confirmed as a Regional Beach. This was formal recognition that the beach and associated coastal area were of high community value. One of the results had been a rise in the value of the coastal land, which had, in turn, increased pressure to optimize use of this land for residential and related purposes rather than the industrial wastewater and water treatment uses for which the land was zoned.

A consortium comprising the state-owned LandCorp and private developers (the Developer) had also been working together to develop the township of Alkimos. The Developer believed that there would be substantial advantages in using

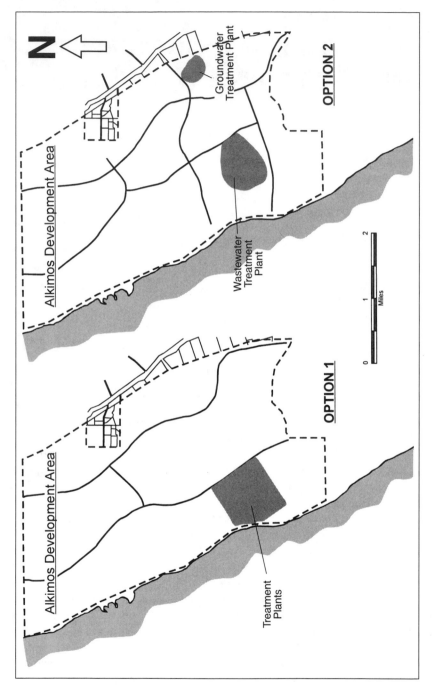

Figure 12.1 Concept scheme plans for location Options 1 and 2 for the wastewater and groundwater treatment plants.

the land owned by the Water Corporation for purposes other than that for which it was zoned. Its proposal involved relocating the proposed wastewater treatment plant to a position approximately 650 yards (600 m) farther back from the coast, reducing the size of the buffer zone, and relocating the proposed groundwater treatment plant some distance farther inland. The objective was to release the higher-value coastal area for greater residential and other community uses. Figure 12.1 shows the original scheme plan (Option 1) and the proposed wastewater treatment plant and groundwater treatment plant relocation sites (Option 2).

The charters of both the Water Corporation and LandCorp included promotion of community benefit. Having reached an impasse on which option to adopt, the two parties agreed to jointly evaluate the economics of relocation in order to assess the costs and community benefits of each. The study was also to determine which party would be responsible for any additional costs and identify potential cost recoveries.

The parties also agreed that the option providing the greatest community benefit would be supported. If Option 2 were to become the favored scheme, it would mean promoting a change to the existing development plan to the Minister of Planning (the appropriate authority within the state government).

SETTING

Organizational Commitment

The study brief required the evaluation of:

- Whether any additional costs incurred by relocation of the wastewater treatment plant and groundwater treatment plant would be adequately compensated by additional community benefits
- The balance between the individual stakeholders' costs and benefits
- Any potential cost recoveries and responsibilities

A benefit-cost analysis had to be carried out in order to assess the possible advantages and disadvantages of Option 2 over Option 1. The analysis had to consider a broad range of events and views and take a holistic view of the impacts (both positive and negative) on the community.

The benefit-cost analysis also had to assess a wide range of engineering, financial, environmental, and societal issues. Consideration of such diverse and often complicated aspects was difficult for a number of reasons, including:

- The significant uncertainty and initial skepticism shown by the Water Corporation and the Developer in trying to quantify community perceptions, reactions, and impacts

- The uncertainty associated with even relatively well-defined issues, such as those associated with such project engineering components as the scope and cost of the works and related infrastructure
- The challenge of quantifying environmental and social issues, particularly in terms of their cost implications
- The different focus, viewpoints, and even language used by advisers in the areas of the environment, the community, and business which complicated the definition and quantification of the relationships between the various issues
- The lack of an established, systematic approach for comparison of such complex options up to that time

Stakeholders

The key stakeholders in addition to the Water Corporation and the Developer were the Shire of Wanneroo/City of Joondalup, the Department of Environmental Protection, Pentland Bay Syndicate, the Ministry for Planning, and Quinns Rock Action Group.

Stakeholder consultation was a key part of the process. Prior to the project, a questionnaire was distributed to the key stakeholders to:

- Explain the total community benefit-cost exercise.
- Ask for advice from the stakeholders on the important community issues with respect to the options.

The questionnaire consisted of two parts:

1. General questions on issues of importance, with the objective of obtaining an appreciation of the key stakeholders' outlook of the impacts of water and wastewater treatment plants on urban development.
2. Site-specific questions to gain data that could be used in the workshop with the Water Corporation and the Developer to compare the total community costs and benefits for the two locations under consideration.

The questionnaires were completed at meetings held with each of the key stakeholders. The key areas of concern were:

- The reduced buffer zones associated with Option 2 with particular emphasis on the increased risk of odors, noise, and visual impacts, and the greater risk to human health and safety. The general feeling was that the smaller the buffer zone, the greater the potential for detrimental impacts, regardless of what technology was employed to manage the impacts.

- The environmental conservation value of larger buffer zones. The proposed buffer around the current location was considered to be environmentally significant as it enabled good protection of vegetation and reduced urban development pressures.
- Restrictions to beach access. Maintenance of unrestricted beach access was considered to be of primary importance.
- That social amenity, environmental, health, and safety benefits exceed any engineering benefits and that they be achieved at minimum additional cost.
- The impact on property value. The general feeling was that the original planned location of the treatment plants would have a more detrimental effect due to their close proximity to the beach.
- Ongoing community costs for the facilities. The survey highlighted a preference for increased initial capital for engineering solutions to reduce ongoing impacts on social, environmental, health, and safety issues.

Issues not considered by the community stakeholder respondents to be important were:

- Impacts on the broader property values
- Light spill from the treatment facilities, as this could be easily controlled with engineering solutions

Assessment Structure

The study primarily comprised probabilistic benefit-cost analysis to compare two options for siting the development's treatment facilities. The approach taken was to compare the additional costs and benefits accrued to the individual stakeholders (the Water Corporation, the Developer, and the wider community) and to the combined stakeholder groups. Figure 12.2 shows a flow chart of the benefit-cost evaluation process.

Although Option 1 clearly had its own set of associated costs and benefits, it was the status quo and was therefore considered to represent the zero cost and benefit case. The benefits and costs derived for Option 2 would then provide a comparison with the default option.

It was also decided to separate the "internal" and "external" stakeholders with respect to assessment of costs and benefits. The internal stakeholders were the Water Corporation and the Developer, while the external stakeholders were the local and regional communities.

A key to the success of this study was the facilitation of the expert panel workshops, which needed to ensure that the panel discussion was structured, was appropriate, was without obvious bias, had direction, and remained focused.

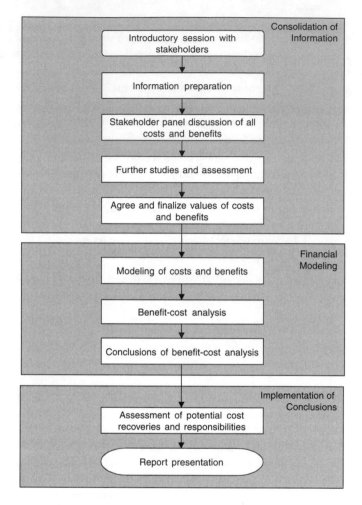

Figure 12.2 **Benefit-cost analysis process flow chart.**

RISK IDENTIFICATION

Expert Panel

The general process of selecting the expert panel members and collecting information in a facilitated workshop was followed for this project. The panel consisted of representatives from the internal stakeholders (Water Corporation and the Developer) and specialist advisers. Members covered a wide range of expertise, including engineering, law, property development, and land valuation. Where necessary, the panel members were able to call on the additional resources of their organizations and specialist consultants to assist the information consolidation process.

Information provided by the panel members needed to be sound and to be accepted by all of the internal stakeholders. Each judgment made by the panel was derived by agreement between individuals with specific expertise in relation to an event in question. For example, increases in land values were discussed and agreed by experienced land valuers appointed separately by both internal stakeholder groups. Each panel judgment, therefore, was provided on an informed basis and was not the product of a "democratic" process where all panel members, regardless of expertise, contributed to (or voted on) the outcome.

Identifying and Quantifying the Risk Events

The panel considered the financial value (benefit or cost) of items associated with public relations, employment, commuting, retail sales and rent, engineering, land development, planning, the environment, social and amenity impacts, health, taxation and risk events. As it is the quantification of the intangible issues involved in this project that sets it apart from the other case studies in this book, quantification of the issues is examined first and in some detail. The readily quantifiable issues (e.g., engineering costs and benefits) have been tabulated without detailed explanation of the basis of their quantification.

Public Relations. Odor. With Option 2, the proposed reduction in buffer area around the WTP would bring more people closer to the plant than would be the case with Option 1. In recognition of this, the design and costs of the WTP for Option 2 were modified to include odor control. However, even with the additional equipment, the closer proximity of residential and commercial areas would mean an increased risk of odor complaints, which in turn could increase the community pressure on the Water Corporation to increase its odor control. As this was not considered viable, an ongoing public relations program was proposed as mitigation. This community consultation program was estimated to have an annual median cost of $40,000, with a 95 percent confidence level ($CL_{95\%}$) cost of $120,000 per year.

In examining this issue, the panel also determined that to provide a balanced comparison of the two options, the screening and grit removal facility for Option 1 would need to be enclosed within a building. This would reduce the likelihood of odor generation from the plant itself to a similar level as that proposed for Option 2, although Option 1 would still benefit from the larger separation distances.

Beach Access. Due to its coastal location, Option 1 restricts and interrupts direct beach access. The greater accessibility of the beach with Option 2 provides a substantial community benefit.

Two measures of benefit were identified:

1. Reduced travel times and distances associated with Option 2 as compared with the indirect beach access alternatives involved with Option 1
2. Negligible beach security cost for Option 2 compared with that required for Option 1

Table 12.1 Option 1—Additional Travel Costs

Item	CL 50%	CL 95%
Regional Population (No.)	200,000	250,000
Affected Population (%)	30	60
Persons per Trip (No.)	3	4
Trips per Year (No.)	2	5
Additional Distance per Trip (miles [km])	12 [20]	16 [25]
Transport Cost ($/mile [$/km])	0.80 [0.50]	1.30 [0.80]

The benefit for Option 2 was calculated as the additional Option 1 costs for each of these components. Table 12.1 presents the calculation of the additional travel costs.

The median travel cost benefit was $400,000 per year. The estimated annual cost of beach security under Option 1 was $140,000.

Community Diversity. Diversity is a measure of community health. An aim for the Alkimos development was to have a varied socioeconomic distribution as this improves community diversity. Greater diversity leads to increased localized employment. A typical employment range is 30 to 70 percent of the regional population. For Alkimos, an employment target of 40 percent was considered realistic.

Local employment also leads to infrastructure benefits, for example, by reducing freeway pressure. A diverse, healthy, and vibrant community provides other gains, such as reduced law and order problems, fewer instances of community protest, less government intrusion, and increased growth.

Option 2 was considered to offer a better layout for encouraging and allowing community growth. With the greater regional population would come increased diversity as compared with that predicted for Option 1. The ballpark estimate of the overall community benefit associated with Option 2 was $1 million (median) and $5 million ($CL_{95\%}$).

Corporate Reputation. Option 2 presents a greater risk to public health due to the storage and use of chlorine at the separate GTP. A chlorine leak would initiate a public relations effort with its attendant costs. Groundwater salinity is also an issue in Western Australia, and salinity affects on the water supply would be another initiating event. The additional costs associated with Option 2 were estimated to be $40,000 (median) to $100,000 ($CL_{95\%}$) per year.

Use of the Buffer Zone. It was recognized that, over time, public pressure to use prime, unutilized land could result in encroachment of development into the buffer area around the treatment plants. Under these circumstances, Option 2 was seen as having a slight disadvantage because of its smaller buffer area. The panel considered that the dollar value of this disadvantage would be minor, and the issue was excluded from the analysis.

Odor Control for Option 1. Due to the large buffer area associated with Option 1, no odor control was proposed for the WTP. On examination, it was felt that odors could still be an issue, and the design was changed to house the screening and grit removal facilities, which were considered the likely primary source of objectionable odors. This change is addressed under the engineering issues.

Recreation and General Amenity. This was covered under the beach access issue.

GTP. No issues could be identified with the GTP that differentiated between the options.

Other Issues. Upon examination, a number of issues identified during the workshops were shown to have the same impact for each scheme. As these provided no differentiation between the options, they were excluded from the analysis. The issues in this category included coastal water quality, groundwater quality, impacts on the surfing reef, development delays due to public opposition, and the public relations components of the options' engineering and design.

Employment. The increased employment achievable with Option 2 was estimated by specialist advisers to the panel. Two firms were engaged for this exercise, and the closeness of their estimates provided confirmation of the results. A median difference in employment of 350 full-time jobs was adopted for the analysis. The 95 percent confidence-level estimate was 400 jobs.

The benefit to Option 2 was calculated as the cost of unemployment (that would occur with Option 1). A rate of $8 per hour was used to calculate the median cost, which for a normal working year of 1,820 hours gave approximately $15,000 per annum. The 95 percent confidence-level estimate was $20,000 per year.

Commuting. Commuting was quantified in terms of environmental costs, accident costs, and time. For the latter, a cost per hour was allocated. The assessment showed a benefit to Option 2, and the results are given in Table 12.2.

The average total employment benefit was calculated at around $7.1 million per year.

Retail Sales and Rent. Specialist advisers to the expert panel assessed the increased trade associated with Option 2. The increases would be generated through the coastal village centers planned for Option 2, as well as through the overall gain of retail trade due to the higher population. The calculated difference in total retail sales and rent over time is shown in Table 12.3.

Table 12.2   Option 2—Commuting Benefits

Item	Benefit (CL 50%, $ per year)
Environmental	559,000
Commuting Accidents	94,000
Time	1,200,000

Table 12.3   Retail Sales and Rent

	Total Sales Difference ($ × million)	Total Rent Difference ($ × million)
Stage 1 (Y2000–Y2005)	6.0	0.6
Stage 2 (Y2006–Y2010)	13.8	1.38
Stage 3 (Y2011–Y2015)	20.8	2.08
Stage 4 (Y2016–Y2020)	25.4	2.54
Stage 5 (Y2021–Y2050)	27.8	2.78

For the analysis, the values shown in the table were reduced by 30 percent to allow for goods and services that were not necessarily specific to the Alkimos region and could therefore be duplicated and provided from outside the region.

Engineering Costs. Because the Option 1 site was chosen as the best location from an engineering perspective, relocation of the treatment plants away from the coast (Option 2) involved either the same or greater engineering costs than those for Option 1. That is, there was no engineering benefit associated with Option 2. The engineering costs are summarized in Table 12.4.

Table 12.4   Engineering Costs

	Cost (Option 2 – Option 1), $ × 1,000	
Item	CL 50%	CL 95%
Site Preparation	3,800	4,600
WTP Construction (including odor control)	11,300	14,100
Aeration Tank Covers	Included as a community cost elsewhere	
Extra Connecting Pipelines	3,100	3,900
Pipeline Easements	No additional cost. Excluded	
Main Sewer Construction	No additional cost. Excluded	
GTP Construction	1,300	1,650
GTP Land Acquisition	Covered elsewhere. Excluded	

Land Development. The land development costs and benefits were determined using an experienced, local land valuation specialist and known development costs. The results are summarized in Table 12.5.

Planning. As shown in Table 12.6, the planning issues were either covered elsewhere under other items contained in the issues register or were deemed to be the same for both Options 1 and 2.

Environment. As shown in Table 12.7 the environmental issues were covered elsewhere under other items contained in the issues register, addressed through mitigation works, or deemed to be the same for both Options 1 and 2.

Table 12.5   Land Development Costs and Benefits

Item		Cost, $ × 1,000		Benefit, $ × 1,000	
		CL 50%	CL 95%	CL 50%	CL 95%
Acquisition	—Water Corp.	4,100	4,500		
	—Developer	No acquisition required. Excluded			
Value Increase	—Water Corp.			16,800	18,900
	—Developer			9,700	14,000
Injurious Affection Payment		Paid. Excluded			
Land Released for Urban Development		Covered in Water Corp. value increase			
Coastal Land Released		Covered in Water Corp. value increase			
General Land Value Increases		Covered in Water Corp. value increase			
Coastal Node Development	—Water Corp.	Not applicable. Excluded			
	—Developer	10,000	10,100		

Table 12.6   Planning Issues Register

Item	Reason for Exclusion
Regional Beach—Community Relationship	Included in Public Relations
Coastal Node Connectivity	Included in Public Relations
Urban Design Flexibility Improvements	Included in Public Relations
Sewage/Water Infrastructure Planning	Same for Options 1 and 2

Table 12.7   Environmental Issues Register

Item	Reason for Exclusion
Increased Odor Impacts	Covered elsewhere—Risk
Human Health Damage (Salinity Risk)	Same for Options 1 and 2
Visual Impacts	Addressed through landform management
Viewscape	Addressed through screening
Environmentally Significant Vegetation	Same for Options 1 and 2
Effluent Reuse	Covered elsewhere

Social Impacts. As shown in Table 12.8, the identified social costs and benefits either were covered elsewhere in the issues register or involved readily quantifiable development costs.

Health Impacts. Table 12.9 shows the outcomes of the panel deliberations on health issues.

Table 12.8   Social Issues

Item	Panel Findings
Impact on Nearby Communities	Covered elsewhere. Excluded
Social Sustainability	Covered elsewhere. Excluded
Community Well-being	Covered elsewhere. Excluded
Southern Coastal Node Building Costs	Development cost of $11.4 million

Table 12.9   Health Issues

Item	Reason for Exclusion
Health Buffer	Covered elsewhere. Excluded
Effluent Reuse	Same for Options 1 and 2. Excluded

Taxation. The outcome of the panel deliberations was that taxation was specifically excluded from the study and hence no allowance was made for this component. It was left to the Water Corporation and the Developer to resolve taxation matters at a later stage.

Risk. The issues identified by the panel showed that the options had limited exposure to risk events. Many of the risk events were managed by modifying the engineering associated with the WTP and GTP (e.g., with the addition of the odor control plant). By modifying the scheme designs, the risk event occurrence costs were transferred to the base cost estimates.

RISK ANALYSIS

Financial Modeling

The model calculated the costs and benefits for the Water Corporation, the Developer, the internal stakeholders (i.e., Water Corporation and the Developer combined), the external stakeholders (community), and all stakeholders combined.

Benefit-Cost Analysis Results

Consolidation of the values input to the model indicated that the costs associated with treatment plant relocation (Option 2) would be substantial. The median engineering cost was around $14.8 million, with land acquisition and public relations making up the bulk of the remainder, which was calculated around $4.5 million.

However, the calculated community benefits associated with Option 2 were significantly larger than these costs. The key community benefits were the savings on beach access ($6 million), improved community diversity (around $10 million), increased employment and reduced commuting costs ($105 million), and increased retail sales and rents ($265 million). The total increase in property values totaled around $26.5 million.

Figure 12.3 provides a summary of the modeling results and lists the estimated benefits and costs for individual stakeholder groups and combinations.

The values in the figure represent a range of dollar values for benefits and costs that reflect different degrees of conservatism. For example, the optimistic estimates are low calculated costs but high calculated benefits. Conversely, the pessimistic estimates are very high estimates of costs but very low estimates of benefit. The planning estimates are considered to be reasonable but conservative estimates of costs or benefits that are suitable for planning purposes.

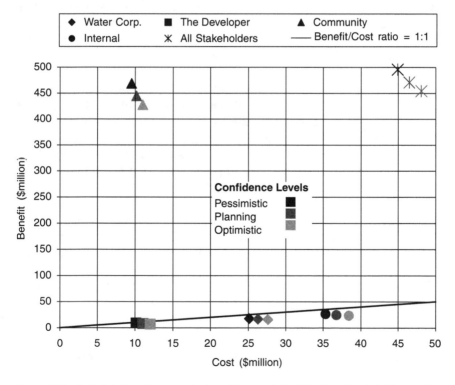

Figure 12.3 Calculated total community benefit-cost relationships for all stakeholders and for each stakeholder group.

Discussion of the study outcomes for each stakeholder and the stakeholder groups follows.

Individual Stakeholders. Figure 12.3 shows that the Water Corporation would have to spend around $20 million to relocate the treatment plants for a benefit of around $16 million (planning level estimates). For the Water Corporation there would be a net cost of around $4 million. The shortfall for the Water Corporation could range from $2 million to $6 million.

Similarly, for the Developer Option 2 would represent a net cost of around $3 million (the benefit of around $8 million is offset by an outlay of around $11 million.) The shortfall for the Developer could range from $1 million to $5 million.

However, the community would be a beneficiary of the relocation. The total community benefit was estimated to be around $375 million compared with the relatively small cost of approximately $9 million—a net benefit of around $365 million.

The benefit-cost relationship in Figure 12.3 also shows the 1:1 benefit-cost ratio. It shows that for the individual, internal stakeholders, the benefit-cost ratio is less than 1.0 (break even) regardless of which combination of benefits and costs is applied. Considering the benefit-costs relationships that apply to the Water Corporation and the Developer, as individual entities there would be no economic incentive to relocate the treatment plants. The community, on the other hand, stands to benefit substantially from the adoption of Option 2.

Internal Stakeholders. When considered together, the internal stakeholders would not achieve a return on the additional investment involved in Option 2. Comparison of the planning level benefits and costs indicates that the internal stakeholders could face a net cost of around $6 million. The cost could range from around $3 million (low-cost, high-benefit case) to around $8 million (high-cost, low-benefit case). In themselves, the potential additional costs provide no incentive for the internal stakeholders to jointly support Option 2.

All Stakeholders. The benefit-cost relationships are dramatically reversed when considered from a much wider community view that includes all stakeholder interests. When all community benefits are taken into account, the benefit of Option 2 is staggering, and society is likely to benefit by around $400 million for a capital outlay in the order of $40 million. There was therefore tremendous incentive for the wider community to ensure that Option 2 was adopted.

IMPLEMENTATION: COST RECOVERY AND RESPONSIBILITIES

The benefit-cost analysis results were used to consider ways of avoiding the negative impacts of Option 2 on the internal stakeholders while retaining the substantial benefits to the wider community. The funding options looked at how to distribute the costs to the stakeholders in some proportion to the benefits accrued. Funding options included:

• Each key stakeholder bears its direct costs, regardless of benefits gained.
• Costs are distributed across the internal stakeholders to restore equitability.
• Obtain a Community Service Obligation (CSO, a state government allocation of funds to advance community projects) to account for the community benefits provided by the key stakeholders.
• Invest in development to obtain funding from profits.

Stakeholders Retain Own Costs

This approach would not provide an outcome acceptable to all parties. The additional costs incurred by each of the internal stakeholders created a strong disincentive to support Option 2, and without the necessary investment, Option 2 could not proceed.

Equitable Distribution of Costs

Equitable distribution of costs among the internal stakeholders would also fail to overcome the shortfall of these parties. Again, the community could gain the potential benefits only if the investment in Option 2 proceeded, but the additional costs were a disincentive to the project no matter how they were distributed to the internal stakeholders.

Obtain a CSO

A CSO passes the project's cost differential to the group that gains by far the greatest benefits—the community. In Western Australia, there were several precedents of CSO payments having been made to provide community benefits. One example involved the relocation of a wastewater treatment plant.

Under a CSO payment, the state government would compensate the Water Corporation and the Developer for the differential costs, which would be the range of $4 million to $8 million and $1 million and $5 million, respectively.

Fund through Development

The last option would involve the Water Corporation and the Developer entering a contractual arrangement with a third party to invest further in the Alkimos development in order to fund the relocation from derived profits. The CEOs of the internal stakeholders decided that they would prefer not to seek funds from the State Government, as at that time the government was under considerable political pressure to increase its spending in other areas. The internal stakeholders therefore decided to jointly invest further in the Alkimos development and to ensure the development was self-funding, to the extent, it was hoped, that the project returned a net revenue.

SUMMARY

This case study clearly demonstrates that substantial financial opportunities can be opened up if so-called nonquantifiable consequences, such as community diversity, amenity, and image, can be valued in dollar terms and used to make decisions that fully take community impacts into account. In addition, the positive study results convinced the stakeholders of the benefits of relocation and, further, strengthened their resolve to enhance community benefit by relocating the treatment plants.

While this case study deals specifically with a community project, social issues are a major component of virtually every project. The ability to quantify the community issues that are generally considered intangible is critical to providing a complete assessment of all pertinent factors on any project. To take this position a step further, experience suggests that most businesses manage the technical risks associated with their core activities very well. However, because they have been unable to do so, companies often neglect to address their social risks. As a result, when the social issues are assessed, they usually are found to pose much greater risks than those well-managed technical risks. The Alkimos case study provides a guide as to how these intangible social risks can be quantified, which then allows them to be managed in the same way that a company manages its technical risk.

13

COMMUNITY SAFETY: TOURISM, NEW ZEALAND

This case study examines:

- Use of nonfinancial consequences to determine risk
- Use of personal injury as the measure of consequence and risk
- Comparison against accepted levels of societal risk

BACKGROUND

This case study examines whether the risk associated with a tourism venture is acceptable to both individuals and society as a whole in terms of commonly accepted risk criteria. While placing a financial cost against the loss of human life or serious injury is accepted and used in certain areas, publicly it remains a controversial practice. By using personal injury as the measure of consequence, this project avoids the controversy while still ensuring robust and valid outcomes from the risk assessment process.

Physical Setting

Meridian Energy Ltd. (MEL) owns and operates the Manapouri Power Station, a hydroelectric power station located in Fiordland, the southwestern region of New Zealand's South Island. The power station is located largely underground and was excavated into solid rock (gneiss and granite). The station was constructed during the latter half of the 1960s using conventional drill and blast mining technology to create the tunnels and voids in which the facility was built. The machine hall is more than 650 feet (200 m) below the ground surface and nearly 500 feet (150 m) below the level of Lake Manapouri. The lower levels of the station are below sea level.

Tourism Venture

The station was built within the Southern Alps, draws water from Lake Manapouri, and discharges via a 6-mile (10-km) tailrace tunnel to Doubtful Sound. The high mountains of the Southern Alps (17 peaks with elevations above 10,000 ft [3,000 m]), deep glacial lakes and fjords provide spectacular natural scenery and sensitive environments that attract tourists from around the world. One of the many tour options offered to visitors of the Fiordland region includes a guided trip through the underground power station.

SETTING

Organizational Commitment

Public safety is a specific component of MEL's Health and Safety Policy. Its stated purpose is "[to] ensure that MEL take appropriate measures to minimize the risk of harm to members of the public who may come in contact with MEL operations."[1] To this end, MEL had recently commissioned a number of technical studies to determine the levels of risk to public safety from various hazards. The overall aim of these and other studies was to guide MEL in deciding whether to allow public tours of the station to continue and, if so, under what conditions. The quantitative risk assessment was commissioned to collate the findings of these various reports and MEL's institutional knowledge into a single, comprehensive document. The purpose of the document was to gauge the level of risk to tourists visiting the station, the determination of which would then lead to rational decisions regarding continuation of the tours.

Stakeholders

The principal stakeholders in the tourist visits to the Manapouri Power Station were:

- The board and shareholders of Meridian Energy (i.e., the government and people of New Zealand)
- The employees of MEL
- The board, shareholders, and employees of Fiordland Travel Ltd. (the company conducting the tours)
- Tourists and visitors to New Zealand generally and those who visit the station specifically
- Contractors and suppliers to MEL

Project Objectives

The objective of the study was primarily to safeguard members of the public from unacceptably high exposure to hazards and incidents that could potentially cause serious injury or death. The subsidiary objectives of the quantitative risk assessment were to combine the existing study data and develop and use any other information held by MEL to:

- Meet the provisions of MEL's Health and Safety Policy.
- Minimize any potential liability to MEL should a visitor(s) to the station be seriously injured or killed.
- Compare the risk to human life against appropriate acceptability criteria to guide MEL in deciding whether to allow public visits to continue.
- Establish or modify practices and rules under which these visits can occur, in order to manage and reduce the risk, assuming the outcome of the previous step indicated that public visits could safely continue.

Risk Assessment Structure

Definition of Personal Injury. Personal injury during a tour of the station could range in seriousness from a minor scratch from inadvertent contact with the unlined rock walls of the underground excavation, through broken bones due to a fall, to a fatality. In setting the context for the project, it was necessary to define the level of personal injury that was to be considered in the assessment.

Minor scratches were not considered to constitute real risk in terms of personal injury. However, a fatality should be prevented to the greatest degree possible. Falls, particularly bad ones, were a gray area, and there was some discussion as to whether they should be included or excluded from the study. It was recognized that falls could occur anywhere; in view of that, MEL had provided stairs, handrails, barriers, and nonskid surfaces, all to appropriate standards. It was therefore concluded that falls would be excluded from the assessment, although the need for MEL to maintain its current practices to minimize the risk of falls was flagged.

For this study, consequence was defined as a serious injury or fatality. Serious injury was defined as a permanent disability or disability/disfigurement requiring long-term care and/or rehabilitation. The study did not differentiate between serious injury and fatality.

Conceptual Structure. The concept developed for the risk assessment structure is shown in Figure 13.1. For each risk event, the total likelihood generally comprised three components, namely:

1. The likelihood of occurrence of the causative incident (e.g., a fire, expressed as a chance per year or a return period [years per event])

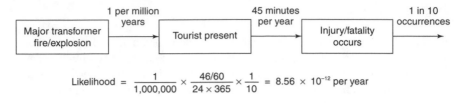

$$\text{Likelihood} = \frac{1}{1{,}000{,}000} \times \frac{46/60}{24 \times 365} \times \frac{1}{10} = 8.56 \times 10^{-12} \text{ per year}$$

Figure 13.1 Example event tree of fatality arising from a transformer failure.

2. The likelihood that one or more visitors would be present (i.e., someone has to be in the vicinity of the fire to be in danger)
3. The likelihood that serious injury or death would occur (i.e., the likelihood that someone close to the fire is unable to escape before being overcome by heat or smoke)

These components were multiplied together to give the overall likelihood of a serious injury or fatality.

Consequence was measured as the number of lives lost (or number of people seriously injured). Where loss of life was concerned, risk was considered using two different measures: (1) individual risk and (2) societal risk.

Individual Risk. For this study, individual risk was the measure of threat to life from the perspective of the person at risk. Individual risk was the risk faced by a single tourist who joined one tour in his or her lifetime and was therefore exposed for the 45 minutes of the tour. Given that the consequence is one particular person's life, for this study incident likelihood and individual risk are equivalent.

Societal Risk. Societal risk was the measure of threat to life from MEL's perspective or from the perspective of society as a whole. Societal risk was the risk faced by any and all visitors to the station. Societal risk was the individual risk multiplied by the total number of visits during the year.[2]

While the study considers only a single consequence (injury/death) for each risk event, consequence magnitude can vary depending on the type of causative incident. For example, one or two people might be hurt if a tour party were caught in a rockfall while walking to the viewing platform, but perhaps a dozen might be injured if a group was on the viewing platform and the platform collapsed. For each identified risk event, societal risk was therefore the product of the annual likelihood and the number of people seriously injured or killed in that incident. The total societal risk is the sum of the individual event risks.

Risk Acceptability Criteria

Acceptability criteria exist for both individual and societal measures of risk. The development of these criteria was based largely on statistical data relating to fatalities associated with common activities such as smoking, driving, and flying. The assumption is that people continue to engage in these activities knowing that by doing so they are placing themselves at risk and that therefore the levels of risk posed by these activities are generally acceptable.

Figure 13.2 shows an F-N chart, which provides a typical presentation of societal risk acceptability criteria. F-N charts plot N, the number of fatalities, against F, the annual frequency of events with N or more deaths.

The curves on this figure are statistically derived and represent the level of risk to which society is exposed. The curves are considered representative of acceptable societal risk. For example, in continuing to choose to fly, society considers that the likelihood of fatalities resulting from aircraft accidents are acceptable.

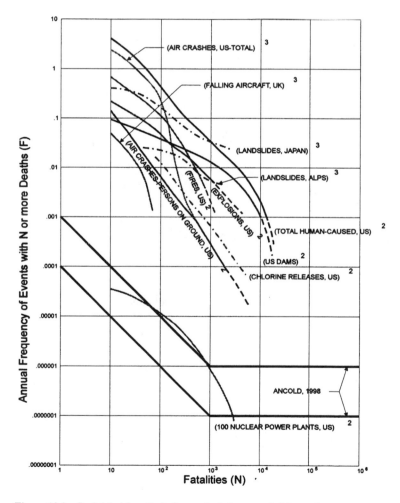

Figure 13.2 Societal risk criteria for a selected range of risk events.

The most conservative sets of curves on Figure 13.2 are those developed by the Australian National Committee on Large Dams[3] (ANCOLD). These values have been derived from existing and proposed criteria in land use planning and the chemical and nuclear industries. The ANCOLD guidelines are used by dam designers to ensure that their designs meet acceptable safety standards and by assessors of existing dams to determine whether a given facility achieves an acceptable level of safety.

For this risk assessment, the ANCOLD guidelines were adopted as the acceptable societal risk criteria. It is worth noting that the risk posed by a dam to a person or community living downstream is essentially an involuntary risk, as compared with the voluntary risk taken by a tourist in electing to engage in a specific activity. Acceptable levels of involuntary risk have been shown to be several orders of magnitude less than the acceptable level of voluntary risk. Therefore, in adopting the ANCOLD guidelines, this assessment provides a conservative set of acceptability criteria.

In this assessment, a risk quotient above the upper of the two ANCOLD curves (the acceptable societal risk limit) was considered to pose an unacceptable societal risk. A risk quotient that fell below the lower of the two curves (the acceptable societal risk objective) was considered to represent an acceptable level of societal risk. The ANCOLD guideline labels the area between the two curves as ALARP (as low as reasonably practicable). The ALARP principle is that risk reduction should be carried out on these events with a risk quotient in this area, provided cost-effective reduction measures can be identified.

Acceptability levels for individual risk tend to be one or more orders of magnitude less than societal risk criteria. For example, ANCOLD suggests a tolerable upper limit for the average individual risk associated with existing facilities (dams) of 1×10^{-5} per year and 1×10^{-4} per year for the individual most at risk. From Figure 13.2, the tolerable upper societal risk limit is 1×10^{-3} per year while the acceptable societal risk is no greater than 1×10^{-4} per year.

RISK IDENTIFICATION

Selection of the Expert Panel

MEL selected the expert panel members to represent those with an in-depth knowledge of the power station, experience in risk assessment, and conducting public tours through the facility. The panel's combined knowledge of the project was used to identify, describe, and quantify the likelihood of occurrence of potential, significant safety hazards posed to visitors to the station. In addition, panel members approached and received information from other MEL employees and contractors with knowledge of specific issues raised in the workshop. Information on the tour frequency, tourist numbers, and time spent on the tours was obtained from the visitors' log book.

Identifying and Quantifying Risk Events

Risk Events and Likelihood. The panel members identified and quantified the risk events in a facilitated workshop. Initial quantification of the likelihood of each causative event and the likelihood of an injury or fatality occurring to people present during the event (the first and third components of likelihood shown in Figure 13.1) was undertaken during the combined risk workshop and was based on:

- Previous technical studies aimed specifically at the public safety aspects of the station
- The consensus of appropriate expert(s) based on best professional judgment
- Historical data (where available)

The expert panel identified 15 risk events, of which eight were later excluded from the risk evaluation due to negligible likelihood or because they were considered management issues rather than risks. A brief summary of the risk register is shown in Table 13.1.

Table 13.1 Summary of Workshop Outputs

	Likelihood of	
Risk Scenarios	*Initiating Event*	*Serious Injury/Fatality*
Overtopping—hydraulic surge floods access tunnel	1.5×10^{-5}	1
Fire—fire/explosion in No. 1 transformer	1×10^{-5}	0.1
Rockfall—rockfall impacts a tour party	Varies by tunnel section—calculated in risk model	
Platform Collapse—seismic load causes buckling	$1/450 = 2.22 \times 10^{-3}$	0.01
Crane Impact—gantry moves over viewing platform	Excluded—negligible risk	
Road Accident—forces bus off road in MEL lease area	1×10^{-2}	0.001
Fall—visitor falls on walkway or stairs to platform	Excluded—as direct cause of fatality is improbable	
Loss of Supervision—pupil wanders from tour group	$1/1,697 = 5.89 \times 10^{-4}$	0.001
Loss of Power—inadequate lighting to enable safe egress	Excluded—negligible risk	
Adequacy of Egress—visitors' ability to climb cable shafts	Excluded—management issue	
Emergency Response—tour leader training	Excluded—management issue	
Wharf Failure—boat collision with wharf	0.001	0.1
Helicopter Landing Pad—unauthorized public access	Excluded—management issue	
Navigation Lights—fail due to inadequate maintenance	Excluded—management issue	
Level Control/Structures—caught by control mechanism or fall	Excluded—management issue	

The likelihood of an individual being present at the time of any of these scenarios occurring was the proportion of time that the person would spend in the station in any given year.

The following exposure times were used:

- Full tour—45 minutes or 8.56×10^{-5} as a proportion of a year
- On viewing platform—30 minutes or 5.71×10^{-5}
- On the wharf—5 minutes or 9.51×10^{-6}

The likelihood of a tour group being present coincident with a causative event (the second component of likelihood shown in Figure 13.1) was derived after the workshop using the average time of the tours (45 minutes) and the number of tour parties per year. The latter was obtained by examining (July 1, 1999, and June 30, 2000) daily data from the visitors' log book for the previous 12 months.

Consequence. The annual numbers of tours and visitors passing through the station derived from the visitors' book also was used to estimate the number of people that could be present during an incident and hence the potential number of lives at risk.

For any given incident, an injury or fatality could occur to some proportion of the total number of lives at risk. Depending on the nature of the incident, this number could vary from one person to all people on the tour. The expert panel estimated the likely number of injuries/deaths for each risk event, and these were expressed as a fraction of the total number of lives at risk.

RISK ANALYSIS

Quantitative Techniques

Rock Fall Event Likelihood. Tourists are driven down the access tunnel by bus, alight, and take a short walk to a viewing platform in the machine hall, then walk back to the bus to be driven out of the tunnel. One of the risk events identified by the expert panel was a serious injury or fatality from a rockfall in the unlined access tunnel or along the pedestrian access walkway between the bus parking area and the machine hall viewing platform. A schematic diagram of the arrangement and the starting assumptions on which the event likelihood was calculated are shown in Figure 13.3.

MEL had commissioned a geotechnical investigation of the tunnel and walkway and had received a draft report giving an assessment of the likelihood of rockfall.[4] This report identified two areas within the access tunnel of differing stability (differing likelihoods of rockfall), which are labeled in Figure 13.3 as "Tunnel" and "Turnaround" (the section of tunnel where the bus turns). The investigation also considered two different sizes of rock: 6-inch (150-mm) diameter being suf-

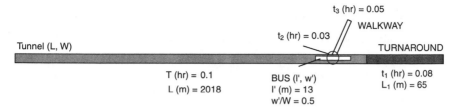

Starting Assumptions:
1. The likelihood of a rockfall is uniform over a year.
2. Vehicle movements and rockfalls are independent events.
3. The total number of buses per day is approximately 4, or annually = 1,222
4. Times are conservatively based on those of the July 12, 2000 site visit.
5. Times are for one-way travel only with the exception of t1, which is for the round trip including turning.
6. When alighting from or boarding the bus (t2), passengers are exposed to falls from 75 and 150 mm rocks*.
7. At all other times they are under protection, and their exposure is to 150 mm rockfalls*.
8. When under walkway, passengers are strung out along its entire length, l/L = 1.
9. Walkway assumed to be 25% of tunnel access width, i.e., w/W = 0.25.
10. The exposure to rockfall while sitting in the parked bus is included in the time of alighting/boarding.
11. The speed of the bus in the access tunnel is 20 km/h.
12. The stopping distance to avoid a collision with fallen rock is assumed to be two bus lengths.
13. The likelihood of a rock penetrating the bus or walkway cover and injuring a passenger is 1%*.
14. The likelihood of a rockfall penetrating the false ceiling in the machine hall is insignificant (assumed = 0).
15. The likelihood of rockfalls for different sections of tunnel is*:

Location	Annual Frequency	
	75 mm	150 mm
Tunnel	5	1
Walkway	0.2	0.04
Turnaround	1	0.2

*Information taken from L. Richards. Draft Report on Manapouri Power Station Public Safety Risk Assessment, June 2000.

Figure 13.3   Schematic of the underground tour during which tourists are exposed to the rockfall hazard.

ficient to penetrate the bus or protective roofing over the walkway and 3-inch (75-mm) diameter being large enough to cause injury in the unprotected area around the bus park.

These data were used to estimate the chance of a serious injury or fatality based on the time tourists were traveling through the tunnel or walking along that walkway and the assessed likelihood of a rockfall of sufficient size to cause personal injury. The method of calculation is shown on Figure 13.4.

Risk Model Description.   The aim of the risk model was to determine the total individual and societal risk to enable comparison with the acceptability criteria. The model did this by:

The likelihood of any one busload being caught by a rockfall (PAV) at any point is determined by the expression:

$$PAV = F * I/L * w/W * t/T$$

where F = Annual frequency of rockfall
I/L = Ratio of bus/person length to total tunnel section length
Bus length includes stopping distance when in motion
w/W = Ratio of bus/person width to total tunnel section width, 0.5
t/T = Ratio of time in tunnel to 1 year, i.e. T = 8,760 hrs

	F	I/L	w/W	t/T	Likelihood of:		
					Impact	Contact	Individual Injury or Fatality
Inward trip	1	1.93E-02	0.5	1.14E-05	1.10E-07	0.013	1.43E-09
Turnaround	0.2	0.2	0.5	9.51E-06	1.90E-07	0.013	2.47E-09
Alighting	6	6.44E-03	0.5	3.81E-06	7.35E-08	1	7.35E-08
Walkway in	0.04	1	0.25	5.71E-06	5.71E-08	0.013	7.42E-10
Walkway out	0.04	1	0.25	5.71E-06	5.71E-08	0.013	7.42E-10
Boarding	5	6.44E-03	0.5	3.81E-06	6.13E-08	1	6.13E-08
Outward trip	1	1.93E-02	0.5	1.14E-05	1.10E-07	0.013	1.43E-09
					PAV = 6.6E-07		**P(I) = 1.41E-07**

The likelihood of no accidents resulting in injury or fatality is given by the expression

$$P(0) = (1 - P(I))^n$$

where n = no. of buses per year

The annual likelihood of one or more accidents resulting in injury or fatality is given by the expression

$$P(>0) = P(A) = 1 - (1 - P(I))^n$$

P(A) = 1.73E-04

Figure 13.4   Calculation of rockfall hazard likelihood.

- Multiplying the likelihood components for each risk event (Columns 2 to 4 in Figure 13.5) to derive a total event likelihood for a single individual (Column 5) (Refer also to the example shown in Figure 13.1.)
- Multiplying this value of likelihood by the consequence of one life to derive the individual risk quotient posed by each event
- Adding the individual event risk quotients to derive a value of total individual risk

Column 1	Column 2	Column 3	Column 4	Column 5	Column 6	Column 7	Column 8	Column 9
Hazard	Likelihood of Event (per year)	Exposure Time for Group/ Individual (per year)	Likelihood of Injury/ Fatality	Likelihood/ Individual Risk	No. of Groups per year	Likelihood per year	Injuries/ Lives per Event	Societal Risk (lives per year)
Overtopping	1.50E-05	8.56E-05	1	1.28E-09	786	1.01E-06	51	5.11E-05

Figure 13.5   Risk model structure example using the overtopping event.

- Multiplying the individual event likelihoods (equal to the risk quotients) by the number of tours per year (Column 6) to provide a measure of the total annual event likelihood (Column 7)
- Multiplying the total annual event likelihood by the number of people injured or killed (Column 8) to provide a measure of the event risk (Column 9)
- Adding the scenario risk values to derive a measure of societal risk

The data were input as distributions, and the threshold method of analysis was applied.

Risk Model Inputs. The inputs derived from the workshop and the visitors' log book are shown in Figure 13.6.

Individual Risk Modeling Results

Figure 13.7 shows the calculated individual risk posed by each of the modeled risk events plotted against a log scale. The profile shows that the road accident event represents the highest risk event (1×10^{-5} lives per year), and that it is more than an order of magnitude higher than the second highest risk event (loss of supervision of tours, 5.89×10^{-7} lives per year).

Comparison against Acceptability Criteria. Figure 13.8 shows the total individual risk quotient (1.07×10^{-5} lives per year) plotted against a number of individual risk acceptability criteria for common activities. From this plot it can be seen that a tour through the station presents a risk approximately equivalent to that of flying. This low level of risk is considered acceptable.

In Figure 13.8 the largest contributor to the total individual risk, road accident, is also shown, along with the total individual risk excluding the road accident event. From this plot it can be seen that the road accident event dominates the total individual risk. It also can be seen that the combined individual risk of all the other events is negligible and is about an order of magnitude lower than the most stringent acceptability criterion.

Sensitivity Analysis. Figure 13.8 also shows that the individual risk quotient associated with a road accident, which is the highest-risk event, is an order of magnitude less than that associated with normal car travel. Intuitively this seems reasonable, particularly given the low volumes of traffic in the remote area of MEL's lease and the low vehicle speeds around the tight, steep site. It may even be an overestimate of the event risk.

However, and more important, the likelihood of this event could be increased by more than an order of magnitude without placing an individual visiting the station at any greater risk than when traveling in a car on a normal road. In other words, even if the likelihood provided by the expert panel underestimated the risk of this event, it probably could still be considered acceptable.

Hazard	Likelihood of Event (per year)	*Exposure Time for Group or Individual (per year)	Likelihood of Injury or Fatality	Likelihood/ Individual Risk	No. of Groups per year	Likelihood per year	Injuries or Lives per Event	Societal Risk (lives per year)
Overtopping	1.50E-05	8.56E-05	1	1.28E-09	786	1.01E-06	51	5.11E-05
Fire	1.00E-05	8.56E-05	0.1	8.56E-11	786	6.73E-08	5	3.41E-07
Rockfall	Refer to "Rockfall" sheet for calculation			1.42E-07	1,222	1.73E-04	3	4.38E-04
Platform Collapse	2.22E-03	5.71E-05	0.01	1.27E-09	786	9.97E-07	13	1.26E-05
Road Accident	1.00E-02	-	0.001	1.00E-05		1.00E-05	25	2.53E-04
Loss of supervision	5.89E-04	-	0.001	5.89E-07	786	5.89E-07	1	5.97E-07
Wharf failure	0.001	9.51E-06	0.1	9.51E-10	786	7.48E-07	3	1.89E-06
TOTALS:								
Total				1.07E-05				7.58E-04
Excluding Rockfall				1.06E-05				3.20E-04
Excluding Road Accidents				7.35E-07				5.05E-04
Excluding Rockfall & Road Accidents				5.93E-07				6.66E-05

Notes: - * Exposure time is not relevant to "Loss of Supervision" or "Road Accident"; the assumption that visitors are present is contained in the event and injury/fatality likelihoods. In both cases the individual risk is the same as the societal risk.

Visitor Information	No. of days	No. of trips/day	No. of buses/day	People/day	People/trip	Total People	No. of School Trips	Pupils/Trip
1 Oct to 15 Dec	76	3	4	116	39	8,816	11	33
16 Dec to 15 Mar	90	3	6	192	64	17,280	10	34
16 Mar to 30 Apr	45	3	5	170	57	7,650	6	39
1 May to 30 Sept	153	1	1	47	47	7,191	20	38
Note: No data for 29 March	364							

Trips per day	2.16		
Trips per year	786	Annual Total Visitors	40,937
Buses per day	3.36	Lives at Risk per Visit	51
Buses per year	1,222		

Annual Total Pupils	1,697
No. of School Trips	47
Lives at Risk per Visit	36

Figure 13.6   Risk model input data.

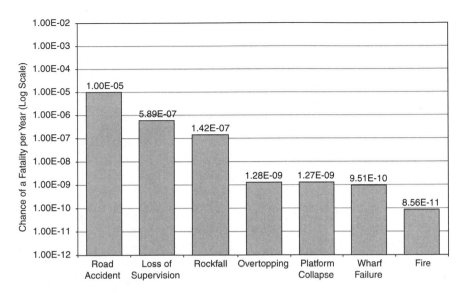

Figure 13.7   Individual risk quotient profile for identified tour risk events.

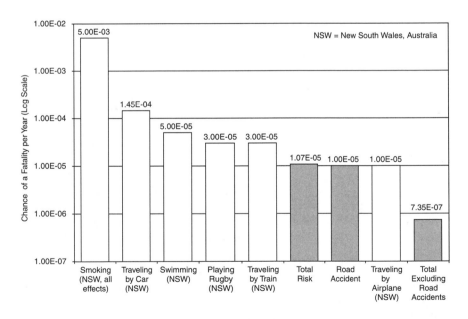

Figure 13.8   Comparison of the individual risk quotients for the total tour risk and the riskiest events against selected individual risk criteria.

The sensitivity analysis also looked at the impact of increasing the second highest risk by an order of magnitude, that is increasing the individual risk quotient associated with the "Loss of Supervision" event from 5.89×10^{-7} lives per year to 5.89×10^{-6} lives per year. The result was an increase in the total individual risk quotient from 1.07×10^{-5} lives per year to 1.6×10^{-5} lives per year. This is less than the risk associated with traveling by train or playing rugby. In summary, even if the likelihood provided by the expert panel underestimated the risk of this event by an order of magnitude, the overall individual risk probably could still be considered acceptable.

An underestimation of the remaining risk events would have less effect on the total individual risk. Therefore, no further sensitivity analyses were run on these events.

Finally, the model calculated the *annual* individual risk for station visitors, which was also the basis for the acceptability criteria. In practice, the large majority of these people would visit the station only once in their lifetime (i.e., would be underground for 45 minutes over a number of decades) rather than 45 minutes per year. It could therefore be argued that the starting assumption for calculating individual risk overestimates the likelihood of serious injury or death by one to two orders of magnitude (assuming a normal life span of, say, 70 years). However, other than noting that the approach taken in this assessment may be conservative, it was considered appropriate and no reduction in the estimate of individual risk was recommended.

Societal Risk Modeling Results

Event Risk and Acceptability. Figure 13.9 plots the calculated likelihood and consequence for each of the risk events on an F-N chart against the ANCOLD curves shown in Figure 13.2. The likelihood (F) and consequence (N, or number of fatalities) for each event are shown at the adopted planning level (the 80 percent confidence level). The error bars show the optimistic and pessimistic estimates of N.

It can be seen that all events fall within the tolerable limit proposed by ANCOLD. Those events below the ANCOLD objective line are considered to fall into the *de minimis* region and represent an acceptable level of societal risk.

Two events, rockfall and road accident, lie in the ALARP region, indicating that risk reduction should be carried out on these events if cost-effective reduction measures can be identified.

Total Risk and Acceptability. Figure 13.10 ranks the total societal risk and the risk associated with each event in descending order. Two additional bars show the total risk excluding each of the two highest-risk events, rockfall and road accident. The bars are included in ranked order and indicate the contribution of these events to the total risk. The ANCOLD guideline values are shown in Figure 13.10 to assist direct comparison with the calculated risk quotients.

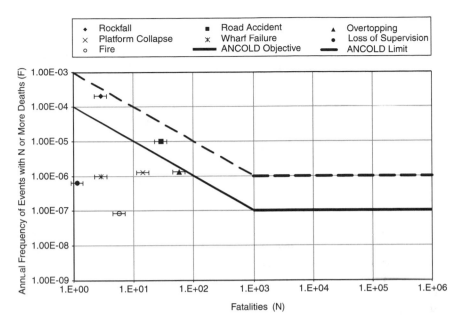

Figure 13.9 Comparison of the societal risk quotient for tour risk events and the ANCOLD guideline criteria plotted as an F-N chart.

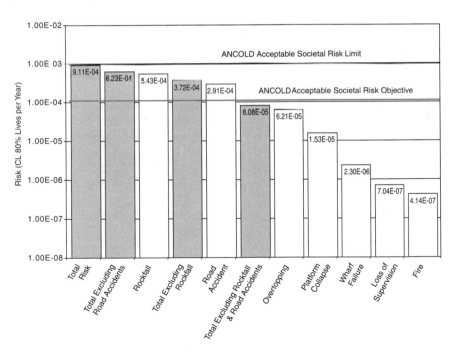

Figure 13.10 Comparison of the societal risk quotient for tour risk events and the ANCOLD guideline criteria for combined and individual events ranked in order of decreasing risk quotient.

As shown on Figure 13.10, both the rockfall and road accident events fall in the ALARP region defined by the ANCOLD risk acceptance criteria. The totals excluding either one of these two events also fall in the ALARP region, while exclusion of both events reduces the total below the ANCOLD objective.

Exposure Profile. The final model output, Figure 13.11, is the societal exposure profile. Each risk event is represented on this profile, ranked in descending order of risk from left to right. The "exposure" shown for each event is the estimated number of visitors who could be seriously injured or killed should the event occur. Exposure is presented at the three confidence levels, optimistic, planning, and pessimistic, adopted for this study. The figure also shows the likelihood associated with each risk event.

Figure 13.11 shows that the highest-risk event poses a threat to between two and four people. Those events that rank second, third, and fourth have higher exposures in terms of lives lost, but, as shown in Figures 13.9 and 13.10, none poses an unacceptable societal risk. Based on the ANCOLD criteria, only the first- and second-ranked events pose sufficient risk to warrant risk reduction measures, and then only if these measures can be shown to be cost effective. The risk associated with each of the other events was considered *de minimis*.

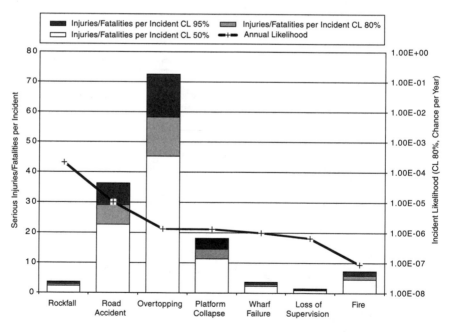

Figure 13.11 Societal exposure profile showing incident likelihood and the number of serious injuries and/or fatalities if the events occur with events ranked in order of decreasing risk quotient.

Sensitivity Analysis. Reducing the estimate of risk event likelihood to the optimistic estimate, rather than the planning level likelihood shown in Figure 13.9, makes no difference to the comparison of the calculated risk and ANCOLD risk acceptability criteria. That is, the rockfall and road accident events remain within the ALARP region of the guideline.

Increasing the likelihood of the highest-risk event (rockfall) by an order of magnitude increased the risk quotient of this event to 1.73×10^{-3} lives per year, slightly above the ANCOLD tolerable guideline value of 1×10^{-3} lives per year. Under this assumption, the total societal risk quotient increased to 4.7×10^{-3} lives per year, which is above the acceptability criterion.

However, the original likelihood adopted for this event was supported by a detailed geotechnical study which suggested that, based on experience at the station over the past 30 years, the input values overestimate rather than underestimate the likelihood of rockfall and hence of serious injury or fatality. On this basis it did not seem reasonable to increase the event likelihood by an order of magnitude. However, it was reasonable to conclude that this event fell into the ANCOLD ALARP region, which indicated that additional risk reduction was required, if cost effective.

Increasing the second highest-risk event (road accident) likelihood by an order of magnitude increased its risk quotient to 2.53×10^{-3} lives per year, which is above the ANCOLD acceptability limit. While the likelihood of a road accident originally derived by the expert panel appeared to be valid when compared with that for normal car travel (as discussed in relation to the individual risk sensitivity analysis), the need to implement some risk reduction measure(s) was indicated.

The effect of increasing the road accident likelihood increased the total societal risk quotient to 3.03×10^{-3} lives per year. This is above the ANCOLD acceptability limit, again confirming that some risk reduction measure(s) should be implemented for this event.

Increasing the third highest-risk event (overtopping) likelihood by an order of magnitude raised the associated risk quotient to 5.11×10^{-4} lives per year, which is below the ANCOLD acceptability limit. The total societal risk quotient increased to 1.22×10^{-3} lives per year, or about the ANCOLD acceptability limit. MEL has already implemented a number of upgrades to its monitoring systems for this event, and no other cost-effective risk reduction measures could be identified. On this basis it was considered that the risk associated with this event was probably acceptable.

Individual and Societal Risk

Individual Risk Results. The individual risk quotient for any tourist visiting the station was calculated as 1.07×10^{-5} lives per year, which is about the same level of risk associated with flying. Based on the results of the sensitivity analysis and a comparison of risk against acceptability criteria derived from statistical data for common activities, the calculated level of individual risk appears acceptable.

Societal Risk Results. MEL had received a geotechnical report that outlined possible risk reduction actions for the rockfall event. Based on the risk assessment, some or all of these measures needed to be implemented if they were cost effective.

The modeling results and sensitivity analysis indicate that some risk reduction measure(s) also should be implemented to reduce the risk associated with road accidents on the lease area. MEL should consider the installation of traffic barriers where the road runs above steep batters, safety run-off areas for runaway vehicles, and more restrictive speed limits.

The societal risk associated with the other events was considered acceptable.

SUMMARY

On the basis of experience with many risk assessments, the risk assessment process seems inevitably to lead to improved project knowledge. This project was no exception. Seventeen issues were identified during the workshop and flagged with MEL to incorporate into its planning and other business systems. The details are not provided here, but in general terms the identified issues covered:

- Staff safety and unauthorized public access
- Structural matters that warranted checking
- Assessment of certain aspects against existing standards and codes
- Routine safety inspections
- Upgrading of alarms and installation of additional safety warning devices
- Modified safety protocols
- Training
- Maintenance obligations
- Additions to MEL's local hazard register

MEL accepted the recommendations of the assessment and at last contact had introduced, or was planning to introduce, a number of initiatives to reduce the traffic and rockfall risks.

Notes

1. Meridian Energy Ltd., 1999. *Health and Safety Plan-Draft.*
2. This is a simplification of the mathematical relationship but is a reasonable approximation for the low-likelihood incidents considered in this study. Strictly speaking, the total likelihood is defined as $1-(1-L)^n$, where L = individual risk and n = number of trips per year.
3. ANCOLD (Australian National Committee on Large Dams), Care of Water Authority of Western Australia, Leederville, Australia. *Guideline on Risk Assessment.*
4. L. Richards, Draft Report of Manapouri Power Station Public Safety Risk Assessment, May 2000.

14

FINANCIAL ASSURANCES: WASTE MANAGEMENT, AUSTRALIA

This case study examines:

- The formulation and structuring of financial assurances
- Rational and justifiable processes for establishing adequate and realistic assurance sums
- The use of probabilistic techniques to quantify environmental risk

BACKGROUND

Boral owns and operates a quarry at Deer Park and proposed to develop a landfill at the site (Boral Western Landfill). The site is situated approximately 12 miles (20 km) west of Melbourne, Australia, and covers an area of 2,600 acres (1,055 ha).

It was proposed that the site be concurrently operated as a quarry and be rehabilitated using modern landfill techniques. The proposal was to operate the site as a sanitary landfill receiving putrescible waste and low-level contaminated soil. Landfill operations would involve six progressive stages that would take place over a 30- to 50-year period. Stages 1 and 2 would offer a combined airspace of 4,700,000 cubic yards (3,600,000 m³), and the landfill would receive up to 315,000 cubic yards (240,000 m³) of waste per year. In total, the site offered up to 8 million cubic yards (6 million m³) of airspace within the intended landfill area (Stages 1 to 6) and would offer in excess of 20 million cubic yards (16 million m³) when quarrying operations are completed.

The Environment Protection Authority of Victoria (EPAV) required Boral to place a financial assurance with respect to the proposed development of the Boral Western Landfill. At that time, the EPAV did not provide any guidance to assist operators in the State of Victoria to develop their financial assurance strategies. Thus, Boral had been given no clear indication of the components that should be covered by the financial assurance. It was assumed that assurance amounts should generally cover the costs of future environmental impairment and aftercare.

The aim of the project was to identify the specific components that should be covered by the financial assurance and suggest fund component amounts that reflect realistic operational and management costs and environmental risk.

Typically for projects of this nature, there is considerable uncertainty associated with the:

- Likelihood of environmental events occurring
- Costs of environmental clean-up
- Extent of environmental damage
- Timing of closure
- Future cost of postclosure care

The method used to determine the above was specifically developed to assist formulation of financial assurances for waste management facilities in a rational and justifiable manner such that assurance sums would be adequate to cover environmental liability in most cases.[1] The method used a probabilistic approach, focused on uncertainty, and quantified environmental risk. By prioritizing risk events, the method identified the specific components to be covered by financial assurances, and the fund amounts reflected a realistic amount of risk. The method had been used previously to develop financial assurance proposals for two other major Australian landfills.

COMPONENTS OF LANDFILL FINANCIAL ASSURANCE

While there were no regulations in Victoria that provide criteria for developing financial assurances for waste management facilities, the 1970 Environment Protection Act does provide for them. The EPAV had produced guidelines for determining financial assurances for Schedule 4 premises (premises that store, treat, reprocess, or dispose of prescribed industrial waste) to cover the cost of sudden and accidental events, disposal of stock, site clean-up, and site audit.[2] However, the guidelines did not cover all of the potential long-term environmental issues associated with landfills.

The U.S. Environmental Protection Agency (EPA) had developed financial assurance criteria for municipal solid waste landfills (MSWLF) that came into effect in April 1997.[3] The EPA regulations require placement of financial assurances for closure, postclosure care, and corrective action. Under these regulations, for any given site, the financial assurances must cover the cost of hiring a third party to:

- Close the site at the point in its operational life when the area to be rehabilitated is at its maximum.
- Conduct postclosure care.
- Undertake corrective action to remediate any events that cause, or have the potential to cause, environmental impairment.

Furthermore, the mechanisms of the financial assurance must ensure that the funds necessary to meet the costs will be available whenever they are needed. In this regard, owners and operators were given the options of establishing a trust fund, a surety bond guaranteeing payment or performance, a letter of credit, insurance, compliance with a local government financial test, or a local government guarantee.

The components of financial assurances required by the EPAV logically cover the main areas of potential public financial exposure.

The financial assurance program put forward by Boral was consistent with EPAV requirements and was composed of three separate elements, based on costs associated with site closure, postclosure operating and management costs (typically for 30 years), and a reasonable cost for corrective action required for potential environmental impairment originating from the site.

Closure Financial Assurance

The Closure Financial Assurance covered the cost associated with environmentally sound closure of the landfill at the planned time or in the event the site owner/operator is unable to continue.

Because the scope of works required to achieve closure changes over time as a project grows from a greenfields site until it is successfully closed by the operator, the value of this component needed to vary over time. Therefore, it was intended that the Closure Financial Assurance amount should be regularly reviewed and the value of the assurance adjusted to reflect the real level of exposure. The fund was calculated on the basis of current dollar value because it could be required at any time within the period between reviews (i.e., there would be no discounting of the closure costs).

Postclosure Financial Assurance

The Postclosure Financial Assurance covered the cost associated with postclosure management of the site. It was calculated on a net present value (NPV) basis, which takes into account the time value of money, because the money would be required over a specified time interval.

Corrective Action Financial Assurance

The Corrective Action Financial Assurance covered the cost associated with environmental risk events that may occur over the active landfilling period and during the period of postclosure aftercare. This component of the financial assurance would be adequate to cover the cost of remediation and further prevention of the high-risk environmental events that might reasonably be considered to occur.

The amounts required for both the Closure Financial Assurance and the Postclosure Financial Assurance were estimated using systematic costing techniques, because the predominant source of uncertainty lay within the cost estimates themselves. This level of uncertainty was handled using probabilistic techniques. The amount required for Corrective Action Financial Assurance was not as straightforward because uncertainty exists, not only with cost, but also with the occurrence of events and severity of impacts. The method used here was developed specifically to account for all aspects of uncertainty to derive a reasonable estimate of such risk cost. For the Boral Western Landfill site, those risk events that comprised 95 percent of the total risk over the project life were defined as the riskiest events and were assumed to occur to determine the Corrective Action Financial Assurance component value.

RISK IDENTIFICATION AND ANALYSIS

The expert panel process was used to identify and describe all of the potential activities and risk events related to the proposed Boral Western Landfill and to derive a comprehensive list of cost items. Consideration of uncertainty and risk events was carried out by a relatively small group of experts (five) with expertise in environmental and design engineering, statutory planning, the law, site operation, and the corporate perspective. Modeling followed the threshold method.

ANALYSIS RESULTS

Closure Financial Assurance

The panel considered that the activities associated with closure would comprise:

- Management and administration (e.g., management time, works supervision)
- Trimming of waste and general earthworks around the site
- Landfill capping with 2 ft (0.5 m) of clay and the same depth of topsoil
- Construction, operation, and monitoring of a gas collection system
- Revegetation of the landfill surface through the application of fertilizer, grass, and plants
- Revegetation of the roads and hardstand areas through the application of fertilizer, grass, and plants
- Disassembly and removal (where appropriate) of site facilities and services
- Site clean-up

Table 14.1 shows the estimated mean costs for each of the closure actions, the assumptions made in deriving the costs, and the time frame applicable to each component.

Table 14.1 Site Closure Costs

Activity		NPV	Year 1	Year 2	Year 3	Year 4
		All costs in $ × 1,000				
Management and Administration						
Management time		$43.60	25	15	5	0
Works supervision		$61.04	35	21	7	0
	Total	$104.64				
Landfill Cap						
Construct Cap 0.5 m clay, 0.5 m topsoil		$200.00	200	0	0	0
Rehabilitate Landfill Surface						
Grassing		$12.78	10	2	1	0
Fertilize		$19.17	10	5	5	0
Planting		$255.31	187.5	37.5	18.75	18.75
	Total	$287.25				
Trim and Earthworks						
Trimming of waste		$15.00	15	0	0	0
Earthworks around landfill		$30.00	30	0	0	0
	Total	$45.00				
Gas Collection						
Construct gas collection system		$320.00	320	0	0	0
Monitor operation of system		$34.44	16	12	8	0
	Total	$354.44				
Rehabilitate Roads and Hardstands						
Earthworks		$60.00	60	0	0	0
Grassing		$7.67	6	1.2	0.6	
Fertilize		$11.50	6	3	3	0
Planting		$215.63	112.5	56.25	56.25	0
	Total	$294.79				
Remove Facilities						
Disassemble site facilities		$30.00	30	0	0	0
Remove services		$40.00	40	0	0	0
	Total	$70.00				
Site Clean-up						
Clean-up		$12.78	10	2	1	0

The total cost of closure was forecast as the probability distribution shown in Figure 14.1. The relatively large difference between the optimistic estimated cost at the 50 percent confidence-level ($1,465,000) and the highly conservative 95 percent confidence-level cost estimate ($2,117,000) indicates a comparatively high degree of uncertainty within the cost estimate. This is because although the panel had a good understanding of the potential type of events, the costs involved

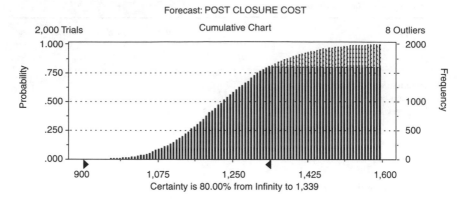

Figure 14.1 **Probability distribution of the forecast cost of landfill closure.**

were difficult to predict. The planning level (80 percent confidence level) cost estimate was $1,729,000.

Postclosure Financial Assurance

The panel considered that the postclosure management activities would be:

- *Management and administration:* Report to management and authorities; manage staff, resources, and task completion
- *Landfill fire:* Monitor for fire, maintain equipment
- *Leachate collection and treatment:* Treatment system operation, maintain sumps, pumps, and disposal system
- *Leachate seepage to surface:* Monitor drainage network, maintain cap
- *Leachate contamination of groundwater:* maintain monitoring bores, collect and analyze groundwater samples, report
- *Gas collection and treatment:* Maintain bores, pipe work, blowers, flare, condensate, and so on; monitor gas composition, instrumentation
- *Gas migration:* Monitor on-site and off-site
- *Rehabilitation (vegetation management):* Monitor and maintain vegetation
- *Rehabilitation (drainage control):* Inspect and maintain drains, regrade drains

Table 14.2 shows the estimated costs for each of the postclosure actions, the assumptions made deriving the costs, and the time frame, where applicable. The total cost of postclosure care was forecast in $NPV as the probability distribution shown in Figure 14.2. The estimated cost at the 50 percent confidence level was $1,229,000, while the 80 percent confidence-level cost estimate was $1,333,000.

Table 14.2 Postclosure Costs

All Cost in $ × 1,000		Operational Costs		Monitoring Costs	
Item	Sub Items	CL 50%	CL 95%	CL 50%	CL 95%
Management and Administration					
	Reporting to Management and Authorities				
	Managing Staff / Resources				
	Managing Tasks Completion	10	16	0	0
Landfill Fire					
	Replace Water Tanks and Pump Equipment				
	Monitoring for Fire	1.5	3	2.5	5
Leachate Collection and Treatment					
	Treatment System—Dilute and Irrigate over Landfill				
	Maintain Irrigation System—Replace pipes				
	Cleaning Sump and Pump	4.5	9	0	0
Leachate Seepage to Surface					
	Monitor Drainage Network—Walkover				
	Repair Erosion in Cap	3	6	1.25	2.5
Leachate Contamination of Groundwater					
	Maintain Monitoring Bores				
	Analysis of Samples				
	Sample Collection and Reporting	5.2	11.5	0	0
Gas Collection and Treatment					
	Maintenance and Repairs				
	Replace Blowers (Yrs 10 and 15)				
	Rebuild Flare (Yr 15)				
	Monitor Oxygen, Carbon Dioxide, and Methane Levels				
	Monitoring Instrumentation	28	0	1.5	5
Gas Migration					
	On-Site Monitoring				
	Off-Site Monitoring	0	0	5	10
Rehabilitation—Vegetation Management					
	Monitor Vegetation				
	Fertilize, replant	5	10	1.25	2.5
Rehabilitation—Drainage Control					
	Inspect Drains				
	Clean Out Drains				
	Regrade sections of drains	4.2	14.4	1.25	2.5

Over a 30-year postclosure period, the actual annual cost would be expected to vary above and below the mean cost input to the model, but the cumulative cost over the period should be similar to the 50 percent confidence-level estimate. Therefore, the 50 percent confidence-level estimate of $1,229,000 was considered to be the most reasonable estimate of the potential postclosure cost and was used for financial planning purposes.

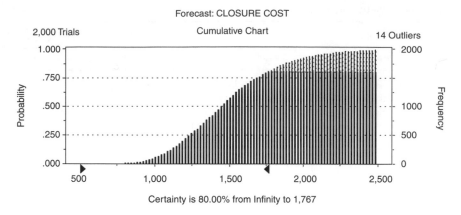

Figure 14.2 Probability distribution of the forecast postclosure cost.

Corrective Action Financial Assurance

The corrective action cost will depend on which risk events actually occur over the project period and their cost. In order to derive a reasonable advance estimate of the corrective action cost, it was necessary to estimate which events posed the most risk over the project period and to calculate the sum of the cost of corrective action for those riskiest events.

Table 14.3 presents a summary of the risk register derived by the panel and indicates whether the risk event was included in the assessment.

The event tree of Figure 14.3 summarizes the panel evaluation of the risk events and their consequences, their likelihood of occurrence at the Boral Western Landfill, and the cost of the required corrective actions. Table 14.4 shows the underlying cost estimates.

Figure 14.4 shows the risk events ranked from highest to lowest (left to right along the horizontal axis) and the event occurrence costs at selected confidence levels (50, 80, and 95 percent confidence levels). The risk associated with the two riskiest events (rehabilitation failure and landfill fire) contributed to around 99.9 percent of the total risk, which exceeded the criterion level of 95 percent for establishing the riskiest events. Therefore, the combined occurrence costs of these two events defined the Corrective Action Financial Assurance component value.

Table 14.3 Summary Risk Register

Leachate discharge to subsurface (included)	Washout (included)
Leachate discharge to surface (included)	Rehabilitation failure (included)
Fire (included)	Waste exceeds limits (included)
Explosion from landfill gas (excluded)	Flora damage (excluded)
Earthquake induced slope failure (included)	Fauna damage (excluded)

ISSUE	Annual Freq	IMPACT	Prob	IMPACT	Prob	CONSEQ.	Prob	Av Cost	High Cost
E1 Liner holes	0.033	Contaminant escape	0.0002	Contam off-site	0.01	Gw remediation	0.1	80	See "Calcs"
E2 Liner disintegration	0.033	Contaminant escape	0.00001	Contam off-site	0.1	Gw remediation	0.1	80	See "Calcs"
E3 Leachate - remediation	0.066	Release to sw	0.0001	Sw contam	1	Remediation	1	10	30
E4 Leachate - livestock	0.066	Release to sw	0.0001	Sw contam	1	Livestock injury	0.0001	10	100
E5 Fire within landfill	0.0003					Firefighting and repair	1	35	300
						Gas system repair	1	15	80
E6 Earthquake slope failure	10E-08					Cap repair	1	30	100
E7 Washout	10E-06					Cap repair	1	30	100
E8 Rehabilitation failure	0.01			Cap erosion	1	Cap repair	1	60	200
					1	Revegetation	1	50	120
				Excess leachate	1	Leachate disposal	1	80	See "Calcs"
C1 Waste exceeds limits	0.001			Gw contam	0.0001	Gw interception	1	80	See "Calcs"

Figure 14.3 Event tree showing major landfill risk events, consequences, and estimated costs.

Table 14.4   Corrective Action Costs

"Calcs" Sheet (all costs in $ × 1,000)
Discount Rate   0.06

Issues E1 & E2—Leachate discharge to subsurface

Interception system cost estimate

# wells	8	
Discharge / well (m3/d)	4	
	CL 50	**CL 95**
Well installation cost	6.25	12.5
Plant infrastructure cost	20	100
Operating costs	0.001	0.003

YEAR	**1**	**2**	**3**	**4**	**5**	**6**	···	**29**	**30**		
	2000	**2001**	**2002**	**2003**	**2004**	**2005**	···	**2028**	**2029**		
	0	0	0	0	70	0	···	0	0	Capital	55
	0	0	0	0	11.68	11.68	···	11.68	11.68	O&M	127
										Cost E1	183

Issue E8—Rehabilitation failure

Leachate volume (m3/d)	5

YEAR	**1**	**2**	**3**	**4**	**5**	**6**	···	**29**	**30**	
	2000	**2001**	**2002**	**2003**	**2004**	**2005**	···	**2028**	**2029**	
	0	0	0	0	0	0	···	0	0	
										Cost E6 2

Issue C1—Waste exceeds limits

Interception system cost estimate

# wells	2	
	CL 50	**CL 95**
$/well	6.25	12.5
Power	1	5
Treatment and disposal	3	10

YEAR	**1**	**2**	**3**	**4**	**5**	**6**	···	**29**	**30**		
	2000	**2001**	**2002**	**2003**	**2004**	**2005**	···	**2028**	**2029**		
	0	0	0	0	12.5	0	···	0	0	Capital	10
	0	0	0	0	4	4	···	4	4	O&M	46
										Cost C1	56

220

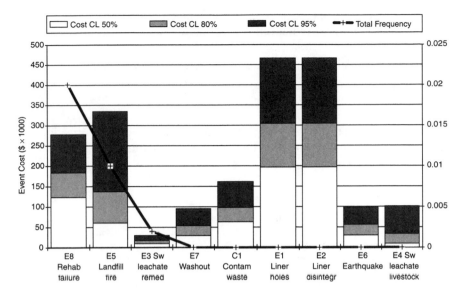

Figure 14.4 Corrective action events exposure profile showing the cost at selected confidence levels assuming risk event occurrence.

The relatively small number of events that contribute a large proportion of the total risk is a typical outcome for many if not most risk assessments.

For the combined cost of the two riskiest events, the relatively large difference between the realistic estimated cost at the 50 percent confidence level ($215,000) and the highly conservative 95 percent confidence-level cost estimate ($546,000) indicates a comparatively high degree of uncertainty within the cost estimate. The 80 percent confidence-level planning estimate of $329,000 was considered to be an adequately conservative yet reasonable estimate of the potential corrective action cost and was adopted.

SUMMARY

A systematic approach was applied to determine appropriate financial assurances for the proposed Boral Western Landfill. The financial assurances for the landfill included components for costs associated with closure, postclosure care, and corrective action against potential environmental impairment. A probabilistic approach to cost estimation was followed, allowing selection of an adequately conservative financial assurance value. The method used was systematic, considered each event in detail, was defensible, catered for inherent uncertainty in cost and occurrence of events, and derived reserve amounts that were likely to be adequate to cover future financial exposure.

In the case of the Boral Western Landfill, Boral proposed that the financial assurance consist of the following component values:

- Closure: $1,729,000
- Postclosure: $1,229,000
- Corrective Action: $325,000

The EPAV accepted the recommended approach and used the information as a basis for negotiating an appropriate financial assurance with Boral.

Notes

1. A. R. Bowden, "A Systematic Method for Determining Appropriate Financial Assurances for Waste Management Facilities," *Proceeding of the 4th National Hazardous and Solid Waste Convention*, Brisbane, Australia, May 1997.
2. Environment Protection Authority of Victoria, "Guideline for Determining Financial Assurance— Schedule 4 Premises," EPA Information Bulletin, Publication 456, June 1995.
3. U.S. Environmental Protection Agency, "Financial Assurance Mechanism for Local Government Owners and Operators of Municipal Solid Waste Landfill Facilities." 40 *CFR* Part 258. *Federal Register*, November 27, 1996 (Volume 61, Number 230) [Pages 60327–60339].

15

INDEMNITY IN PERPETUITY: MINING, NEW ZEALAND

This case study examines:

- Strategy development of an innovative solution to financial assurance where none previously existed
- Development of the structure and quantum of a postclosure bond
- Making use of the time value of money

BACKGROUND

Mining and the Environment

How Mining Can Pose an Environmental Threat. Mining involves the excavation and placement in engineered structures of a large quantity of soil and rock, a portion of which contains elevated concentrations of metals such as gold, silver, copper, zinc, iron, and manganese. If liberated into the environment, many of these metals have the potential to cause significant environmental damage. For example, if silver, copper, and zinc enter a stream in dissolved form, they can be toxic to aquatic plants and animals at very low concentrations; at higher concentrations they can render water unsafe to drink for stock or humans.

The metals are present in the rock in chemical forms that are practically immobile. However, oxidation of these minerals changes the metal compounds to forms that are soluble in water, which allows the metals to be leached from the rock. The oxidation process can also produce acidic conditions, which themselves can pose an environmental threat and can exacerbate the leaching of metals from the rock. These are natural processes that occur wherever mineralized rock is exposed to air and water. But in nature they tend to occur very slowly as erosion and other mechanisms expose fresh rock.

Excavation of rock during mining exposes it to atmospheric oxygen. In addition, the blasting and excavating breaks the rock, increasing the surface area exposed to the air and hence the opportunity for it to oxidize. For the metal-rich rock (ore), size reduction and increase in potential oxidizing surface is further pronounced during the gold extraction process, which involves grinding the rock to a fine sand. The changes wrought by mining mean that oxidation of the minerals contained in the mined rock and tailings (ground rock from which the gold and silver has been extracted) potentially can occur many times faster than occurs naturally. Notwithstanding this increased rate of oxidation, it is a process that could last for centuries before all of the mined rock oxidizes.

Residual, Long-Term Environmental Risks. Modern mining techniques involve safely disposing of the waste rock and tailings in engineered structures and provision of compacted soil or water covers. These covers are designed to exclude contact between the mineralized rock and air; the aim is to control the rate of sulfide oxidation and minimize the potential threat posed by the oxidation by-products to the environment. In spite of the attention given to the safe, long-term disposal of these materials, some residual risk to the environment remains that damage to the water or soil covering media could produce acid conditions and/or enable release of soluble metals. If this were to occur, the effects could continue for a considerable period (decades or even centuries) and could impose a significant cost on the local or regional community to mitigate or remedy.

A lesser long-term risk is posed by tailings storage facilities. Tailings are disposed as a slurry, often behind an engineered embankment (the tailings dam). The clay, silt, and fine sand that comprise the tailings are slow to release the slurry water trapped between the particles, and when initially placed, tailings can flow like a heavy liquid. Also, the tailings liquor can contain elevated concentrations of toxic chemicals used for processing, such as cyanide. These process chemicals liberate the gold and other metals from the ground ore. The cyanide and dissolved metals in the tailings liquor have the potential to cause significant impairment if released into the environment.

For these reasons, an uncontrolled discharge of semiliquid tailings and tailings liquor could flow over a large area and cause extensive property and environmental damage.

However, over time the tailings consolidate in a tailings storage as their own weight presses the water from between the particles. As the water content of the tailings decreases, they gain strength and change from a liquid to something more like soil. In this latter state they cannot flow. Also, the toxicity of the tailings liquors reduces as cyanide, which is unstable under normal conditions, decomposes to less toxic compounds and water quality within the tailings impoundment improves. Therefore, the risk posed by the tailings dam and contents gradually reduces to a level where it is no longer of concern, and this can happen over a relatively short time (a period of years).

Martha Mine Project

Physical and Legal Setting. Waihi Gold Company (WGC) has operated its Martha Mine in New Zealand since 1987. This open-cut gold mine is situated near the center of the rural town of Waihi, the pit perimeter being only 600 feet (180 m) from the central business district.

The Martha Mine operates under New Zealand's rigorous environmental legislation, the Resource Management Act 1991 (RMA). Within this challenging environmental and political situation, WGC has run a successful mine by acting sensitively and sympathetically to both the natural environment and the community, and through applying industry best practice.

As a result of the best practice methods applied during the mine's operating period, there was a high expectation that it will pose an acceptably low level of long-term risk to the environment once mining ceases and the site is rehabilitated. However, some residual risk to the environment will remain; damage to the water or soil covers could produce acid conditions and/or enable release of soluble metals.

Extended Project. In 1998 WGC applied for consents under the RMA to extend the Martha Mine for a further seven years past year 2000, which was the planned and consented end of mine life. Under the RMA process, and before any consents are granted, applicants are required to demonstrate to a high degree of certainty that they can operate and close a project in a manner that ensures acceptable, and often minimal, adverse environmental impacts. In addition, the RMA allows the regulators to impose bonds or other financial securities on the applicant company against nonperformance of environmental obligations contained in the consent conditions.

Traditional Bonding Approach. Prior to 1998 when WGC lodged the consent applications for its mine extension, the New Zealand regulators imposed bonds on mining companies to cover site rehabilitation. The purpose of these "rehabilitation bonds" was to provide financial security that the regulators could call on to fund site closure in the event that the mining company becomes either unwilling or unable to rehabilitate the site to an appropriate standard. WGC had already posted a rehabilitation bond that would remain in place until the site was completely rehabilitated.

Origin of Postclosure Securities. In August 1997 the office of the Parliamentary Commissioner for the Environment produced a report entitled, *Long Term Management of the Environmental Effects of Tailings Dams*, that recognized the potential enduring environmental risk posed by remnant mine sites. The report recommended steps to enable the imposition of postclosure bonds (or equivalent financial instruments) that last beyond the period covered by the rehabilitation bonds. The objective of these postclosure bonds was to indemnify the people of

New Zealand against the potentially large costs for preventing or remediating future adverse environmental effects originating from mining that could arise following mine closure and the departure of the mining company. The postclosure securities were to exist in perpetuity.

The Challenge. WGC was the first mining company in New Zealand (and possibly in the world) faced with the need to establish a perpetual postclosure bond. WGC accepted the principle of such a bond, but the structure and scope of such an instrument had not, at that stage, been determined, and WGC was naturally reluctant to commit to such an open-ended concept. The regulators were also struggling to define exactly what they expected of a postclosure security. The impediments faced by the regulators and by WGC were the lack of:

- A definition for the meaning of "perpetuity" and hence the term to be covered by the security
- A rational method of assessing what events needed to be covered by the security
- A means of determining an appropriate quantum that was both realistic and adequate

The antimining and environmental lobby groups were also unable to adequately define the basis for establishing a quantum "in perpetuity," although in their view the security needed to be extremely large. The lobbyists were calling for a quantum in excess of $100 million.

SETTING

Project Context

Unlike many projects, initially the project context was not defined. Both WGC and the regulators understood the objective of the postclosure security and accepted it in principle. However, at the outset of the project neither party understood the means by which the security could be structured and calculated.

Stakeholders

In addition to the local stakeholders, the stakeholder group for this project was very broad. If the regulators did not impose a postclosure security, or if an imposed security was inadequate, the New Zealand government would be forced to fund the remediation of any future environmental impairment arising from the closed mine site. The potentially wide impacts were equivalent in nature to the U.S. Superfund sites, which were, however, of a very much larger scale. The stakeholders were therefore WGC and the government and citizens of New Zealand.

Project Objectives

The purpose of the proposed postclosure security was to adequately indemnify the taxpayers and rate payers of New Zealand against potential future costs associated with any residual site risk.

Target Audience

The decision-making authority in this case consisted of relevant regulators who, acting as the representatives of the New Zealand public, could approve or reject the proposed security. If approval were to be withheld, WGC would be unable to proceed with its mine extension.

Strategy Overview

Definition of Closure and Postclosure. One of the first steps in developing the strategy was to define a time line for the project and determine the mechanics of when and how the postclosure security could be established and used. WGC identified two key project phases and defined the end points of each. These were:

Phase	*End-Point Descriptor*	*Expected End-Point Date*
Operations	Cessation of mining	2007
Aftercare	Regulatory approval that the site is in a safe, stable, self-sustainable state equivalent to that of the land adjacent to the site; defined as "closure"	2017

The completion of closure defined the start of the postclosure period. It was defined as the point in time when the residual risk posed by the site became low enough to be considered acceptable by the regulators. The 10-year aftercare period was thought to be conservative because WGC had used best practices throughout the operations period. However, in determining closure, the 10-year term was less critical than the attainment of defined success criteria, and the actual time could potentially vary by several years either side of the current prediction.

Liability Cut-off. The attainment of closure was critical to the postclosure security strategy. Once achieved, WGC expected to be released from any further liability associated with the site. To facilitate its release, a charitable trust has been established. The trust will, once the site is closed, manage the tailings storage facilities and Water Treatment Plant and take title to the land on which they stand. The Trust will also take title to the lakeside park, and maintain it for use by the general public, and be responsible for the monitoring and maintenance of the proposed pit lake. At that time, WGC would provide the trust with a sum of money (the capitalization sum) sufficient to fund the trust's management and maintenance activities in perpetuity.

During the operations period (i.e., until the trust became established), WGC was required to post a capitalization bond, the quantum of which is equivalent to the capitalization sum. In the event that WGC defaulted from its responsibilities, the regulators would call on the rehabilitation bond to fund site closure, then use the capitalization bond to fund the trust.

Security Components

The capitalization sum needed to be adequate to enable the trust to pay for:

- Trust operating expenses
- Insurance premiums
- Remediation of uninsurable events

Trust Operating Costs. The first component of the capitalization sum (and hence the capitalization bond) covered the cost of operating the trust, which included:

- Contractor/employee salary, equipment, and overhead to undertake and manage the monitoring and maintenance tasks
- Expenses associated with the routine land management and maintenance tasks, such as drain clearance, revegetation and fertilizer, pest/weed control, structure inspections and surveys, removal of trees from the cap, and repair of minor damage to the capping layer over the waste rock
- Environmental monitoring costs
- Trust administration

Insurance Premiums. Insurance generally covers two areas: (1) third party and (2) industrial and special risk (ISR). Third-party insurance was readily available, relatively inexpensive, and was required as a matter of course. Third-party insurance was part of the trust operating costs but was split from this component of the bond to allow clear identification of the insurance commitment.

ISR usually provides insurance against sudden failure events, and the amount of cover is best determined through a risk assessment process.

Remediation of Uninsurable Events. Events that are gradual and/or cause environmental impairment are usually prohibitively expensive to insure or are effectively noninsurable. Identification of the risk events and the quantification of their likelihood and remediation costs required a risk assessment approach in order to establish a rationally derived quantum for this component of the capitalization sum.

The types of events covered by this component included mitigation of issues such as acid drainage and seepage, degraded surface water, and pit-lake water quality.

Risk Assessment Strategy

The aim of the risk assessment project was to:

- Define a meaning for "perpetuity"
- Establish a rational method of assessing which risk events needed to be covered by the security
- Provide a means of determining a realistic and adequate quantum

DEFINITION OF "PERPETUITY"

An agreed definition of "perpetuity" was crucial to the development of a successful bond strategy. Without this, lawyers for both WGC and the regulators were having difficulties drafting the bond and other consent conditions. Furthermore, the management of WGC feared that a negotiated bond quantum may be unrealistically large and too large to fund reasonably. WGC felt that the issue was heading for a stalemate.

The solution offered by the risk analyst, and immediately accepted by WGC and the regulators, relied on using the concept of the time value of money. For accountants and others working in the financial arena, the concept of discounting is well understood and accepted practice, although its application to define "perpetuity" was new.

How time affects the value of money, and how it was applied to this project, is best demonstrated by the following example.

- Assume a risk event occurs on the first year following closure that requires $10,000 per year in perpetuity to mitigate.
- Assume also that the available annual interest rate on an investment is 4 percent above inflation (defined here as the real rate of return). This is a realistic if somewhat conservative assumption. For example, if the current annual inflation rate is, say, 2 percent, banks generally offer interest rates around the 6 to 8 percent range. If the inflation rate increases to 5 percent, interest rates would be expected to rise to around 10 percent. Thus, the real rate of return is independent of inflation.
- To provide a sum of money today capable of paying the $10,000 per year for site management in perpetuity requires an investment equal to $10,000 for this year, plus $10,000 less one year's interest at 4 percent for next year, plus $10,000 less two years' interest at 4 percent for the following year, and so on.
- Due to the effect of compounding interest, the investment required today to fund one year of mitigation in the future becomes progressively smaller as the term of the investment increases.

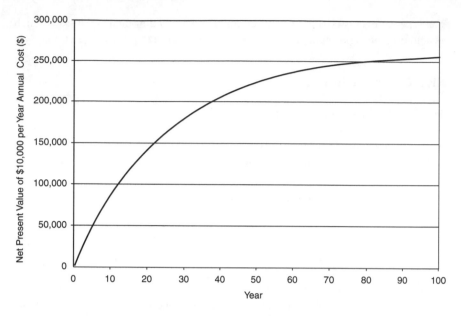

Figure 15.1 Definition of perpetuity at 4% per year rate of return showing the reducing rate of increase in net present value with increasing time.

- This effect is clearly illustrated in Figure 15.1. It shows that an investment today of a little over $250,000 is sufficient to provide $10,000 per year for a period of 100 years and that the additional investment required today to fund subsequent years is insignificant.

An alternative explanation sees $250,000 invested today and $10,000 withdrawn to pay for mitigation this year. Over the year, interest on the remaining $240,000 increases the investment back to $250,000, ready for the withdrawal of the next $10,000 for the second year. This cycle can be repeated each year in perpetuity as the fund is self-sustaining.

Using this approach, and a real rate of return of 4 percent per year, "perpetuity" can be defined as a period of 100 years.

RISK IDENTIFICATION

Selection of the Expert Panel

The WGC's section managers formed the expert panel. The disciplines represented were mining, tailings dam construction, environmental, milling, water treatment, and engineering. The panel also drew on specialist expertise from outside the company, particularly in the areas of the law, geotechnical engineering, geochemistry, hydro-geochemistry, hydrogeology, and water treatment.

Risk Register

In the workshop, the panel identified all of the risks associated with the operation. The risk register included operational and site closure risks as well as postclosure risks. Only the latter were of relevance to the postclosure security. However, the operational and closure risks were retained and later incorporated into other risk management strategies (e.g., the environmental management system and the rehabilitation and site closure plan).

Table 15.1 provides a summary of the credible risk events following appropriate mine closure and sign-off by the regulators. As can be seen by comparison with the excluded risk events summarized in Table 15.2, the number of residual risks following closure was minor, a reflection of WGC's operational best-practice approach and its comprehensive mine closure plan. Many of the risk events listed in Table 15.2 were excluded because they existed only during mine operation and closure activities and/or were improbable or inconsequential following closure.

Postclosure Risk Events

The postclosure risk events that were included in the analysis, and their assessed likelihood and occurrence costs, are described in the following sections.

Item 1: Pit Wall Instability. Due to the design of the pit wall slopes and its inherent conservatism, a sudden catastrophic failure was not considered realistic. The risk event therefore assumed a gradual failure and formed part of the uninsurable risk component of the capitalization sum.

Table 15.1   Summary Risk Register—Included Events

PIT

Pit Wall Instability—	Lake Discharge—
1.1. Pump House	7.2. Outlet structural integrity
Lake Water Quality—	
8.1. Acid generation	

WASTE DISPOSAL AREA

36. Collection Pond—Water Quality	40. Tailings Bypass Seepage
41. Waste Rock Bypass Seepage	42. ARD Perimeter Bund
43. Catastrophic Release of Tailings	44. Seepage Release
60. Tailings Pond Water Quality	

Table 15.2 Summary Risk Register—Excluded Events

PIT

Pit Wall Instability	Dust	Settlement/Rebound	Groundwater Effects
1.2. Effects on the town—public safety	2.1. Noncompliance	3.1. Damage to pump house	4.1. Water levels/water supply availability
1.3. Effects on the town—property damage	2.2. Soil contamination	3.2. Damage to buildings	4.2. Contamination
1.4. Buffer-area failure		3.3. Damage to services	
Blasting	Noise	Lake discharge	Lake Water Quality
5.1. Noise	6.1. Noncompliance	7.1. Flooding	8.2. Aquatic biology
5.2. Pump House	6.2. Unachievable noise standards imposed		8.3. Public amenity/health
5.3. Vibration			
5.4. Fly rock			
9. Lake filling takes longer than expected	10. Regulatory change to discharge standards	Hazardous materials storage/handling	Noise Bund
		11.1. Fuel and solvents	12.1. Acid Rock Drainage (ARD)
		11.2. Explosives	12.2. Instability
13. Uncontrolled spring flow during/following lake filling	Damage to historical/heritage features	15. Rehab failure	
	14.1. Mine manager's residence		
	14.2. Grand Junction refinery building		
	14.3. Grand Junction power house and boiler house foundations		

PROCESS PLANT

Noise	Dust	18. Minewater Pipeline Burst	22. Collection Pond Pipeline Burst
16.1. Conveyor	17.1. Conveyor	19. Decant Pipeline Burst	23. Bridge Failure
16.2. Mill	17.2. Lay-down areas	20. Tailings Pipeline Burst	
16.3. Noncompliance	17.3. Stockpiles	21. Seepage Pipeline Burst	
	17.3.1. Crop damage		
	17.3.2. Amenity		
	17.3.3. Human health		

17.3.4. Soil contamination
17.3.5. Noncompliance

WTP Spills
24.1. Chemical spills
24.2. Tank/clarifier collapse
25. WTP Discharge Quality Out of Spec

CIP Spills
26.1. Chemical spills
26.2. Tank collapse
27. Materials Storage and Handling

Ore Stockpiles
28.1. Soil contamination
28.2. Groundwater contamination
28.3. Surface water contamination
29. Mill Collection Pond Discharge
30. Contaminated Soil
31. Hazardous Materials Storage/Handling
32. Regulatory Change to Discharge Standards
33. Conveyor Tunnel Collapse
34. Insufficient WTP Capacity
35. Unacceptable Air Emissions

WASTE DISPOSAL AREA

37. Collection Pond—Sediment Discharge
38. Perimeter Drain Failure

Contractor's Workshop
39.1. Contaminated soil
39.2. Solvents, fuel spill
39.3. ARD from pad
45. Embankment Damage
46. Overtopping
47. Wildlife Health
48. Rehab Failure
49. Noise—noncompliance
50. Tailings Dust
51. Waste Rock Dust
52. Dust Control
53. Regulatory Change to Discharge Standards
54. Hazardous Materials Storage/Handling
55. Tailings Ponds Significantly Bigger than Planned
56. Flood Erosion Damage at Embankment Toe
57. Insufficient NAF Material for Liners/Capping
58. Unable To Achieve Liner (Zone A) Permeability Spec.
59. Unable to Achieve Capping (Zone G) Permeability Spec
61. Terrestrial Flora and Fauna Impacts on Rare and Endangered Species

OFF-SITE

62. Contractor Accident
63. Traffic
64. Bulltown Rd Tip
65. Visual Impact Unacceptable
66. Road Stopping Not Approved
67. Degradation of Receiving Environment by Other Activities
68. Community Opposition to Project
69. Carbon Dioxide Discharge Unacceptable
70. Decrease in Property Value
71. Charitable Trust Cannot Be Established

All pit wall designs during the mine's operation are peer reviewed, which was considered to reduce the risk associated with failure. However, a low likelihood remained that some gradual slumping of the pit wall could occur sometime in the future. The critical section in terms of consequence was in the vicinity of an old Cornish pump house that had heritage protection and needed to be protected against subsidence-related damage that could affect its structural integrity.

On the advice of WGC's pit design specialist, as an additional safeguard it was proposed to undertake engineering works in the pit in the vicinity of the pump house to buttress the wall in this area. These works further lowered the likelihood of slumping close to the old pump house.

The panel estimated that the frequency of pit wall slumping of any magnitude anywhere in the pit would be 1 in 1,000 years. The probability that this would occur in an area that could affect the pump house was estimated at 1 in 100 and that the trust would be required to fund remedial works, 1 in 10. This gave a total estimated frequency of 10^{-6} per year (or 1 chance in a million years).

Should slumping occur in the vicinity of the pump house, its gradual nature would enable remedial measures to take place before structural damage occurred. Remedial works might include piling between the pump house and the pit perimeter or underpinning the foundations. A cost estimate of $1.5 million was allowed for this work.

Under the worst-case scenario, relocation of the pump house may need to be considered. This was estimated to cost $3 million.

On the assumption that relocation was required, it was thought that some operating and maintenance costs could be incurred, and that additional monitoring of the pit wall in the vicinity of the pump house would be required. These costs were assumed to continue throughout the study term (100 years postclosure) and were estimated at the median value and the 95 percent confidence level to be $2,000 and $4,000, and $2,000 and $5,000, respectively.

Item 7: Pit Lake Outlet Structural Integrity. Waihi's average annual rainfall is about 7 feet (2.1 m). It was proposed that the pit would be rehabilitated as a lake and will discharge via a piped outlet to an adjacent stream. Maintenance, or replacement, of the outlet structure and tunnel was assumed to be required during the postclosure period. This was a base cost.

During the postclosure period, there will be a risk that the proposed lake outlet tunnel and associated structures could be damaged, for example, as a result of an earthquake. This was an ISR insurance risk.

As underground structures are less susceptible to earthquake damage than aboveground structures, the likely consequence was that some maintenance of the works would be required. The estimate of cost to undertake this work was $80,000.

At worst, the tunnel might need to be rebored and the inlet and outlet structures replaced. A cost of $400,000 was assessed for this case.

Under either scenario, additional annual costs of $2,000 and $5,000 (at the median and 95 percent confidence limits, $CL_{95\%}$) were expected.

The frequency of this risk event was 1 in 1,000 years, or 0.001 per year.

Item 8: Pit Lake Water Quality. The risk was that, contrary to the current predictions, quantity and quality of runoff from the pit walls could lead to degradation of lake water quality. This risk event formed part of the gradual, uninsurable risk component.

The estimated frequency that the actual runoff quality could be significantly worse than predicted is 1 in 1,000 years. Assuming that the water quality would be significantly worse than anticipated, the panel assessed that there was a 1 in 100 probability that this would result in an unacceptable lake water quality (unusable for aquatic biota and/or the community). The overall likelihood of this risk event occurring was then 10^{-5} per year (1 chance in 100,000 years).

Possible mitigation actions include:

- Pumping river water into the lake continuously to dilute the effects of acidic runoff
- Capturing acidic runoff on the benches and diverting it to treatment
- Adding lime to recirculated lake water
- Pumping and treating lake water discharge at the WTP prior to discharge
- Partially emptying the lake following treatment, then remediating the unoxidized pit wall rock to reduce or remove the contaminant at source
- Scaling, or mining out of, the unoxidized pit wall rock

The consequential cost estimate assumed that the adopted option would be pumping and treatment at the WTP prior to discharge. As the WTP would be left to the trust, the costs relate to treatment and maintenance. An annual sum of between \$37,000 (median) and \$58,600 ($CL_{95\%}$) was allowed. Additional monitoring at \$3,000 and \$4,000 per year was allowed.

Item 36: Collection Pond—Water Quality. Collection ponds collect runoff from the waste rock disposal areas during placement and prior to rehabilitation as a safeguard against elevated soluble metals concentrations. If the water quality requires it, collected runoff is pumped to the WTP for treatment prior to discharge.

One of the success criteria that WGC must attain before closure was that collection pond water quality must be at least equal to that of runoff from the surrounding farmland. Water quality in the ponds relies primarily on successful completion of rehabilitation on the tailings embankment and waste rock disposal structures. Once successfully rehabilitated, the risk of poor water quality occurring in the ponds is reduced significantly. However, the panel felt there remained a low likelihood that collection pond water quality could deteriorate over time. The estimate of frequency for this issue was 10^{-4} per year (1 in 10,000 years). This was a gradual, uninsurable risk component.

In the unlikely event that collection pond water quality did degrade, this water would need to be collected and treated. The WTP was to remain available as a contingency to events of this type. Therefore, the consequential costs relate to pumping, treating, and plant maintenance for which an annual total of \$100,000 (median) and \$200,000 ($CL_{95\%}$) was allowed.

Item 40: Tailings Bypass Seepage. Seepage of tailings liquor escaping through the floor of the tailings storage facility and under the tailings embankment could have adverse environmental effects. This was part of the gradual, uninsurable risk component of the capitalization sum. The potential for bypass seepage from the tailings is limited by the:

- Low permeability of the tailings, which decreases further with time due to consolidation
- Natural containment provided by the generally low permeability bedrock, particularly the weathered bedrock
- Upward groundwater gradients

Even if bypass seepage did occur, the expected minor amount reaching the local streams and rivers was not expected to be detectable following dilution. In summary, the likelihood for potential bypass seepage was low. The expert panel assessed this as 10^{-5} per year (1 chance in 100,000 years).

Assuming bypass seepage did occur, the solution would be to selectively grout areas of concern or to install cut-off drains or collection wells and to collect and treat seepage prior to discharge. Cost estimates at the median and $CL_{95\%}$ were assessed to respectively be $50,000 and $100,000 to provide cut-off drains and ancillary equipment and $30,000 and $60,000 per year for treatment.

Item 41: Waste Rock Bypass Seepage. This event is similar to that of tailings seepage, but the origin of the water is rain leaching through the waste rock before it is covered. The event was part of the gradual, uninsurable risk component of the capitalization sum. The potential for bypass flow of seepage from the potentially acid forming (PAF) waste rock is limited by:

- Use of a compacted clay liner beneath the PAF waste to limit seepage losses
- Use of a compacted clay cap on the embankment to limit recharge and hence driving head within the embankment and on the clay liner
- Reduction of permeability over time due to consolidation and unsaturated conditions
- The seepage collection system
- The natural containment provided by the low-permeability bedrock, particularly the weathered bedrock
- The upward groundwater gradients

Even if bypass seepage were to occur, the expected minor amount reaching the local streams and rivers was not expected to be detectable following dilution. In summary, the likelihood for potential bypass seepage is low. The expert panel assessed this as 10^{-5} per year (1 in 100,000 years).

Assuming bypass seepage were to occur, the solution would be to selectively grout areas of concern or to install cut-off drains or collection wells and to collect and treat seepage prior to discharge. Cost estimates at the median and $CL_{95\%}$ were assessed to be $50,00 and $100,000 to provide cut-off drains and ancillary equipment and $30,000 and $60,000 per year for treatment.

Item 42: Acid Rock Drainage Perimeter Bund. The perimeter road and bund around the tailings and waste rock storage facility was built of waste rock excavated from the pit early in the licensed project. At this time, there was little that could potentially cause acidic runoff, so the likelihood of the bund containing such material and hence causing an acid rock drainage (ARD) problem was considered remote. This event was part of the gradual, uninsurable risk component of the capitalization sum. The expert panel assessed the likelihood of the bund containing PAF material as 1 in 100 years. Assuming the bund does contain PAF material, it was considered that the compaction undertaken during construction would effectively seal it from exposure to the atmosphere, reducing the probability of it producing acid to 1 in 1,000. Then, assuming that acid production occurred, the panel felt that there was a 1 in 2 chance that the release would be of sufficient quantity, and of such poor quality, that there would be adverse environmental effects. The overall likelihood was then 5×10^{-6} per year (1 in 200,000 years).

In the event that acid drainage from the bund occurred, the leachate would need to be collected and treated. Cost estimates at the median and $CL_{95\%}$ were assessed to be $5,000 and $10,000 to install a collection system and $2,000 and $5,000 per year for treatment.

Item 43: Catastrophic Release of Tailings. Based on advice from specialist geotechnical engineers, a sudden release of tailings due to an embankment failure was considered inconceivable. Therefore, it was concluded that on technical grounds, this event should be excluded from further consideration.

However, it was also acknowledged that the event was of particular interest to the regulators and the public. For this reason the event was ultimately retained in the assessment.

A sudden release of tailings would be an insurable (ISR) risk. WGC received advice confirming that insurance would be available to the trust and that an indicative premium cost was around $45,000 per year, which would provide a significant level of cover (up to $50 million).

The proposed rehabilitation concept for the facility was to reduce the tailings pond water level to promote negative pore pressures in an outer annulus of tailings and to promote desiccation of this zone to increase tailings strength. The primary purpose was to enable the placement of capping over this zone of the tailings. The development of higher-strength tailings around the impoundment, and the consolidation provided by the capping itself, will increase tailings strength and hence reduce both the probability and consequence of a sudden release, even in the inconceivable event of a breach of the embankment.

Over the longer term, as the tailings continue to consolidate, they gain strength. As this occurs, their ability to flow decreases. For the purpose of this assessment, based on the tailings strength alone (and ignoring the expert opinion about the improbability of embankment failure), a period of 50 years was assumed as the maximum term this risk could exist.

Given all of the above, it was considered that the event had a negligible likelihood of occurrence of 10^{-6} per year (1 chance in 1 million years). To provide an estimate of remediation cost following a tailings release, some estimate of the release volume was required. For the purposes of this assessment only, a release of 1.3 million cubic yards (1 million m^3) was assumed, resulting in a total cost of around $12 million to cater for recovery, transfer and placement of tailings, embankment repair, cultivation, compensation, and upstream and downstream remediation. On the basis of this assumption, the ISR insurance policy would need to provide $12 million cover for this risk event.

Item 44: Seepage Release. This issue relates to release of tailings liquor or waste rock leachate as a result of failure of the underdrainage system (i.e., it differs from the issue of bypass seepage addressed in items 40 and 41). It was an insurable component of the capitalization sum.

The event was estimated to have a frequency of 4×10^{-5} per year (1 in 25,000 years). If this event occurred, it would necessitate the installation of a collection system and treatment of collected seepage prior to discharge to the river. The median cost for the collection system was estimated at around $32,000, with annual treatment costs being $8,400 per year.

Item 60: Tailings Pond Water Quality. One of the success criteria that WGC must attain before closure is attained is that the water quality of the pond on top of the rehabilitated tailings storage facility must be suitable for discharge to the local river (i.e., meets U.S. Environmental Protection Agency water quality standards after mixing). After cessation of mining, water quality in the ponds will improve as the tailings mass consolidates and the rate of upward release of pore fluid declines.

After the pond water achieves an acceptable discharge quality, subsequent deterioration would require a change to the pond inflow quality (e.g., for the tailings go acid). Based on the expert specialist advice obtained by WGC, the natural geochemical stability of the tailings means that there is very little likelihood of them going acid even if exposed to the atmosphere for extended periods. The expert advisers felt that the proposed rehabilitation strategy, which has crushed limestone added to the tailings during the final few months of deposition, would eliminate such risk. However, the expert panel felt that a conservative approach should be adopted and that this event should remain within the assessment, albeit with a low likelihood. The estimate of frequency for this event was 10^{-4} per year (1 chance in 10,000 years). The cost to treat the pond discharges through the WTP prior to discharge was estimated at $30,000 to $60,000 per year. This event was a gradual, uninsurable risk component of the capitalization sum.

RISK ANALYSIS

Quantitative Techniques

The threshold method of risk modeling was used for the risk assessment, but with some minor modifications.

Risk Quotient. Rather than produce a risk profile that ranked all of the risk events by descending order of risk quotient, the events were subdivided into two groups; ISR and Gradual. The ISR group contained the sudden events that were insurable. The Gradual group contained those events that resulted in environmental impairment and were assumed to be uninsurable.

Risk Cost. For each group, the risk cost was calculated as the sum of the occurrence cost of the highest-ranked risk issues that contributed to 95 percent of the total risk quotient for that group. The ISR group risk cost was used to explain and negotiate the ISR insurance requirements to WGC's insurance broker. The annual premium then was used to calculate this component of the capitalization sum.

For the Gradual group, the risk cost was synonymous with the capitalization sum quantum for that component and was adopted directly.

Risk Event Occurrence. The risk model developed for this project simulated random occurrence of the risk events over time. In addition, the event occurrence cost was discounted over time. The aggregated values over the full model run produced a distribution that accounted for uncertainty associated with both the cost and timing of the event occurrence.

When dealing with low-likelihood residual risk events such as existed in this case, assuming that all of the events do occur during the 100-year term provided a conservative estimate of risk cost. However, as in this case where few events contributed to the risk cost, the discounting inherent in this method potentially underestimated the occurrence cost if an event occurred early in the project term. For example, an event with an occurrence cost today of $100,000 has a net present value of $14,600 if it were to occur in 50 years' time (assuming the 4 percent per year real rate of return). If the latter sum was used to establish the capitalization sum quantum, and if the event then occurred much earlier in the project term, the funds available to address the scenario would be inadequate. The regulators were aware of, and sensitive to, this potential problem.

While there were a number of strategies to overcome this difficulty, a conservative approach was indicated by this precedent-setting project. Accordingly, the approach taken was to assume that the risk events occurred at the earliest possible time. For many of the events, this meant occurrence in the first year following closure. For the water quality–related events, a delay of several years was allowed. The reason was that, by definition, water quality must be good for WGC to attain closure, and due to the volumes involved and mechanisms by which quality could subsequently deteriorate, the events could not conceivably occur for some time.

The outcome of this approach was indeed conservative, but the advantage was that the regulators accepted the method and the results it produced with minimal debate.

Modeling Results

ISR Insurance Component. The results of modeling for the ISR insurance component produced a sum equivalent to the annual insurance premiums that would be paid to realistically cover the occurrence of sudden events. Figure 15.2 shows that two risk issues (pit lake outlet and waste seepage release) were the two riskiest events and accounted for approximately 96 percent of the total project risk for the ISR insurance events. The combined occurrence cost of these events was therefore the risk cost. However, as insurance for sudden and accidental environmental events was widely available, the risk cost was not used directly in the derivation of the capitalization sum. Instead, discussions with WGC's broker identified an annual premium offered by the insurance industry, and this was used to calculate the ISR insurance component.

Even though the risk quotient for the catastrophic tailings release event lay below the risk cut-off, as Figure 15.2 shows this event dominated the exposure profile. From a technical standpoint, this event could be excluded, but it was retained for political reasons. The outcome of the discussions with the insurance industry was that ISR insurance to cover $12 million for catastrophic tailings release was around $45,000 per year (but for the same premium up to $50 million could be purchased). This level of cover would be more than adequate for the riskiest events.

The estimated net present value of an annual ISR premium of $45,000 per year, discounted over the 50 years that the potential for a tailings release event was assumed to exist, was $960,000.

Gradual Risk Component. Figure 15.3 shows the key information used to derive the gradual risk component of the capitalization sum. Figure 15.3 shows that the riskiest issues (waste collection pond quality and waste rock bypass) contribute to almost 94 percent of the total project risk for all the issues.

The calculated risk cost for the events shows a moderate degree of uncertainty where the estimate varies from $2.997 million (optimistic, $CL_{50\%}$) to $5.281 million (pessimistic, $CL_{95\%}$). The planning ($CL_{80\%}$) estimate of the risk cost is $3.977 million. The exposure profile chart of Figure 15.3 shows that the calculated risk cost would also be able to cover the occurrence of all individual issues lower down the risk profile.

On the basis of the modeling results, the gradual risk component of the capitalization sum was set at $3.977 million.

Public Liability Insurance Component. The public liability insurance component of the capitalization sum was equivalent to the annual insurance premiums

ISSUE	Liability / Insurance	PROJECT RISK	ANNUAL RISK	Cost CL 50%	Cost CL 80%	Cost CL 95%	PROJECT Frequency	% Cumulative Risk	
Pit Lake Outlet	ISR risk	12.89703979	0.128970398	140.92	248.51	463.64	0.1	90.39%	Riskiest
Waste Seepage Release	ISR risk	0.77938824	0.008118628	202.97	217.54	233.69	0.00384	95.85%	Events
Waste Catastrophic Fail	ISR risk	0.592451958	0.011849039	11,864.47	12,386.75	12,869.02	0.00005	100.00%	

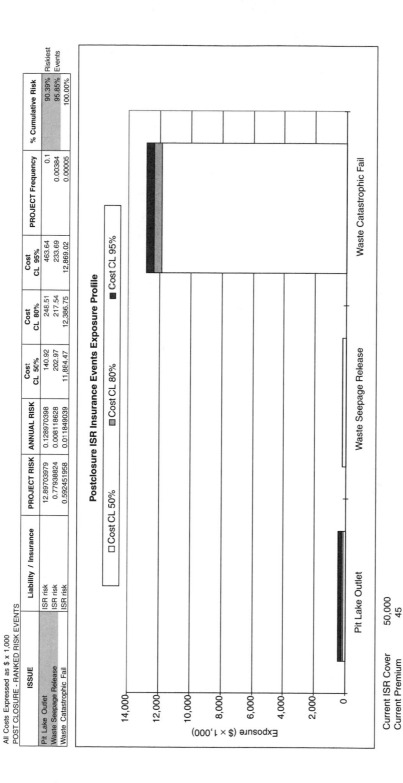

Figure 15.2 Occurrence cost of insurable (ISR) postclosure events if the risk events occur.

Current ISR Cover 50,000
Current Premium 45

ISSUE	Liability/Insurance	PROJECT RISK	ANNUAL RISK	Cost CL 50%	Cost CL 80%	Cost CL 95%	PROJECT Frequency	% Cumulative Risk	Riskiest Events
Waste Coll Pond Quality	Gradual risk	20.84170361	0.217101079	2150.081627	3070.336856	4351.640244	0.0096	68.17%	
Waste W/rock Bypass	Gradual risk	7.845559687	0.078455597	770.0979491	1078.869357	1526.658937	0.01	93.83%	
Waste Tailings Bypass	Gradual risk	0.784555969	0.0078455556	784.0646308	1092.551973	1541.663213	0.001	96.39%	
Pit Lake Quality	Gradual risk	0.620984847	0.006468592	648.9016475	852.4990239	1097.384336	0.00096	98.42%	
Waste Pond Quality	Gradual risk	0.3	0.003	29.79944131	42.98176627	59.73693642	0.01	99.40%	
Pit Wall Pumphouse	Gradual risk	0.15509704	0.00155097	1528.396594	2165.304602	2983.203382	0.0001	99.91%	
Waste Perimeter ARD	Gradual risk	0.026985199	0.000269852	55.52840839	85.87479011	130.3709727	0.0005	100.00%	

GRADUAL ($x1,000)

COMPONENT	Optimistic	Planning	Pessimistic
Sum	2,997	3,977	5,281
Risk	0.321	0.418	0.551

GRADUAL ($x1,000)

	Amount Req'd
Sum	3,977

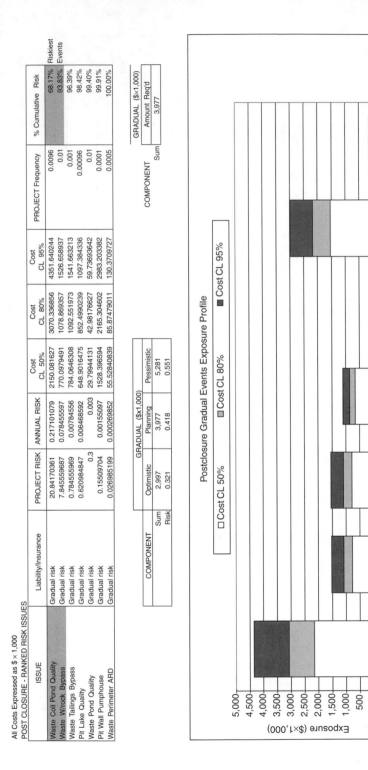

Postclosure Gradual Events Exposure Profile

□ Cost CL 50%   ▨ Cost CL 80%   ■ Cost CL 95%

COMPONENT

Exposure ($×1,000)

Figure 15.3 Occurrence cost of uninsurable, gradual postclosure events if the risk events occur.

that would be paid to realistically cover third-party claims. No specific issues were identified that would require public liability insurance. However, it was recognized that the trust would be managing land and would encourage public access. It was therefore assumed that the trust would require a standard public liability cover and that the capitalization sum would need to provide for that insurance.

Third-party, or public liability, insurance to cover property damage and injury was widely available at the time. Annual premiums of around $5,000 were typically required for policies with $5 million of cover. The net present value amount required to provide these premiums in perpetuity was estimated to be $127,000.

Postclosure Base Costs. The estimated annual base costs to cover land management, monitoring, and remedial action averaged around $20,000. The net present value of this annual expenditure in perpetuity totaled $549,000.

Summary

Table 15.3 shows a consolidated summary of the capitalization sum to be vested with the trust at the time of its establishment at closure. The total sum of $5.613 million would allow the trust to undertake its land management and maintenance responsibilities in perpetuity.

Table 15.3   Capitalization Sum Components ($ × 1,000)

Component	Amount Req'd 2017	Cover
ISR Insurance (premiums)	960	50,000
Gradual Risk Issue Costs	3,977	na
Public Liability Insurance (premiums)	127	5,000
Postclosure Base Costs	549	na
TOTAL	5,613	na

IMPLEMENTATION AND RISK REDUCTION

When the bond proposal was put to the regulators, the bond strategy and quantum were accepted without challenge. The capitalization bond became one of the matters appealed to the Environment Court by objectors to the extended project, and so the strategy and quantum subsequently underwent legal and technical examination within the court situation. At the hearing, the regulators supported adoption of WGC's proposal without change. Opponents to the project offered no contrary technical or other evidence that justified making significant modifications to WGC's proposal. In his decision, the judge chose to round the quantum up to $6 million, and WGC posted a capitalization bond of this amount.

The extended project consent conditions allowed for the bond (and capitalization sum) to be reviewed annually. These reviews will account for any changes to the operation that might influence the risk assessment inputs and outputs, inflation, plus any other issues that could affect the bond amount. The review process provides WGC with the opportunity to look at and reduce its postclosure risk profile. It is hoped that, over time, this focus will enable the very reasonable capitalization sum to be further reduced.

SUMMARY

The WGC had a regulatory obligation to estimate and provide a postclosure assurance to indemnify the people of New Zealand against the cost of mitigating potential environment impairment arising from its rehabilitated mine site at any time in the future.

Application of the RISQUE method has led to development of a postclosure assurance strategy and determination of an adequate and realistic value to the satisfaction of the regulators.

An agreed definition of "perpetuity" was crucial to development of the successful assurance strategy. Using the concept of the time value of money, the risk analyst demonstrated that perpetuity could be defined in financial terms, a solution immediately accepted by WGC and the regulators.

16

CORPORATE REPORTING AND INSURANCE: RESOURCE PROCESSING, UNITED STATES

This case study examines:

- Application of the RISQUE method to achieve compliance with corporate reporting regulations and guidelines
- Balance sheet recovery of contingent liability
- Using sound risk management processes to improve the bottom line
- Development of insurance strategies

BACKGROUND

U.S. Corporate Reporting: Staff Accounting Bulletin 92

Regulatory pressure is increasing for public corporations to disclose potential contingent liabilities through the corporate reporting process. Contingent liabilities are losses that can be anticipated to arise if particular events occur.

The aim of corporate reporting of contingent liability is to protect the interests of current and potential shareholders by informing them of potential liabilities that could have a material effect on corporate assets and operations and to maintain fairness in the marketplace. In addition to disclosure of the dollar value of contingent liability, the regulators require discussion of uncertainties affecting estimates and how management has handled, and proposes to handle, these liabilities and uncertainties.

Reporting Requirements. Legislation has been in place since June 1993, with release of the U.S. Securities and Exchange Commission (SEC) Staff Accounting Bulletin 92 (SAB 92), which requires disclosure of environmental and product liabilities. In 1994 the SEC signaled its intention to enforce SAB 92 and to target several types of corporation thought to have significant environmental liabilities. The organizations targeted were operating in oil and gas, pulp and paper, chemicals, and property and casualty insurance companies.

SAB 92 is the SEC interpretation of existing securities and accounting regulations and is a "full-disclosure" concept. SAB 92 requires a financial report containing comprehensive disclosure of:

- Actual assets and liabilities
- Potential liabilities: present and future
- Potential recoveries: present and future
- Secondary and derivative liabilities and assets
- Footnotes that present detail on methods used to derive the sums disclosed
- Narrative discussion, in Management's Discussion and Analysis (MD&A), of the uncertainties associated with events and potential and proposed solutions

SAB 92 has several specific requirements in relation to the disclosure of contingent environmental and product liabilities. It requires separate disclosure of a potential liability and a related potential recovery. It is not acceptable simply to disclose the net liability. SAB 92 requires discussion of uncertainty, specifically, the uncertainties affecting the precision of the estimates and the uncertainty associated with a corporation's legal responsibilities regarding the liabilities. Finally, SAB 92 requires substantial discussion both of the balance sheet impacts of potential environmental events and of management of the potential liabilities.

SAB 92 requires that corporations that are publicly traded in the United States must disclose environmental liabilities that are "reasonably possible to occur." They also must include in the financial statements those liabilities that are "reasonably probable" to occur and have a "material" effect on the assets and profits of the corporation in question.

Impacts of Changes. All corporations that are publicly traded in the United States are affected by SAB 92. The ruling not only includes U.S.-based companies registered on U.S. exchanges but also non-U.S. corporations trading registered issues on U.S. exchanges, and non-U.S. corporations trading American Depository Receipts (ADRs) in the United States. SAB 92 therefore has far-reaching impacts on many corporations beyond the boundaries of the United States.

The impacts of SAB 92 are also likely to extend, indirectly, to corporations around the world, because regulators in a growing number of countries are showing an increasing interest in introducing similar corporate reporting regulations. In addition, in some countries corporate professional organizations are proactively introducing voluntary corporate reporting procedures.

Prior to SAB 92, it was acceptable for corporations to disclose only those liabilities that they knew about and that were current. A typical statement would have

Table 16.1   Impact of SAB 92

Prior to SAB 92	Post-SAB 92
Highly variable reporting practices	Relatively uniform reporting practices
Disclosure of few, if any, contingent liabilities	All material liabilities are reported
Tendency to report minimum values	Reporting of minimum values is generally not allowed
Reporting of net value (liability minus recovery)	Net value reporting is not allowed
No explicit treatment of uncertainty	Explicit treatment of uncertainty is required
Little or no MD&A	Extensive footnotes and MD&A are required in the financial statements
Disclosure had little or no effect on the balance sheet	Disclosure can potentially have a major effect on the balance sheet

been: "We know of no contingent liabilities that are material." An important impact of SAB 92 is a shift in the burden of discovery. Now corporations can claim "no material effect" only if they can state: "We have identified and measured all of our contingent liabilities that are reasonably likely to occur, and have determined that none are material, outside of those disclosed here."

As a consequence of SAB 92, corporations must take positive action to evaluate their operations (e.g., through environmental audits), quantify the liabilities (and their uncertainties), and then make a determination as to materiality.

Table 16.1 summarizes the impact of the introduction and enforcement of SAB 92 on the characteristics of corporate reporting.

The potential consequences of noncompliance with SAB 92 are:

- Increased scrutiny and investigation
- Notices of noncompliance and violation
- Fines for violations of reporting regulations
- Suspension of trading
- Market effects from news of SEC scrutiny or enforcement actions

The following case study was originally based on a confidential assessment of third-party exposure to environmental impairment. The events and liabilities presented here are not the actual results of the assessment; the results have been modified to reflect the risk profiles of typical, large industrial corporations. The name of the corporation is confidential; therefore, the generic "The Company" is used herein to refer to the corporation.

Case Study Introduction

The Company had substantial financial interests in approximately 10 operating companies at over 30 sites located around the world, in the United States,

Australia, Indonesia, Taiwan, and New Zealand. The Company was engaged in mining, mineral processing, and manufacturing.

The Company's corporate risk manager needed to gain a quick, comprehensive understanding of The Company's environmental and third-party liability with respect to substantial sudden and gradual environmental events. This information was required to restructure the corporate environmental and third-party liability insurance strategy. Prior to this assessment, the corporate risk manager had no way of assessing whether the current insurance cover was adequate.

The Company was also required (under SAB 92) to report corporate environmental and contingent liability on the balance sheet. The Company had been a leader in applying new technology to enable it to better manage the environment and its business.

RISK IDENTIFICATION

Panel Process

The Company selected an expert panel to identify the key environmental events at each site that could lead to substantial environmental remediation and/or third-party claims. The panel members worked together for one week at the commencement of the project. During that time they reviewed the available information, became aware of the project aims, understood the project methodology, and established the appropriate roles and responsibilities of panel members. After the first week the panel members worked individually on preparation of information in a predetermined format. The role of the risk analyst was to coordinate panel contributions, ensure consistency of approach, and perform subsequent risk analysis.

The expert panel consisted of the business manager, a mining industry environmental specialist, a manufacturing industry environmental specialist, and corporate legal counsel. Where additional information was needed for specific events, individual panel members consulted with Company operations personnel. The panel members were generally familiar with many of The Company sites. In cases where the panel members had little or no firsthand knowledge of particular sites, the panel experts compared what they knew of The Company site activities and conditions with their experience of similar activities carried out in similar environments elsewhere in the world.

The available information on site conditions varied in quality and comprehensiveness from site to site. Information for some sites consisted of detailed environmental audit reports and backup data. For other sites, a selection of technical reports, such as engineering reports, groundwater studies, and environmental incident reports, were available. In a few cases, the only information available was a brief project summary and background photographs drawn from published annual reports.

Nature of Risk Events

The panel identified 235 key events that were entered into the risk register. Each event was classified as either a sudden or gradual occurrence to assist with the later determination of an insurance strategy. Sudden risk events were considered by panel members to be accidents, generally involving low probability and high consequences (i.e., tanker collision, fire, or explosion). Gradual risk events are representative of the more classic cases of pollution and usually had relatively high likelihoods of occurring. Typical gradual risk events were leakage from an underground storage tank and seepage of leachate from a hazardous waste dump to the groundwater.

The panel members estimated the annual frequency of each event, median and high estimates of occurrence cost, and estimates of the most cost-effective management steps that could be taken to prevent the event from further occurring.

Panel Conclusions

The risk events identified by the expert panel included issues such as:

- Stormwater discharges to surface water
- Wastewater discharges to surface water and sewer
- Soil and groundwater contamination from aboveground and underground storage tanks (ASTs and USTs); landfill leachates; stockpiles; tailings seepage; drum disposal; waste disposal; PCB releases; chemical, oil, and solvent spills
- Pollution from air emissions of heavy metals, particulates, oxides of nitrogen and sulfur, methane, carbon dioxide
- Transport and off-site disposal of wastes
- Noise
- Fuel and chemical transport accidents
- Asbestos handling
- Degradation of sites of cultural or heritage significance
- Chlorine and fluoride emissions
- Refinery waste storage
- Cooling water discharges
- Mine water discharges
- Tailings dam failure
- Acid rock drainage (ARD)
- Concentrate spillage during transport

The types of remediation requirements that were considered by the panel included:

- Documentation of the nature and occurrence of the event
- Hydrogeological and hydrological assessment
- Groundwater recovery and treatment
- Development of alternative water supplies
- Public relations and community consultation
- Leak detection and soil remediation (both in situ remediation and dig and dispose)
- Water and wastewater treatment works design, installation, and operation
- Monitoring, upgrading of facility and equipment
- Installation of containment structures
- Drainage improvement
- Response plan preparation and implementation
- Vegetation and soil rehabilitation
- Spill clean-up
- Alternative waste management and disposal
- Dredging (or excavation) and disposal of contaminated sediments

Risk Management Criteria

During the project, the panel members defined several criteria that assisted with interpretation of the modeling results and provided guidance in developing risk management strategies. The criteria were:

- A risk quotient of $20,000 per year was used as the cut-off threshold between the riskiest events and those that posed a low risk.
- Risk event occurrence costs of $500,000 and less were considered manageable under operational contingencies and therefore did not require specific management action.
- Sudden risk events were considered separately from gradual risk events and were assumed to be insurable.
- All gradual events with an annual likelihood of occurrence of less than 0.5 were considered to be risk events (i.e., there was a possibility that the event would not occur in future) and therefore would be potentially insurable.
- Similarly, all gradual events with an annual likelihood of occurrence of 0.5 or greater were assumed to occur and were therefore assumed not to be insurable due to their high likelihood of occurrence.

RISK ANALYSIS

Risk Modeling

The main features of the risk model that were specific to this project were:

- The costs of consequences of each risk event were divided into two categories, third party and environmental impairment.
- Third-party consequences included costs of claims by third parties for human health damage, stock and fishery loss, regulatory penalties, property damage, consequential loss, and some environmental damage.
- Environmental impairment consequences included the cost of remediation and reasonable works to prevent, or restrict the impact of, further occurrences.
- The risk quotient was calculated using a conservative estimate of the combined cost of all consequences at a conservative confidence level (CL 80 percent).
- The events were ranked by risk and risk profiles were generated, which showed both the event risk quotient and the financial exposure to each event.

Separate risk profiles generated by the model were:

- Sudden events (third party and environmental impairment)
- Insurable gradual events (third party and environmental impairment)
- Uninsurable gradual events

Sudden Events

A total of 66 sudden events was identified by the panel. Figure 16.1 shows the risk quotient and exposure profile of all sudden risk events ranked from highest to lowest risk. The profile shows that a relatively small number of risk events have risk quotients that are effectively identifiable on the profile.

A total of 20 events have risk quotients above the risk cut-off criteria set by the panel ($20,000 per year); the other 46 events have comparatively minor to negligible risk quotients. Of the 20 riskiest events, 10 have risk quotients above $200,000 per year.

The exposure profile of Figure 16.1 shows the 10 or 12 highest-risk events present, on average, approximately $2 million of exposure at the planning confidence level. This compares with an exposure of approximately $3 million for the next 20 risk events with material exposure.

For the 12 highest risk events, the representative pessimistic estimate of exposure is approximately $4.5 million compared with $7 million for the next 20 most risky events.

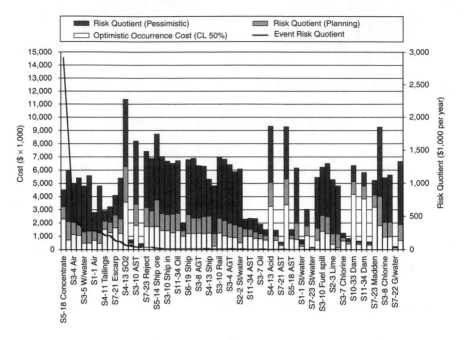

Figure 16.1   Sudden event exposure profile showing the occurrence cost of events ranked in order of decreasing risk quotient.

The exposure profile of Figure 16.1 also shows that there is considerable uncertainty in the estimates of the potential exposure to sudden risk events. This is illustrated by the large range in value between the optimistic and pessimistic costs, the pessimistic estimate often being two to three times greater than the estimated optimistic cost.

Figure 16.2 is a cumulative risk profile that shows the cumulative exposure and the cumulative percent risk for risk-ranked events. This figure shows that the most risky 12 events are responsible for approximately 93 percent of the total risk presented by all sudden risk events.

Insurable Gradual Events

Panel members identified a total of 73 insurable gradual events. Figure 16.3 shows the risk quotient and exposure profile of all insurable gradual risk events with the events ranked from highest to lowest risk. The risk quotient profile shows that the risk posed by the insurable gradual events is substantially greater than that posed by the sudden events.

The profile shows that 50 risk events, approximately two-thirds of identified insurable, gradual risk events, have risk quotients that are greater than the $20,000

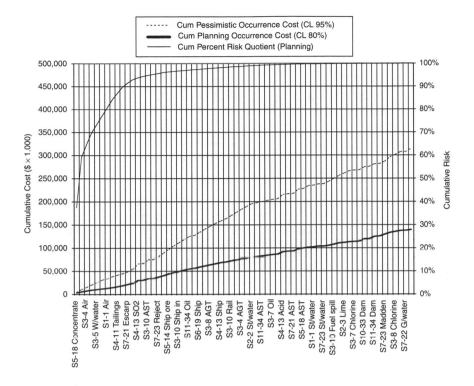

Figure 16.2   Sudden event cumulative graph showing the progressive contribution of risk events to total risk and occurrence cost with events ranked in order of decreasing risk quotient.

per year risk threshold. The six most risky insurable gradual events have risk quotients above $600,000 per year. In addition, the top 20 risk events have risk quotients greater than $200,000 per year. Figure 16.3 also clearly indicates that approximately one-third of insurable gradual risk events (22 events) show negligible risk quotients of less than $20,000 per year.

The exposure profile of Figure 16.3 shows that risk events within the group of the most risky 18 or 20 events generally present more exposure than events within the next 20 or so most risky events. At the planning confidence level, approximately 10 of the most risky 20 events present approximately $6 million exposure compared with approximately $1 million for many of the next 20 risk events. In addition, a representative pessimistic estimate of the exposure for 10 of the most risky 20 events is approximately $10 million compared with $3 million for the next 20 most risky events.

The exposure profile of the figure also shows that there is considerable uncertainty in the estimates of the potential exposure to sudden risk events.

Figure 16.4 is a cumulative risk profile that shows the cumulative exposure and the cumulative percent risk for risk-ranked events. It shows that the most risky 20

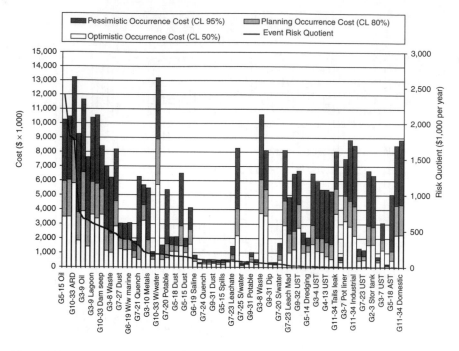

Figure 16.3 Insurable gradual events exposure profile showing the occurrence costs for events ranked in order of decreasing risk quotient.

events are responsible for approximately 82 percent of the total risk presented by all insurable gradual risk events.

Uninsurable Gradual Events

Uninsurable gradual events were identified as those events with some uncertainty of occurrence but with likelihoods so high (greater than a 50 percent chance per year) that it can reasonably be assumed that they would occur.

Figure 16.5 shows a combined risk and exposure profile of the 96 uninsurable gradual events. The risk quotient posed by every one of the uninsurable gradual events is greater than the $20,000 per year risk threshold that was selected to define the riskiest insurable events (both third party and environmental impairment). The lowest risk quotient of the uninsurable gradual issues was $90,000 per year.

The figure shows that the shape of the risk profile is very similar to that of the exposure profile, mainly due to the way in which the uninsurable risk events are defined. There is little difference between the risk quotient and the exposure to

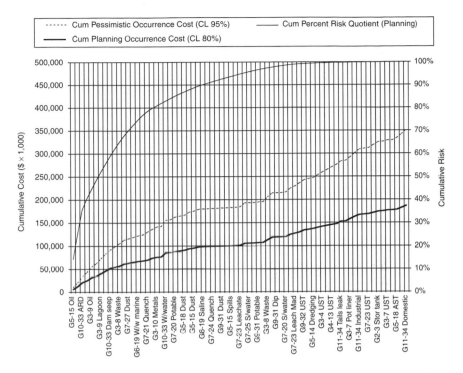

Figure 16.4 Insurable event cumulative graph showing the progressive contribution of risk events to total risk and occurrence cost with events ranked in order of decreasing risk quotient.

third-party and environmental impairment liability at the planning level of confidence because all of the uninsurable events have very high likelihoods of occurrence (greater than 50 percent per year).

The exposure profile of Figure 16.5 shows that there is substantial uncertainty in the estimates of the potential exposure and substantial financial exposure to uninsurable gradual risk events.

Four events each present in excess of $20 million of exposure (planning confidence level) to environmental impairment liability. A pessimistic estimate of exposure to each of the top two events is approximately $80 million.

Approximately 15 events each exhibit exposures of between $5 million (planning level of confidence) to $10 million (pessimistic confidence level). Furthermore, an additional 20 events could, from a pessimistic perspective, each incur $10 million liability. These events, however, present less exposure at the planning confidence level (approximately $3 million to $5 million).

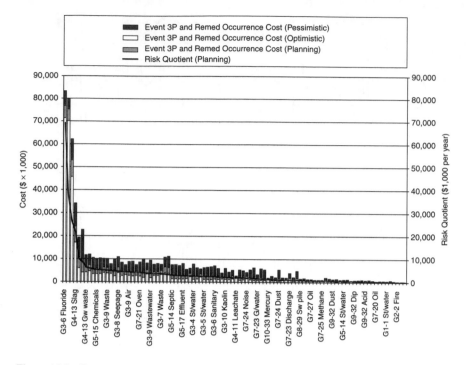

Figure 16.5 Occurrence costs of gradual, uninsurable events shown at three selected confidence levels with events ranked in order of decreasing risk quotient.

STRATEGY DEVELOPMENT

Where possible and cost effective, risk treatment can be achieved by transferring risk through insurance. Where risk transfer is not an option, risk reduction strategies need to be developed. Usually, there are a number of options and methods for reducing the likelihood of occurrence of the risk event to negligible levels, the exposure of the events to sums that can be taken up as operational contingencies, or both.

The strategy developed by the risk manager in this case study was confidential and was based on different dollar values from those presented here. The following risk reduction strategy is therefore an example of how the results of the RISQUE method can be interpreted and used to develop strategy.

Transfer of risk via insurance can be achieved using a wide range of instrument types and opportunities. Where purchased insurance is preferred over self-insurance, cover is possible using instruments such as:

- Sudden and accidental insurance, including industrial and special risk insurance (ISR)

- Finite risk insurance
- Third-party insurance
- Environmental impairment liability (EIL) insurance

The event types and exposures that were evaluated in this case study were required by the risk manager, presumably because of the nature of insurance cover readily available to The Company. The nature of cover was therefore apparently dependent on whether the risk events were sudden or gradual.

In addition to the risk and exposure profiles of Figures 16.1 through 16.4, various risk relationships were specifically generated and used to assist with strategy development. The risk relationships considered the cumulative cost for events, cumulative risk quotient for events, event prevention cost versus occurrence costs, and cumulative prevention costs compared with cumulative occurrence costs for risk events.

The costs and types of insurance cover to be discussed are provided for illustrative purposes only and are based on general current practice within the insurance industry but are not based on quotations. The types of cover described and the indicated rates to determine premium cannot be used or relied on for any other purpose.

Furthermore, the insurance options are based on a rudimentary understanding of the insurance industry and instruments. An experienced insurance broker would be able to generate a more sophisticated and appropriate strategy and also take advantage of specific market conditions. For example, an occasional bargain becomes available when substantial amounts of coverage move in and out of syndication for short periods of time and require placement. Taking advantage of the occasional bargain can represent large savings.

The basic strategy developed for insuring sudden and insurable gradual events was similar, and was to obtain a standard insurance policy plus a cap insurance policy. The standard policy would cover the conservative but realistic planning-level estimate of occurrence cost for all of the riskiest sudden events (those with a risk quotient greater than $20,000 per year). The cap insurance policy would cover the much less likely chance that the actual cost of claims would be greater than the planning cost (as represented by the pessimistic level estimates of cost). Under this strategy it was assumed that the cost of obtaining cap insurance would be less expensive than for normal insurance.

Insurance of Sudden Events

For purposes of the case study, it was assumed that ISR insurance would be readily obtained for the sudden risk events. ISR insurance covers first-party remediation and third-party claims for personal injury, property damage, consequential loss, fishery and livestock losses, and environmental damage. Liability associated with statutory penalties was excluded because transfer of risk for penalties is illegal in most countries; therefore, penalties are usually excluded from most policies.

The ISR insurance strategy summarized in Table 16.2 is based on interpretation of the risk and exposure profile of Figures 16.1 and 16.2, which show a plot of the cumulative relationships between cost of occurrence of risk events and overall risk presented.

The strategy assumes the deductible (or excess) on the policy to be $500,000 per event as The Company would be able to absorb risk costs up to this value within its operating contingencies.

A representative estimate of the exposure cost (planning confidence level) for each of the 12-highest risk events is approximately $2.0 million. The planned cover of $2.5 million per event should also be adequate to cover the occurrence of any one of the risk events contained within the risk profile. Cover is provided for 10 events, as it is considered extremely unlikely that all 12 events would occur.

Figure 16.2 shows that the estimated planning cost of the riskiest sudden events is approximately $25 million, which means the total cover should be adequate to cover most occurrences. The figure also shows that the riskiest events are responsible for around 93 percent of the total sudden event risk. Therefore, the standard ISR policy covers the vast majority of the risk presented by the riskiest events.

As current standard rates for ISR insurance appear to be around 0.3 to 0.8 percent per year, a standard policy premium rate of 0.6 percent per year has been assumed, giving an annual premium of $150,000.

Figure 16.1 shows that a representative estimate of the exposure cost (pessimistic confidence level) for each of the 12 riskiest events is between $2.5 million and $7.5 million. With the standard policy providing up to $2.5 million per event, cap insurance cover of up to $5 million per event should be adequate to cover the very conservative cost of any one of the risk events contained within the risk profile. The figure shows that the estimated pessimistic cost of the riskiest sudden events is approximately $50 million, which is equivalent to the planned cap insurance cover. Premiums for cap insurance have been assumed at half that for the standard cover (i.e., 0.3 percent per year), meaning the annual premium for this policy is $150,000.

Under this strategy, the total liability covered by sudden event insurance will be $75 million.

Table 16.2   ISR Insurance Strategy

	Primary Policy	Cap Insurance
No. of Events	10	10
Deductible/Event	$0.5 million	—
Maximum Cover/Event	$2.5 million	$5 million
Total Cover	$25 million	$50 million
Estimated Maximum Exposure	$25 million	$50 million
Premium —Rate	0.6% per year	0.3%
—Cost	$150,000 per year	$150,000 per year

Insurance of Gradual Events

For purposes of the case study, it was assumed that EIL insurance would be readily obtained for the insurable gradual events. A summary of the strategy is given in Table 16.3. As with ISR insurance, this strategy was developed from interpretation of risk and exposure profiles and plots of the cumulative relationships between risk event occurrence costs and overall risk. The reasoning behind the strategy was similar to that used for the ISR insurance cover.

Because of the higher risk associated with the EIL insurance component, the assumed premium rate for the standard policy is 6 percent per year, which is 10 times greater than that assumed for the ISR cover. The total liability covered by EIL insurance will be $120 million.

Table 16.3 EIL Insurance Strategy

	Primary Policy	Cap Insurance
No. of Events	10	10
Deductible/Event	$0.5 million	—
Maximum Cover/Event	$6 million	$6 million
Total Cover	$60 million	$60 million
Premium —Rate	6% per year	3%
—Cost	$3.6 million per year	$1.8 million per year

Management of Uninsurable Gradual Events

Interpretation of Results. Ninety-six risk events were identified as being effectively uninsurable. The total estimated cost (at the planning confidence level) of third-party claims and environmental remediation for all of the uninsurable, high-likelihood gradual risk events was $480 million. A pessimistic estimate of the combined financial liability for the uninsurable risk events was approximately $740 million. Clearly, The Company needed to reduce the financial exposure by carrying out risk reduction actions that either would effectively prevent the events from occurring or would reduce the cost of the consequences should those events occur.

For each of the uninsurable risk events, the expert panel considered the most cost-effective risk reduction measures that could reasonably be taken. A profile of the cost of the identified prevention measures and the concomitant financial liability for each uninsurable risk event is plotted on Figure 16.6. Both sets of cost estimates are presented at the planning level of confidence. The profile shows that most of the prevention costs are substantially lower than the costs that would be incurred if the events occurred.

Figure 16.7 shows more clearly the relationships between prevention costs and occurrence costs for the riskiest 26 uninsurable risk events. It shows that the two

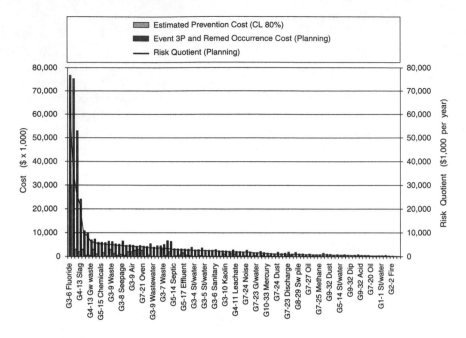

Figure 16.6 Prevention and occurrence costs of gradual uninsurable events ranked in order of decreasing risk quotient.

events with the highest financial exposure (both air pollution issues) present an exposure of around $75 million each, and the estimated planning cost to prevent each event is approximately $30 million. It is easy to conclude that The Company should invest $60 million to reduce an imminent financial exposure of around $150 million, which represents good value for the environmental dollar. If the funds were unavailable for both prevention actions to be carried out immediately, then the fluoride emission event should be addressed first as it is more risky and more likely to occur.

Figure 16.7, in conjunction with Figure 16.8 (which shows a comparison of the cumulative prevention and occurrence costs of all the uninsurable events), shows that for a relatively small additional cost ($5 million), the total exposure of $228 million associated with the top four events could be reduced. Additional gains in reducing financial exposure could be made by spending a further $5 million (total of $70 million) to lay off $260 million, which is the exposure to the top eight uninsurable risk events.

Figures 16.7 and 16.8 would be used to develop a rational, cost-effective risk reduction strategy for the uninsurable risk events.

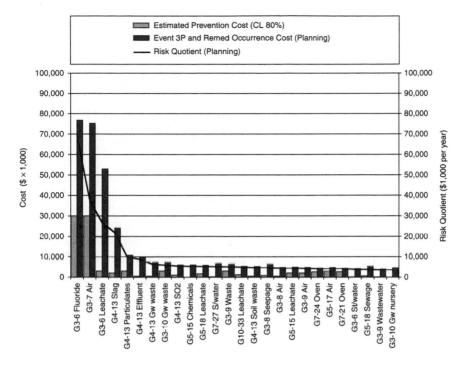

Figure 16.7 **Prevention and occurrence costs of the riskiest gradual uninsurable events ranked in order of decreasing risk quotient.**

Strategy for Uninsurable Risk Events. The general risk reduction strategy would be to:

- Immediately create a management reserve of $480 million. This is the planning level estimate of exposure for all uninsurable events. It is considered reasonable to use only the planning confidence-level estimates, because the 80 percent confidence level is conservatively high and the uncertainty of cost variation is mitigated by the relatively large number of events that are assumed to occur. For example, for every occasion where a cost greater than average is incurred, it could reasonably be expected that another event would incur a cost below the median.
- Plan ultimately to spend approximately $111 million to reduce $480 million of exposure.
- For the next reporting period, budget to spend $70 million to reduce the $260 million of exposure to the eight riskiest events.
- In the subsequent reporting periods, budget to spend $41 million to reduce the remaining $220 million of exposure associated with the remaining uninsurable events.

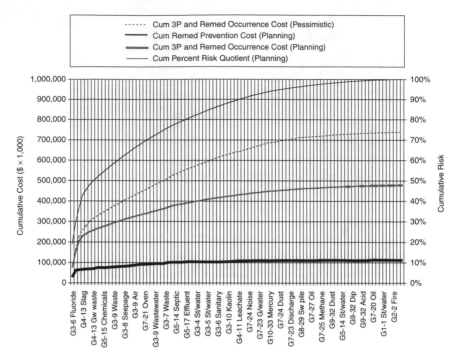

Figure 16.8 Comparison of cumulative prevention and occurrence costs of gradual uninsurable events showing that the cumulative prevention costs are less than the estimated occurrence costs.

DISCLOSURE: SAB 92

Balance Sheet Reporting

Individually, the financial liabilities derived from all of the identified risk events are generally not material. However, when the financial exposure is considered in aggregate, each of the classified risk event groups (sudden: $75 million; gradual: $120 million; and uninsurable risk events: $480 million) constitute material contingent financial liability.

The Company's financial statements for the current year would include disclosure of contingent liabilities for that year. For the current-year financial statement, The Company would book an overall contingent liability of $675 million but would recover $185 million through insurance and include $5.7 million for deductibles (premiums). The Company therefore would reserve $495.7 million. It would be able to comply with legislation and state: "We have identified and measured all of the contingent environmental liabilities that are reasonably possible to occur. We have assessed their significance and beyond those liabilities declared here, we know of none that will have a material effect."

Corporate reporting legislation requires a description of the contingent liabilities and any associated recoveries and deductibles and justification of the current and proposed actions in the MD&A.

Management's Discussion and Analysis

The risk reduction strategy just developed would be discussed in the MD&A. Tables 16.4 to 16.7 summarize the overall risk reduction strategy for the following

Table 16.4 Current Financial Year

Event	Liability ($ × million)	Risk Transfer or Reduction Costs ($ × million)	Recovery ($ × million)
Sudden Environmental Impairment	75	0.3	70
Gradual Environmental Impairment	120	5.4	115
Gradual, Uninsurable Environmental Impairment	480	—	—
Book	675	5.7	185
Reserve	$495.7 million		

Table 16.5 Financial Year 2

Event	Liability ($ × million)	Risk Transfer or Reduction Costs ($ × million)	Recovery ($ × million)
Sudden Environmental Impairment	75	0.3	70
Gradual Environmental Impairment	120	5.4	115
Gradual, Uninsurable Environmental Impairment	480	70	260
Book	675	75.7	445
Reserve	$305.7 million		

Table 16.6 Financial Year 3

Event	Liability ($ × million)	Risk Transfer or Reduction Costs ($ × million)	Recovery ($ × million)
Sudden Environmental Impairment	75	0.3	70
Gradual Environmental Impairment	120	5.4	115
Gradual, Uninsurable Environmental Impairment	220	40	220
Book	415	45.7	405
Reserve	$55.7 million		

Table 16.7   Financial Year 4

Event	Liability ($ × million)	Risk Transfer or Reduction Costs ($ × million)	Recovery ($ × million)
Sudden Environmental Impairment	75	0.3	70
Gradual Environmental Impairment	120	5.4	115
Gradual, Uninsurable Environmental Impairment	—	—	—
Book	195	5.7	185
Reserve	$15.7 million		

three years. Figure 16.9 shows the planned trends over the subsequent nine years in reduction of contingent liability, annual and cumulative costs of recoveries, and the benefit of expenditure in reduction of contingent liability. Figure 16.9 shows the very substantial benefits that would be gained over a period of four years, where the total contingent liability of almost $700 million before starting this exercise is planned to be reduced to approximately $16 million.

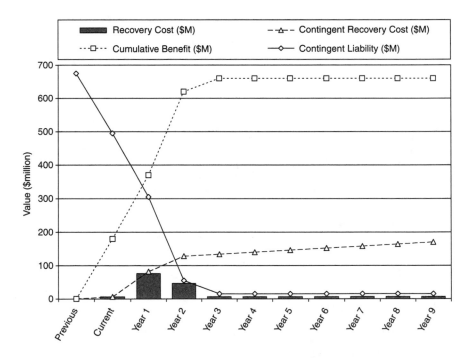

Figure 16.9   Planned recovery of contingent liability showing the anticipated schedule of recovery and the ranked, early reduction of liability.

SUMMARY

The case study demonstrates that there are substantial benefits to be gained from utilization of the RISQUE method to comply with statutory corporate reporting requirements or voluntary reporting. Key advantages of the method are:

- The approach follows a systematic, transparent procedure to ensure that all of the material contingent liabilities are considered.
- The approach is logical and consistent and, therefore, defensible.
- Contingent liability is clearly reported in dollar terms.
- Compliance with corporate reporting regulations and guidelines is clear and comprehensive.
- The focus is on balance sheet recovery of contingent liability.
- A diverse range of potential recoveries and risk management options is explored.
- Insurance strategies are more likely to be well conceived, cost effective, and genuinely reduce corporate exposure to contingent liability.

17

ASSET MANAGEMENT: WATER, NEW ZEALAND

This case study examines:

- Risk analysis and management strategy development for a large number of assets
- Interpretation and simplification of large volumes of detailed information into a format most usable for achieving the project objectives
- Use of release modes as a simplifying measure of consequence
- Advantages of preparation prior to workshops
- Quantification of environmental, community, and political risks
- Development of risk acceptability criteria
- Systematic development of cost-effective risk reduction actions to meet risk acceptability criteria

BACKGROUND

Metrowater owns and operates 102 wastewater pumping stations in Auckland City, of which 90 are sewage pumping stations. The remaining 12 stations pump stormwater or combined sewage and stormwater. Many of the stations are located close to environmentally sensitive areas, such as coastal waterways and aquifers. Metrowater had identified the pumping stations as being critical assets and commissioned the risk management study to identify which sewage pumping stations posed the greatest risk in terms of operational and environmental consequences should any failure event occur.

The corporation's objectives for the study were to:

- Identify and document the existing management, technical systems, and procedures currently used by Metrowater to control risks.
- Identify and quantify the main risk contributors at each of the pumping stations.

- Rank the pumping stations in order of the risk each poses.
- Develop risk treatment options and risk acceptance criteria.

Metrowater's overall objective in commissioning this study and pursuing the risk treatment actions resulting from the risk analysis was to reduce the frequency and impact of sewage overflows from the pumping stations.

A quantitative risk analysis was required to ensure that the pumping stations were fully evaluated in a consistent manner and that a comparative ranking of the risk posed by each station was provided. To enable effective risk management, for each pumping station the study outcomes needed to clearly identify the risk quotients of each of the factors contributing to the overall pumping station risk.

The input information was collected during a series of workshops. The expert panel was drawn from key Metrowater staff, all with direct operational and management experience with Auckland's sewerage reticulation and most with many years of service. The panel members were selected to ensure that all the relevant operating and management knowledge could be collected and included in the study inputs.

The key stakeholders were identified as:

Metrowater	Auckland City Council
Metrowater employees	(Metrowater's owners)
Auckland ratepayers	Auckland Regional Council (the
Residents living adjacent to the stations	environmental regulators)
Community and specific interest groups	Harbor users
	Groundwater users

PROJECT SETTING

Sewerage System Characteristics

Metrowater's files held a considerable volume of detail about each pumping station's characteristics, equipment, and operation, although many of these records were out of date to varying degrees. In addition, a database contained the overflow records of the sewerage system. While a good understanding of the system characteristics and its operation was required to complete the risk analysis, this significant volume of information needed to be distilled into a manageable format.

The general system characteristics derived from Metrowater's records are summarized in the following sections.

Pumping Station Operation. Sewage pumping stations are required in the Auckland city region to pump sewage from houses and buildings into the city's sewerage network and ultimately into a regional sewerage collection and treatment scheme. The number of houses serviced by each pumping station ranges from five to 150, with most pumping stations servicing around 20 houses. Most of the pumping stations are located at relatively low elevations near the coast.

Sewage flow from the catchment varies substantially. Average dry weather flows (ADWF) vary from less than 95 gallons per hour (gal/hr) (0.1 liters per second [L/s]) to around 11,400 gal/hr (12 L/s). For approximately 60 percent of the pumping stations, ADWF is less than 475 gal/hr (0.5 L/s). A small proportion (around 10%) have ADWF in excess of 2,850 gal/hr (3 L/s).

Maximum flows also vary substantially from station to station, from less than 950 gal/hr (1 L/s) to almost 57,000 gal/hr (60 L/s). Approximately 50 percent of the pumping stations have maximum flows of less than 1,900 gal/hr (2 L/s), and only 10 percent of stations have maximum flows of greater than around 14,300 gal/hr (15 L/s).

Pumping station catchment area also varies substantially, from less than 2.5 acres (1 ha) to 740 acres (300 ha). Around 80 percent of pumping stations have catchment areas of less than 25 acres (10 ha), and all stations (bar three) have catchment areas less than around 74 acres (30 ha).

As expected, there is a strong and significant relationship (p <<0.001 that the relationship is due to chance) between catchment area and ADWF. Maximum flows coincide principally with large rainfall events.

Emergency storage capacities vary considerably, so storage time before station overflows occur can be less than one hour up to approximately 110 hours. Around seven pumping stations have close to, or less than, the minimum storage requirement of four hours at ADWF required by the regulatory authority, the Auckland Regional Council. Approximately 40 percent of the pumping stations have storage times between five and 10 hours, and around 20 percent of stations have storage times greater than 20 hours.

Pumping station overflow records between July 1997 and October 1999 show that there were 69 recorded overflows. Of these, 13 were fault induced and the rest (56) were rain induced. Pumping stations E10, W07, and H04 had the most frequent overflows, with nine, eight, and seven events, respectively. Eight other stations (E01, E03, W26, H03, H05, T11, W01, and W20) recorded more than two overflows. One or two overflows were recorded at another 11 pumping stations.

The duration of rain-induced overflows ranged from 0.1 to 15 hours, with a mean duration of 2.8 hours. In 50 percent of cases, the overflow duration was less than two hours; in 80 percent of cases, it was less than four hours; and in 90 percent of cases, the duration was less than six hours.

Rain-induced overflows were 1.5 times more common where the emergency storage time was less than eight hours (34 overflow events), which occurs in one-third of the pumping stations. Rain-induced overflows were approximately 10 times more common (51 events) in catchments of over 12 acres (5 ha) than in smaller catchments. Approximately one-third of all catchments are over 12 acres (5 ha).

Tables 17.1 and 17.2 summarize key overflow statistics.

Table 17.1   Overflow Frequency

Overflow Type	Fault Induced	Rain Induced	
		Catchment <12 acres	Catchment >12 acres
Pumping Station No.	102	70	32
No. of Events	13	5	51
Likelihood (per station/yr)	0.056645	0.031746	0.722222
Return Period (years)	17.7	31.5	1.4

Table 17.2   Overflow Duration

	Overflow Duration (hrs)	
	Fault Induced	Rain Induced
Minimum	0.1	0.1
Mean	5.25	2.8
CL 50%	2	2
CL 80%	6	4
CL 90%	13	6
Maximum	23	15

Failure Mechanisms. Initial appraisal of the nature, location, and operation of the pumping stations indicated that four potential mechanisms could lead to substantial sewage overflows. The two most common mechanisms were pump stoppage, leading to sewage overflow from the emergency storage tank, and failure of the rising main, most likely rupture, leading to sewage release somewhere along the alignment of the rising main. Other, less likely mechanisms were undercapacity pumps and sewage backflow to the water supply system (e.g., via the water supply hose in the pump house).

Preliminary identification was carried out of potential events that could trigger the failure mechanisms. Table 17.3 was prepared as an initial guide to the expert panel and shows a summary of trigger events for each release mechanism.

Sewage Overflow Impacts. The preliminary evaluation carried out prior to the first workshop indicated that although the impacts of sewage release to the environment would be complex, the assessment of impacts for each pumping station could be made relatively simple due to commonality of settings for many of the stations. For example, effluent discharge from many of the pumping stations would enter the foreshore and the near-shore marine environment. For other, more inland pumping stations, the principal impact of effluent discharge would be on the quality of the underlying groundwater system. For the remainder, it was considered that the discharge would be collected in the stormwater system some dis-

Table 17.3   Summary of Trigger Events for Release Mechanisms

Pump Stoppage	Rising Main Failure	Pump Inadequate	Backflow
Equipment fault	Pipe failure	Infiltration	Valve failure
Seismic event	Seismic event	Illegal dumping	Operator error
Vandalism, sabotage	Vandalism, sabotage		Design, construction
Land subsidence	Land subsidence		
Blockage (e.g., silt, debris)	Blockage (e.g., silt, debris)		
Impact (e.g., truck collision)	Impact (e.g., truck collision)		
Power failure			
Fire			

tance from the coast and although ultimate discharge would be to the marine environment, the effluent would be substantially diluted by stormwater prior to discharge, thus reducing the impact on the receiving environment.

It was anticipated, and later confirmed at the workshops, that the engineering and clean-up consequences of sewage overflows resulted in only minor cost impacts. The major consequences would result from environmental impacts and from community and political reactions. Table 17.4 summarizes the key impacts assessed for the marine discharges. Many of the same events and impacts also applied to the groundwater system.

Pre-Workshop Preparation.   The preliminary understanding of the operation and potential impacts of the pumping stations led to the following conclusions:

- The attributes (e.g., trigger events, failure mechanisms, and impacts of sewage overflow) that must be considered in the risk assessment were very complex and would be difficult to manage if each pumping station were to be considered separately in relation to all attributes. There was a practical need to group the pumping stations (and if possible) to simplify the risk assessment.

Table 17.4   Key Overflow Impacts

Environmental Impacts	Community Impacts	Political Impacts
Public health damage	Visual amenity	Operational interference
Fauna damage (e.g., shellfish)	Recreational amenity	Opposition to consents
Ecosystem damage	Reputation damage	Lost future opportunity
Damage to fisheries	Community opposition to future developments	Withdrawal of revenues and subsidies
Clean-up		Overdesign of remedial solutions
Regulatory fines		
Property damage		

- The pumping stations could be grouped on the basis of nature and sensitivity of the receiving environment and the likely volume of an overflow.
- Using these groupings, it was possible to identify a few specific release modes and to assess the likelihoods and consequences associated with each. In this way, the large number of pumping stations and their consequences could be made manageable.
- Information was then prepared to help focus the expert panel on appropriate outcomes, thereby maximizing value from the panel members' time.

Management Procedures in Place

Metrowater was aware of the failure pathways and the potential impacts on the community and the environment. As part of its normal risk management procedures, it had implemented a number of management actions to reduce exposure to risk events.

The existing risk management actions included:

- Installation of a comprehensive telemetry system to monitor pumping station operations
- Establishment of a rapid response team that was on call on a 24-hour basis
- Installation of a standby pump at all pumping stations
- Establishment of an emergency management plan to ensure generator availability in the event of power failure
- Regular field inspections of plant operation and condition
- Implementation of a comprehensive maintenance schedule
- Progressive upgrading of emergency storage capacity
- Implementation of a community consultation process

Risk Assessment Structure

The risk posed to Metrowater by any pumping station is equal to the likelihood (annual probability) of a sewage overflow occurring, multiplied by the cost of the entire range of consequences. The key tasks of the panel were to:

- Identify the potential mechanisms that could trigger effluent release to the wider environment.
- Estimate the likelihood of a release (considering the available overflow response time at each station).
- Identify and estimate cost ranges of the potential consequences of sewage release from each pumping station.

The risk assessment structure relied on the simplified release mode approach to quantify the input data, from which was calculated the risk posed by each of the 90 sewage pumping stations, allowing each station to be prioritized in order of risk. In addition, the structure retained the detail of each trigger mechanism to assist development of a staged risk reduction strategy.

Numerical Inputs. The schematic diagram of Figure 17.1 indicates the input information that was required from the panel to develop the risk model. It shows that the likelihood of Event 1, which was overflow due to pump stoppage, was equal to the sum of the likelihoods of all trigger mechanisms (i.e., power failure, equipment failure, etc.) that could lead to Event 1. Similarly, the likelihood of Event 2, which was the release of sewage due to rising main failure, was equal to the sum of the likelihoods of all release mechanisms (i.e., pipe failure, vandalism, etc.) that could lead to Event 2.

Figure 17.1 shows that regardless of release mechanism (pump or rising main failure), any effluent would be released to the same environment and therefore would have effectively the same consequences.

Figure 17.2 is a flow chart that indicates (for the two main release mechanisms only) the process the panel needed to follow to perform its key tasks. The flow chart shows that the panel had to determine how sensitive each of the receiving environments (swimming beach, harbor, groundwater, and stormwater) would be to an influx of sewage. The panel then needed to determine, for each sensitivity class, what volume of overflow would constitute a significant sewage flow result-

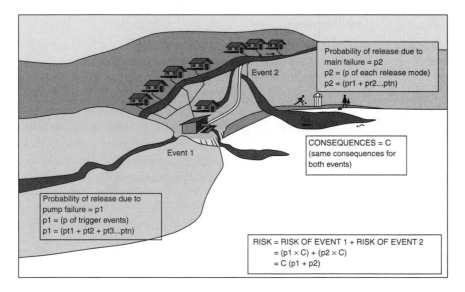

Figure 17.1 Risk calculation schematic showing the relationship between likelihood of release, the consequences, and the calculation of risk quotient.

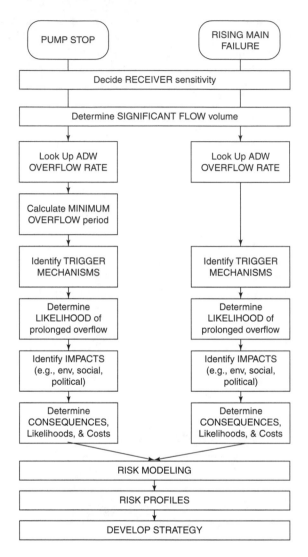

Figure 17.2   Flow chart describing the process used to quantify the likelihoods and consequences of sewage overflows.

ing in substantial environmental damage and/or strong community reaction. For example, a release of several hundred gallons of sewage to a moderately sensitive environment, such as Manukau Harbor, may not be considered a significant spill. However, the same volume at an extremely sensitive receptor site, such as a swimming beach, could possibly be considered a significant discharge.

Having defined the volume of a significant release into a given receiving environment, the minimum allowable period of overflow could be calculated for a specified rate of sewage flow (e.g., the ADWF). The panel would then be in a position to evaluate the likelihood of an overflow lasting longer than the minimum period for each trigger mechanism.

Similarly, for each receiving environment (classified according to sensitivity), the panel could consider the nature of significant effluent discharges and identify specific impacts (e.g., damage to fish, community outcry, and political backlash) and their potential consequences (e.g., compensation, remediation, public relations, and business losses).

The information that the panel provided would then be used as input to the risk modeling process.

RISK IDENTIFICATION AND QUANTIFICATION

Expert Panel

The fields of expertise represented by the panel members were:

- Engineering
- Pumping station operations
- Corporate communications
- Finance and Accounting
- Customer relations
- Geology

Panel Discussions

The panel met on two occasions to generate the input required for the risk analysis. Once the analysis results were available, a third workshop was held at which the panel used the modeling outputs to develop the risk reduction strategy.

During the first panel workshop, the risk assessment process was explained and the panel members were informed of the information required from them. The members then identified the key stakeholders, decided receiver sensitivities, and estimated significant overflow volumes. In the remaining time available, they completed assessment of the trigger mechanisms, impacts, and consequences for release from a number of representative pumping stations. During the second workshop, panel members completed assessment of the receiving environment sensitivity and trigger of the mechanisms for each of the remaining pumping stations.

Receiver Sensitivities and Significant Flow Volumes

The water supply aquifer was considered extremely sensitive because sewage overflowing from a pumping station would move directly to the groundwater supply. The panel considered that even if only a very small volume of sewage was released, it would be noticed by the public and would cause substantial reaction due to the potential health hazard to the potable water supply. A significant release to the water supply aquifer was considered to be 50 gal (200 L).

Swimming beaches were considered to be highly sensitive to sewage release due to obvious visual presence, recreational contact, and loss of beach amenity. Other aquifers occur within the area. Although they are mostly of potable standard, they have not yet been developed as water supplies. These other aquifers were also considered to be highly sensitive due to their future water supply potential. A significant release to the swimming beaches and other aquifers was considered to be 530 gal (2,000 L).

The harbor areas, used predominantly for fishing and recreation, were considered to be moderately sensitive due mainly to visual impacts rather than, for example, the potential for recreational contact. A significant release to harbor areas was considered to be 5,300 gal (20,000 L).

Stormwater, or the stormwater reticulation, was considered to be sensitive (the lowest sensitivity category) because considerable dilution by stormwater would occur prior to ultimate discharge of the effluent to the coastal environment. A significant release to stormwater was considered to be 35,000 gal (130,000 L).

Table 17.5 summarizes the receiver sensitivities and significant overflow volumes determined by the panel.

Table 17.5   Receiver Sensitivities and Significant Flow Volumes

Receiving Environment	Sensitivity	Significant Sewage Release (gal)
Water supply aquifer	Extremely sensitive	50
Swimming beach/other aquifer	Highly Sensitive	530
Harbor	Moderately sensitive	5,300
Stormwater	Sensitive	35,000

Identification of Trigger Mechanisms

The panel recognized that, notwithstanding the design, operations, and maintenance efforts that have been applied to the pumping station system to reduce the amount of risk, there remained some residual risk that failures leading to substantial sewage release would occur in future. Accordingly, the panel identified a range of mechanisms that could trigger release of effluent, either as overflow or as a result of rising main failure.

Overflow Triggers. The following trigger mechanisms were considered to have the potential to lead to uncontrolled overflow from pumping stations:

- *Equipment fault:* Pump stoppage due to mechanical breakdown, failure of sensor probes, telemetry system failure. The potential for equipment failure was reduced by installation of backup pumps at each station, round-the-clock monitoring of telemetry information, and regular maintenance schedules and periodic operational inspections.
- *Power failure:* Unscheduled power outages are relatively common due to the combined effects of events such as provider failure, vehicle accidents, and inclement weather. The likelihood of extended pump stoppage due to power outage was reduced by installation of generator power plugs and development of a comprehensive emergency generator plan.
- *Impact:* A number of pumping stations were constructed below ground surface. These pumping stations usually had a surface-mounted electrical control box, which was, in many cases, exposed to collision with passing traffic. Some control boxes were protected by steel or concrete bollards. In some cases there was potential for a vehicle to crash through the protective bollards (where present), thus causing equipment failure that could lead to sewage release. This event would cause a major failure, resulting in the potential release of substantial volumes of sewage effluent.
- *Fire:* There was some potential for fire to break out in a pumping station (mainly due to some kind of electrical failure). Such a fire could cause a wide range of damage. The likelihood of major fire was reduced by the absence of fuel material within the pumping station.
- *Flooding:* In cases where the pumping stations were located in low-lying areas of the topography, there was some potential for flooding to cause equipment failure leading to substantial downtime.
- *Tide:* In some cases the pumping stations were located in close proximity to the shore zones and had some potential to be flooded by the tide. Conditions that promote tidal flooding of stations included "king tides" and strong onshore winds.
- *Blockage:* Deposition of silt and debris in the pump wells was ongoing, and there was potential for this material to be entrained within the pumps and cause mechanical damage (e.g., to impellers), which would cause pump failure. The likelihood of blockage was reduced by scheduled cleaning of pump wells.
- *Vandalism/sabotage:* Many of the pumping stations were relatively isolated from view or human activity, and there was potential for vandals to break into the pump houses and damage equipment. The likelihood of vandalism was reduced by construction of steel security fencing, security doors, and enclosure of equipment.
- *Seismic event:* There was some potential for earthquake activity to cause damage to equipment, emergency storage, pipes, and pump house that could lead to release of sewage.
- *Land subsidence:* In some cases, pumping stations were located in areas with some potential for geotechnical instability. A geotechnical failure (subsidence

or landslide) could lead to a sewage release. In many cases the likelihood of release was reduced by design and sound construction of the pumping station facilities.

- *Volcanic activity:* There was some minor potential for volcanic activity to cause sewage release.

- *Coastal erosion:* Some pumping stations were located close to shore, where wave action under certain circumstances could undercut the pumping station foundations and cause sewage release.

Rising Main Failure. The following trigger mechanisms were considered to have the potential to lead to uncontrolled overflow from rising mains:

- *Pipe failure:* Rising mains could rupture due to structural failure, corrosion (where applicable), or joint failure.

- *Impact:* There was some potential for pipework to be ruptured during unrelated earthworks activities or, in the case of unburied pipes, by collision with a truck or digger.

- *Vandalism/sabotage:* In cases where pipes were on the surface, there was some potential for vandalism and sewage release.

- *Blockage:* Silt or other debris could potentially cause a blockage in the rising main, leading to pressure buildup and pipe rupture.

- *Seismic event:* Earthquake activity could rupture the rising main.

- *Land subsidence:* Geotechnical failure had potential to rupture the rising main in some cases.

Likelihood of Prolonged Overflow

In each case where a potential trigger mechanism was considered to be applicable, the panel estimated the likelihood that sewage release would be sustained for longer than the relevant minimum period of uncontrolled release.

Impacts and Consequences

The expected impacts of sewage release and their subsequent financial consequences were determined by the panel according to the sensitivity of each receptor (extremely sensitive, very sensitive, moderately sensitive, and sensitive). The panel also evaluated, for each receptor, the severity and likelihood of causing each of the potential impacts. The key impacts and consequences were listed in Table 17.4, and a brief discussion on the outcomes of the workshops on each follows.

Environmental Damage. The following impacts and consequences of environmental damage were identified:

- *Public health:* The panel considered that a member of the public could become ill from contact with, or ingestion of, sewage if swimming in a contaminated beach area, or if a person were to fall into contaminated water from a boat. Direct contact by the public could result in a claim or series of claims for compensation. Another impact of sewage release could be lodgment of a claim that fish contaminated with sewage from a release had been eaten and had caused human health problems. Metrowater's public liability insurance provided $10 million cover per case, which panel members thought was more than adequate to cover claims against it. The major consequence was therefore related to the cost of mounting a legal defense against such claims. A median cost of $100,000 and a high estimate of around $200,000 were adopted.
- *Fauna:* There was limited potential for damage to fauna by domestic sewage released from a pumping station, but this did not preclude a claim against Metrowater for the overflow. It was considered unlikely that a successful claim could be made. However, Metrowater still would need to mount a legal defense, which was assessed as costing around $100,000 on average, with a high estimate of around $200,000.
- *Ecosystem:* Damage to the ecosystem was not considered a reasonable impact of pumping station overflow.
- *Fishery:* Commercial fisheries were not common in any of the receptor environments, and damage to a fishery was not considered a reasonable impact of pumping station overflow.
- *Clean-up:* Significant overflows (as described in Table 17.5) of sewage to beach or foreshore environments would require effective clean-up. However, effective clean-up of overflows into marine environments was not considered practical and therefore would not be required. Where required, the cost of clean-up could be around $2,000 on average, with a high estimate of around $5,000.
- *Regulatory fines:* There was potential for Metrowater to be fined for sewage overflows. Fines would be more likely where regulators considered management to be substandard or where there was a previous history of overflows and/or warnings from the regulators. The cost of fines could be around $30,000 on average, with a high estimate of around $50,000.

Property Damage. Substantial damage to property was not considered a reasonable impact of pumping station overflow and was excluded from further consideration.

Community Reaction. The following social issues were identified:

- *Amenity:* This was a key consideration with respect to sewage overflows and had the potential to cause substantial adverse public reaction. The key events were impairment of visual and recreational amenity. It was considered that where Metrowater responded effectively to overflows with urgency there would be little exposure to substantial community reaction. However, in circumstances where a spill remained in evidence for some time (e.g., a few days), Metrowater could expect a rapid escalation of adverse community reaction. Metrowater's response would be to conduct a focused public relations campaign explaining the circumstances of the release, the actions taken, and future actions to be taken to reduce the potential for further occurrences. The cost of a public relations campaign could be around $2,000 on average, with a high estimate of around $5,000.

- *Reputation:* Overflows had considerable potential to damage Metrowater's reputation. The most effective response would be to conduct a broad public relations campaign explaining the circumstances of the release, the actions taken, and future actions to be taken to reduce the potential for further occurrences. The cost of a public relations campaign could be around $10,000 on average, with a high estimate of around $20,000.

- *Opposition to future developments:* Adverse community reaction following a sewage release from a pumping station could potentially lead to public opposition to future resource consent applications (not necessarily related to sewage events) made by Metrowater. The opposition probably would be centered on the public perception of Metrowater's past environmental performance. Public objection to resource consents would most likely result in expenditure of greater-than-budgeted costs involved to obtain the resource consents. The additional cost of obtaining resource consents could encompass several applications and could be around $100,000 on average, with a high estimate of around $400,000.

- *Major civil disobedience:* Under circumstances where members of the public felt that the frequency and impact of overflows was intolerable, individual members of the community could engage in acts of civil disobedience. In the context of Metrowater pumping stations, civil disobedience could take the form of not paying water rates. Not only could Metrowater end up forfeiting the rates; more important, it would incur legal costs to recover the fees and would need to mount a public relations campaign to restrict further civil disobedience. The cost of legal resources and a public relations campaign could be around $100,000 on average, with a high estimate of around $300,000.

- *Cultural impact:* Sewage release to coastal waters had substantial potential to cause adverse reaction of Maori and other ethnic communities. Under these circumstances there was potential for claims seeking compensation for damages. The consequences of defending the claims in the Environment Court and implementing a well-conceived and executed public relations campaign was estimated to be around $20,000 on average, with a high estimate of around $100,000.

Political Reaction. Issues related to political reaction to uncontrolled sewage discharge were:

- *Operational interference:* Political reaction to ongoing overflows could take the form of political directives to take greater external control over Metrowater. Such actions could include closing beaches, making changes to by-laws, and intervention in Metrowater's governance (changes to the board, threats of closure, staff firings, or redundancy). The consequences of political intervention would include additional administration costs (i.e., staff time in justification and preparing reports), lost productivity due to change in focus, loss of corporate memory, training of new staff, and redundancy and termination payments. Combined with a public relations campaign to explain the changes, the cost of this impact was estimated to be around $100,000 on average, with a high estimate of around $400,000.
- *Revenues/subsidies:* The panel initially considered that a potential benefit could arise from sewage overflows through special funding from the national government to help fix the problem. However, on closer examination this was not considered a realistic expectation and it was excluded from further consideration.
- *Consents:* Refusal of Metrowater consent applications in wider areas was not considered a reasonable impact of sewage release from pumping stations and was excluded.
- *Lost future opportunity:* In the event of frequent or extremely large overflows, there existed a possibility that Metrowater would be dissolved and its service function revert to the Auckland City Council. This extreme action would incur substantial administration costs and difficulties with respect to security of the existing Metrowater debt. The cost of lost future opportunity could be around $5 million on average, with a high estimate of around $6 million.
- *Overdesign:* In response to continued overflows, political pressure could potentially be placed on Metrowater for higher design standards for new pumping stations, upgrading of existing facilities, or even replacing specific pumping stations with a totally new facilities. The cost could be around $100,000 on average, with a high estimate of around $300,000.

Likelihood of Impacts and Consequences

Table 17.6 shows the likelihoods of the identified impacts for each of the four receptor environments.

Table 17.6   Likelihoods of Impacts for Receptor Environments

Impact		Receptor Sensitivity			
		Extremely	Very	Moderately	Sensitive
Environmental	Public	0.01	0.1	0.000001	0.000001
	Fauna	—	0.001	—	—
	Ecosystem	—	—	—	0
	Fishery	—	—	—	—
	Cleanup	1	—	—	—
	Fines	0.01	0.01	0.001	0.001
	Property	—	—	—	—
Community	Amenity	1	0.01	0.001	0.001
	Reputation	1	0.01	0.0001	0.0001
	Opposition	0.1	0.02	0.01	0.01
	Disobedience	0.001	0.0001	0.001	0.001
	Cultural	0.00001	0.1	0.0001	0.0001
Political	Interference	0.02	0.1	0.01	0.01
	Consents	—	—	—	—
	Opportunity	0.000000001	0.000001	0.000001	0.000000001
	Overdesign	0.02	0.01	0.01	0.01

RISK ANALYSIS

Model Inputs

For each pumping station, the panel provided the following inputs:

- Likelihoods of all trigger mechanisms leading to sewage overflow
- Likelihood of consequences occurring assuming overflow occurs
- Cost of the consequences of each impact of overflow

Calculations

Cost of Consequences for Each Receptor Environment. For each receptor environment, the model calculated the risk posed by each impact (by multiplication of likelihood by cost) and assumed that the costs of the riskiest impacts were incurred. The riskiest impacts were defined here as those with a calculated risk quotient of greater than 1.0. The combined cost of the riskiest consequences is shown in Table 17.7.

Risk Posed by Each Pumping Station. For each pumping station, the event risk quotient was calculated by multiplication of the combined annual frequency of trigger mechanisms leading to overflow by the estimate of combined cost of the consequences of a release.

Table 17.7   Median Cost of Sewage Release Consequences

Receptor	Consequential Cost ($ × 1,000)		
	Optimistic	Planning	Pessimistic
Extremely Sensitive	410	590	850
Very Sensitive	780	1,020	1,400
Moderately Sensitive	280	490	770
Sensitive	280	500	790

Risk Profiles

Figure 17.3 shows the calculated risk posed by each pumping station, with the pumping stations ranked in order of decreasing risk. The risk profile in the figure was the key output of the risk assessment process and was used as the basis for development of Metrowater's risk reduction strategy.

This figure shows that less than approximately one-quarter (19) of the pumping stations presented substantially more risk than the remaining 71 stations. The nine riskiest pumping stations show risk values of greater than approximately $60,000 per year. The next group of 10 pumping stations each presented a risk more than twice that of the bulk of the remaining stations.

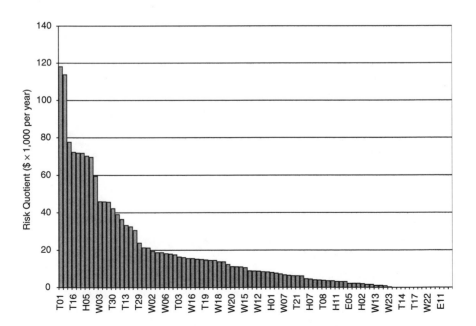

Figure 17.3   Initial risk profile showing the pumping stations ranked in order of decreasing risk quotient prior to the implementation of any risk treatment actions.

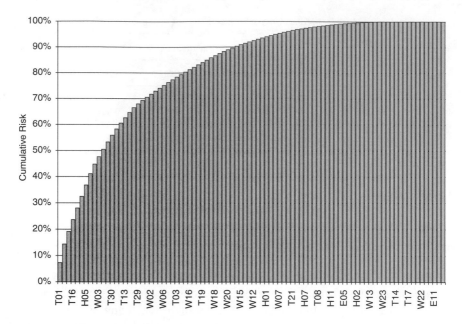

Figure 17.4   Initial cumulative risk profile showing the pumping stations ranked in order of decreasing risk quotient prior to the implementation of any risk treatment actions.

The cumulative risk profile of Figure 17.4 shows the cumulative risk as a percentage of the total. From this figure it can be seen that the riskiest nine pumping stations were responsible for 43 percent of the total risk posed by all of the pumping stations combined. The riskiest 19 pumping stations together posed almost 70 percent of the total risk. The remaining 71 pumping stations were responsible for only 30 percent of the total risk posed by all of the pumping stations.

RISK REDUCTION STRATEGIES

The risk management strategy stage of the study involved:

- Development of risk acceptance criteria
- Development of risk treatment options designed to reduce risk to acceptable levels
- Determination of the extent that the strategy reduces overall risk
- Demonstration of the benefits created by implementation of the strategy

Risk Acceptance Criteria

Corporate Risk Acceptance. The acceptance of financial risk by organizations is an individual matter. Risk acceptability is dependent on the:

* Financial capacity of the organization to absorb the consequences of risk
* Level of conservatism of the decision makers
* Amount of risk inherent in the business activities normally undertaken by the organization
* Diversity of the business
* Extent to which risk can be transferred or reduced

Furthermore, given a choice, senior managers of most organizations would aim to continually reduce risk rather than to set risk acceptance criteria and then maintain those levels of risk once achieved. Risk reduction through the continuing implementation of risk management is therefore, in effect, a never-ending process. In most risk management strategies, large reductions in risk are achievable relatively early in the risk management process, after which there are progressively diminishing returns from expenditure of each risk management dollar. In the risk management process there comes a point where risk reduction ceases to be cost effective. That is, the cost of risk reduction is greater than the potential exposures presented by the residual risk.

Clearly, then, no guidelines or rules determine the acceptability of risk for a given organization. The acceptability criteria and threshold at which risk reduction is no longer required need to be developed on an organization-specific basis.

Metrowater Pumping Station Risk Acceptance. As Metrowater had no existing risk acceptability criteria, the overall approach was to establish an initial and appropriate level of acceptability for use as a risk reduction target in this study. The expectation was that, over time, this target may be refined as Metrowater's appreciation of risk increased. The adopted approach was based on Metrowater's initial perception of risk and its level of comfort with respect to specific pumping stations.

When asked, panel members indicated that the perceived risk posed by the pumping station presenting the least risk (T18) was very low and was considered to be clearly acceptable. The calculated risk for pumping station T18 was negligible, at $0.6 per year. The panel was asked the same question for pumping stations presenting progressively increasing risk according to the risk profile in Figure 17.3. At a point along the profile where the risk posed by an individual pumping station was around $20,000 per year, panel members started to become uncomfortable about the level of risk. Pumping stations with risk quotients of $30,000 per year or more were identified as clearly posing unacceptable risk. A conservative approach was taken and the acceptability criterion was set at $20,000 per year. Figure 17.5 shows the acceptability criterion plotted on the risk profile and its relationship to the risk posed by each of the pumping stations.

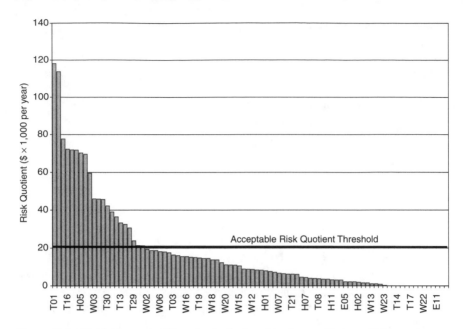

Figure 17.5 The "risk acceptability criterion" selected by the panel below which pumping station risk was considered acceptable for the time being.

Risk Treatment Options

Risk treatment may seek to reduce likelihood or consequence, or both. Examination of the treatment options available to Metrowater indicated that engineering solutions seemed to be the most appropriate to address reduction of likelihood of sewage overflows, while community-related actions were appropriate to reduce the consequences.

The identified engineering solutions included:

- *Increasing pumping station storage capacity:* This action would provide more time for Metrowater response teams to take action to prevent uncontrolled overflows.
- *Improved monitoring:* Monitoring could be improved by installation of landline systems to back up the existing telemetry monitoring system, which would increase the likelihood of timely detection of pumping station equipment failure.
- *Installation of audible alarms:* Provided the alarms were set at appropriate levels and did not become a public nuisance, this action would increase the likelihood of detection of high effluent levels in the pumping station storage and allow time for action to prevent overflows.

- *Upgrading pumps:* In some cases pump upgrades would substantially reduce the likelihood of sewage overflow due to pump failure.
- *Installation of bollards:* Protective bollards would reduce the potential for pumping station failure due to collision by vehicles.

Community solutions included:

- *Involvement:* Public involvement in responding to an audible alarm, for example, would not only reduce the likelihood of a spill but would make the public aware of its responsibilities in reducing the impacts of sewage overflows. Under these circumstances, where the community accepted part of the responsibility, the public would be less likely to react against Metrowater (provided the company responded appropriately to community requests).
- *Education:* Introduction of an appropriately designed and implemented public education program would make the community more aware of the need for pumping stations, the inherent risks involved, and the measures being taken to reduce the risk. If the public understood these events, it was felt that adverse public reaction and its consequences would be less likely.

Risk Reduction

Starting with the riskiest pumping station (T01) and working down the prioritized list, the panel considered the actions that should be taken to reduce pumping station risk quotient to the acceptable level of $20,000 per year. The panel needed to:

- Identify the main contributors to risk at each pumping station.
- Identify the effects of actions on reducing pumping station risk.
- Assess the cost of carrying out the actions.

Strategy Development Process. The process the panel followed in relation to pumping station T01 is provided to demonstrate the procedure followed with all of the pumping stations having a risk quotient above the acceptability criterion.

The panel first reviewed the trigger mechanism likelihoods and identified that pump stoppage due to equipment and power failure was the most likely event that could lead to an overflow from T01.

The panel also reviewed the current conditions related to pumping station T01 and concluded that the installed emergency storage capacity was less than indicated on the original data sheets due to subsequent quadrupling of house numbers in the connected catchment. Consequently, the panel considered that the available emergency storage time would be around four hours, which was only marginally acceptable.

Furthermore, pumping station T01 was a difficult site to access, particularly when the response team had very little time to get to the station.

The panel concluded that the first action required was to substantially reduce the likelihood of power failure (frequency of 0.1 per year). The most cost-effective action was to provide extra storage, at a cost of $50,000 (median) to $100,000 ($CL_{95\%}$). The extra storage would allow more time in which to connect an emergency generator. This action would reduce the likelihood of overflow due to power failure by a factor of 10. On rerunning the risk model with the proposed improvement, the panel found that the calculated risk was still in excess of the target $20,000 per year.

The panel then concluded that purchase of a long generator cable would overcome the difficulty of generator access to the pump house. The cable would be permanently stored in the pumping station and would cost an estimated $1,000 to $2,000. It was considered that provision of the spare cable would further reduce the likelihood of power failure leading to sewage release by a factor of 2. Rerunning of the model with both actions showed that although substantial risk reduction would be achieved, the risk posed by T01 would remain greater than the target.

The panel then focused attention on the next most likely trigger mechanism, equipment failure (frequency of 0.05 per year). The panel felt that construction of an access track would facilitate emergency repairs to equipment and would increase the time available to carry out repairs or replacement. The estimated cost of access track construction was $20,000 (median) to $35,000 ($CL_{95\%}$). The access track would reduce the likelihood of sewage overflow from T01 due to equipment failure by a factor of 50. Rerunning the model with all of the above risk reduction actions included showed that the calculated risk was $20,200, which was considered to effectively meet the risk acceptability target.

Overall Risk Strategy. Table 17.8 shows the set of prioritized risk management actions required to reduce the risk posed by the nine highest-risk pumping stations to an acceptable level.

Figure 17.6 shows a comparison between the current risk posed by each of the pumping stations and the risk expected to be presented by the 25 most risky pumping stations after implementation of the risk management strategy shown in Table 17.8. With few exceptions, the proposed risk management actions generally reduced the risk posed by individual pumping stations to less than one-half of the acceptability criterion, which comprehensively achieved the desired level of risk reduction. Depending on availability of funds, Metrowater could decide at some future date either to review the risk management strategy or to develop another strategy to reduce pumping station risk even further.

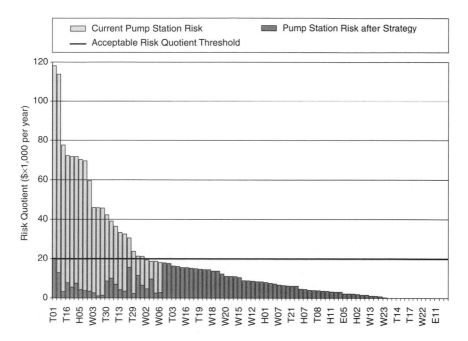

Figure 17.6 **Risk profile showing the expected risk quotient before and after implementation of selected risk treatment actions.**

Benefit-Cost of the Risk Reduction Program

Figure 17.7 shows the progressive median cost to implement the risk reduction strategy and also shows the financial benefit of the strategy. Financial benefit was defined as the exposure that would be effectively reduced by the proposed risk management actions. The resultant benefit-cost relationships could be used to plan budget expenditure.

The figure shows that expenditure of around $1.2 million would effectively reduce around 40 percent of the current risk (the nine riskiest pumping stations) and reduce exposure by around $9.4 million. Expenditure of a further $300,000 would address the 16 next highest-risk pumping stations and reduce risk exposure by a further $11.6 million.

The benefit-cost analysis demonstrated that the proposed risk management actions were very cost effective and expenditure could be planned to address the highest-priority pumping stations according to availability of funds.

Table 17.8 Prioritized Risk Management Actions: Cost and Effect

Pump Station	Action	Cost ($ × 1,000)		Trigger Addressed	Likelihood Reduction	Cumulative Cost ($ × 1,000)
		CL 50%	CL 95%			CL 50%
T01	Provide extra storage (10 m × 2 m dia)	50	100	Power fail	10	50
	Standby long generator cable	1	2	Power fail	2	51
	Construct access track	20	35	Equipment fail	50	71
E13	Replace the current pumps with Flyte pumps	50	70	Equipment fail	10	121
	Replace PLC with new switchboard	15	20	Equipment fail	10	136
	Install an audible alarm	2	3	Power fail	100	138
T05	Install an audible alarm	2	3	Equipment fail	20	140
	Provide extra storage (10 m³)	60	100	Power fail	100	200
	Install bollards	2	4	Impact	100	202
T16	Install an audible alarm	2	3	Equipment and power fail	10	204
	Provide extra storage (10 m³)	60	100	Power fail	100	264
H08	Install an audible alarm	2	3	Equipment and power fail	20	266
	Provide extra storage (6 m to 8 m deep)	175	250	Power fail	100	441
T07	Install an audible alarm	2	3	Equipment fail	10	443
	Provide extra storage (18 m³)	90	140	Power fail	100	533
H05	Install an audible alarm	2	3	Equipment fail	20	535
	Provide extra storage	150	200	Power fail	100	685
H06	Install an audible alarm	2	3	Equipment fail	20	687
	Provide extra storage	175	200	Power fail	80	862
T02	Install flow sensors	35	60	Pipe	100	897
	Install an audible alarm	2	3	Equipment and power fail	20	899
	Install link to T01, auto shutoff, dedicated landline	20	30	Equipment fail	20	919

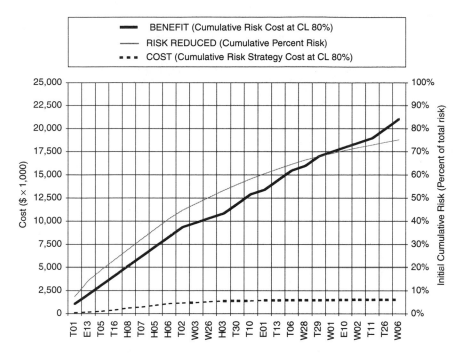

Figure 17.7 Benefit-cost relationships expected to be gained by implementation of the selected risk treatment actions.

SUMMARY

The following benefits and conclusions were derived from the Metrowater case study:

- The existing practices to control pumping station risks were identified.
- The main contributors to risk at each pumping station were identified and quantified.
- The pumping stations were ranked in order of risk.
- Sufficient information was collated and generated to enable development of a systematic, defensible, prioritized strategy to reduce the risk posed by the pumping stations.
- Appropriate risk acceptance criteria were determined.
- Risk treatment options designed to reduce risk to the acceptable levels were identified.

- The extent to which the strategy reduced overall risk was determined.
- The benefits created by implementation of the strategy were demonstrated.

Applying the above approach to any asset management endeavor is likely to generate a similar set of conclusions, thus using the RISQUE method provides a useful and cost-effective approach to developing an asset management program.

GLOSSARY

This glossary defines the meaning of technical terms as they have been used in this book. Other literature may use and define these terms in different ways.

acceptable risk: Risk that may be accepted without further treatment because its likely consequences are negligible, or the risk cannot be avoided or transferred, or the costs of doing so would be too high.

ALARP (as low as reasonably practicable): The principle that risks should be evaluated against the costs of reducing them; measures then must be taken to reduce or eliminate the risks unless the cost of doing so is obviously unreasonable (grossly disproportionate) compared with the risk and the benefit derived by treating the risk.

asset: In engineering and commerce terms, usually refers to a capital cost item. In security, insurance, and loss control, usually refers to an item that if (accidentally) lost would cause a loss.

base cost: The cost of construction, operation, and other committed costs over the project life. Base cost may be expressed in either current dollars without account for the time value of money or can be discounted back to current dollars net present value.

benchmarking: A process improvement tool for comparing and adopting processes better performed by another organization.

brainstorming: Generating ideas about a topic without screening, and listing them without criticism from anyone.

capital estimate: A quantification and presentation of the monetary resources (investment costs or dollars) required to achieve a business objective.

chance method: An alternative method of calculating risk cost. The chance method assumes that a risk event occurs according to its probability of occurrence. For example, the cost of a risk event with an 80 percent chance of occurring will be included in the risk cost calculation in 80 percent of trial simulations.

CL 50% or **50th percentile:** The 50 percent confidence level for a range or distribution, or that value which should not be exceeded in 50 percent of occurrences. It is the median value. Often considered to be an optimistic estimate with respect to cost.

CL 80% or **80th percentile:** The 80 percent confidence level for a range or distribution, or that value which should not be exceeded in 80 percent of occurrences. Often considered to reflect the corporation's level of conservatism with respect to cost. It may be the value used for planning purposes.

CL 95% or **95th percentile:** The 95 percent confidence level for a range or distribution, or that value which should not be exceeded in 95 percent of occurrences. Often considered to be a pessimistic estimate with respect to cost.

common mode failure: Refers to the simultaneous failure of multiple components or systems due to a single, normally external cause such as an earthquake or fire. It is used to distinguish discrete failures of individual components or systems due to defect arising locally within that component or system.

confidence level or limit: The probability that a reported value will not be exceeded, expressed as a percentage; for example, the 95th percentile confidence limit would not be exceeded in 95 percent of cases.

consequence: The outcome of a risk event expressed qualitatively or quantitatively, being the actual or potential degree of severity of loss, injury, disadvantage, or gain. A range of consequences may be associated with a risk event.

consequence threshold: A financial cost to a project or organization that would not be material to the organization or could marginally be absorbed by the usual operational contingency. The consequence threshold for a risk assessment of a business line within an organization may be, for example, $100,000. In contrast, the consequence threshold for an organization-wide business risk assessment could be $2 million.

consequential cost: The cost associated with a risk event, assuming it occurs. Also referred to as the exposure or occurrence cost.

contingency planning: Preparing to handle a given circumstance that may arise in the future.

core risk: The risk that is considered to form an inherent part of the business environment, for example, variation in product price.

cost (i): Of activities, both direct and indirect, involving any negative impact, including money, time, labor, disruption, goodwill, political, and intangible losses.

cost (ii): Base cost or risk cost reported in current dollars or dollars net present value.

cost distribution: A probability distribution of cost.

critical success factors: Aims, objectives, or outcomes that a stakeholder regards as critical for project success.

damage control: Procedures designed to minimize severity of loss.

decision tree: A risk analysis technique for describing random processes and computing the probability of a given occurrence using a tree diagram.

Delphi approach or technique: A technique for obtaining an independent opinion on a topic by consulting with subject matter experts.

dependence: The correlation or linkages between uncertain variables that must be estimated for accurate quantitative risk analysis.

discount rate: The annual rate (expressed as a percentage) used for discounting future cash flow that represents the rate of inflation or the interest rate of a competing investment. The discount rate is used to calculate the net present value of an investment by a series of future payments and income.

environmental hazard: An event or continuing process, which, if it occurred, will lead to circumstances having a potential to degrade, directly or indirectly, the quality of the environment in the short or long term.

environmental risk: A measure of potential threats/hazards to the environment that combines the probability that the events will cause or lead to degradation of the environment and the severity of that degradation.

event: An incident or situation that occurs in a particular place during a particular interval of time.

event number: An identifier assigned to a risk event; for example, Corp 1-12, PCB contaminated oil stockpile leading to tank replacement and remediation.

event tree: A hazard identification and frequency analysis technique that employs inductive reasoning to describe the potential outcomes that may arise from an initiating event. The fundamental principle of the event-tree process is to unravel a relatively complex event to derive a sequence of simpler component events, whose probabilities and consequences have a better prospect of being estimated using available data or judgment.

exposure profile: Shows the financial exposure that would be derived from occurrence of each risk event.

failure (risk): A cessation of function that has consequences (usually meaning death, injury, or damage) beyond a component or entity merely becoming unavailable to perform its function.

fault: The inability of an entity to perform its required function, resulting in unavailability. May be a nonperformance against some defined performance criterion. Can also be referred to as a breakdown failure.

fault tree analysis (FTA): A hazard identification and frequency analysis technique that starts with the undesired event (failure) and determines all of the ways in which it could occur. Probability of occurrence is quantified in this process. Fault trees are presented graphically.

feasibility: The phases of a project when a determination is made as to whether there is a practical alternative to current operations.

FMEA (fault modes and effects analysis): A procedure by which potential failure modes in a technical system are analyzed.

FMECA (fault modes, effects, and criticality analysis): An extension of an FMEA, in which each failure mode identified is ranked according to the combined influence of its likelihood of occurrence and the severity of its consequences.

frequency: The probability of an event occurring, expressed as number of occurrences over time (i.e., the project life). For example, a likelihood of occurrence of 1 in 100 years is equal to a frequency of 0.01 per year, or 0.1 over the project life of 10 years.

gap analysis: Analysis of the difference between a defined set of performance criteria and actual performance.

hazard: A threat or source of potential harm or danger or a situation with a potential to cause loss, an event that might lead to an uncontrolled release of energy or material, with on-site or off-site consequences for people, buildings, plant, equipment, material, animals, or the environment.

hazard identification: Process of recognizing that a hazard exists and defining its characteristics.

HAZOP (hazard and operability study): A structured approach for identifying hazards, operational problems, or deviations from designed performance in a process.

heuristics: A risk analysis technique using a rule of thumb.

incident: An unplanned event or situation that occurs in a particular place during a particular interval of time, which should provide an alert to the risk management system. This can be a failure of a control system; or a near miss; or having potential for injury, ill health, damage, or other loss.

individual risk: The frequency at which an individual may be expected to sustain a given level of harm from the occurrence of specified hazards.

insurance: A method of transferring risks by financial means.

likelihood: The probability or frequency of occurrence of a risk event.

log normal distribution: A probability distribution that has no upper limit, all values are greater than zero, most of the values fall at the lower end of the range, and the logarithm of the variable is normally distributed.

long-term annual discount rate: Also known as the real rate of return, that is, the rate at which a chosen measure discounts the future value of a sum or series of payments. For example, a real rate of return of 4 percent per year may represent the difference between return on investment and the rate of inflation. (See **discount rate**).

loss: The embarrassment, harm, financial loss, legal, or other damage that could occur due to a loss event. Any negative consequence, financial or otherwise, including death, injury, damage loss, or breach of statute. It may lead to a claim and/or court proceedings.

loss control: Any conscious action intended to reduce the frequency or severity of accidental losses.

management reserve: An estimated sum of money required over the project life to cover the costs of incidents (risk events). Synonymous with risk cost.

monitor: To check, supervise, observe critically, or record the progress of an activity, action, or system on a regular basis in order to identify change.

Monte Carlo simulation: A frequency analysis technique that generates expected values from a random value for an appropriate probability distribution in a mathematical model. Monte Carlo simulation calculates numbers not as single numbers but as cost distributions. The results are expressed as a range of possible outcomes together with the likelihood of each outcome. (Also known as simulation by random sampling).

net present value (NPV): Today's value of an investment over a specified period of time, using a discount rate and a series of future payments and incomes.

normal distribution: A probability distribution where the values are evenly distributed on either side of the mean, values are more likely to be in the vicinity of the mean than far away, and two-thirds of the values lie within one standard deviation (the average distance of values from the mean) of the mean.

optimistic cost: Normally considered to be the 50 percent confidence level, which represents an optimistic estimate within a cost distribution.

organization: A company, firm, enterprise or association, or other legal entity or part thereof, whether incorporated or not, public or private, that has its own function(s) and administration.

peripheral risk: The risk that is associated with noncore aspects of a business.

pessimistic cost: Usually considered to lie within the 90 to 99 percent range of confidence levels, which represent a pessimistic estimate within a cost distribution.

planning: A management process for determining what steps to execute, assigning who will perform those tasks, and verifying when they must start and stop.

planning cost: Usually considered to lie within the 70 to 85 percent range of confidence levels, which represent a conservative but realistic estimate within a cost distribution.

probability: The likelihood of an event occurring measured by the ratio of specific events or outcomes to the total number of possible events or outcomes. Expressed on a decimal scale from 0 to 1, with 0 indicating an impossible event or outcome and 1 indicating an event or outcome is certain.

probability distribution: A set of all possible events and their associated probabilities that describes the uncertainty of data within the set.

project manager: Responsible person within an organization for ensuring that the risk management process is followed and that appropriate information is provided to decision-makers.

proportional risk profile: Shows how much risk each event, or a group of events, contributes to the total risk presented by all risk events.

qualitative risk assessment: An analytical process that uses qualitative (descriptive) measures to describe the likelihoods and consequences of risk events, which usually are brought together as a risk matrix. The qualitative measures are tailored to meet the needs of the specific application under evaluation. The qualitative risk matrix differentiates risk on a relative basis (e.g., high, medium, and low).

quality: Conformance to a set of requirements that, if met, results in an organization, service, or product that is fit for its intended purpose.

quantitative or quantified risk assessment (QRA): An analytical process that attributes values to the full suite of likelihoods and consequences arising from risk events. Risk is expressed as the product of likelihood and cost. Estimates of consequence can be made using any consistent measure—dollars, number of lives lost, and so on—depending on the nature of the application. Quantitative engineering risk assessments often measure risk in terms of frequency and number of potential lives lost. Business applications usually use monetary measures to define risk. Estimates of likelihood are made in terms of event frequency (e.g., annual frequency or frequency over the period of a specified project) and/or probability of occurrence if the event occurs.

ranked risk profile: Ranked risk profiles clearly indicate relationships such as the relative magnitude of risk for each event and show which events are the riskiest and those that are the least risky.

real rate of return: Also known as the long-term annual discount rate, that is, the rate at which a chosen measure discounts the future value of a sum or series of payments. For example, a real rate of return of 4 percent per year may represent the difference between return on investment and the rate of inflation.

reliability: The probability that an item will perform a required function under stated conditions for a stated period of time.

residual risk: That which remains beyond the identified, managed risks. For example, residual risk is the risk that remains after the project managers have addressed the core risk events that are associated with their project or business activity.

resources: The human, physical, and financial assets of an organization.

risk: A notion consisting of an intrinsic combination of two components: the likelihood of an event occurring in the future and the consequences if the event occurs.

risk (speculative): Generally, risk deliberately accepted for a perceived benefit.

risk acceptance: An informed decision to accept the consequences and the likelihood of a particular risk.

risk analysis: Systematic use of available information to determine how often specified events may occur and the magnitude of their consequences. Quantitative risk analysis involves quantification and modeling of the probabilities and consequences for each substantive risk event.

risk analyst: Specialist (usually a consultant) in risk assessment and strategy development, employed to develop and facilitate the risk management process.

risk assessment: The study of decisions subject to uncertain consequences; the overall process of risk analysis and risk evaluation.

risk aversion: Risk management is predicated on the worst-case scenarios while simultaneously trying to address all risk situations.

risk avoidance: An informed decision not to become involved in a risk situation. Decision-makers take action to avoid one or more threats or hazards.

risk control: Identification and implementation of measures, or controls, to treat (lessen or avoid) the impact of a threat/hazard to a process, asset, resource, or project.

risk cost: A reasonable estimate of the combined cost that will be incurred over a specified future time period due to the occurrence of risk events. Risk cost usually is calculated as the cost of consequences for the riskiest events and expressed as a distribution or range of cost rather than a single-point cost estimate.

risk cutoff or threshold: A value of risk (the risk quotient) that determines which of the risk events are to be included in the riskiest issues.

risk engineering: The application of engineering techniques to the risk management process.

risk evaluation: The process to determine risk management priorities by comparing the level of risk against predetermined standards, target risk levels, or other criteria.

risk event: An environmental, statutory, engineering, or other event that has been identified during the risk assessment as having some likelihood of occurrence and that could have some potential detrimental effect should it occur.

risk exposure: The impact of a threat on a product, system, or project.

risk financing: The methods applied to fund risk treatment and the financial consequences of risk events.

risk identification: Systematic listing of risk events and their causes and determination of what, how, and why events can happen.

riskiest events: Those (usually relatively few) events that contribute to the bulk (usually around 90 to 95 percent) of the aggregate risk for each scheme. The measure of risk of each event that exceeds the "risk threshold."

risk management: The process of planning, organizing, directing, and controlling the resources and activities of an organization in order to minimize the adverse impacts of accidental losses to that organization at least possible cost.

risk map: A graph that shows the probability of a risk event occurring plotted against the consequences (e.g., financial cost or lives lost).

risk perception: How people perceive threats.

risk profile: An assessment that shows the relationships between risk events and how the total risk is distributed among the risk events.

risk quotient: The product of occurrence frequency of a risk event and its consequences (cost). While expressed as dollars, this measure is not a real dollar value as its derivation includes the frequency of occurrence of the risk event. Also referred to as long-term risk, expected cost, risk factor, risk level.

risk reduction: A selective application of appropriate techniques and management principles to reduce either likelihood of occurrence of a risk event or its consequences, or both.

risk register: Derived from information provided by the expert panel, it is a tabulation of all risk events identified throughout the course of a risk assessment. The risk register lists risk events (grouped by type); provides a brief description of each event; indicates the likelihood of occurrence and the potential cost range (at the mean and 95 percent confidence limit); whether each event has been included in, or excluded from, the risk model; and a reason for their inclusion/exclusion.

risk retention: Intentionally or unintentionally retaining the responsibility for loss or financial burden of loss within the organization.

risk threshold: The value of the risk quotient that separates the riskiest events within a risk profile from the remainder. The risk threshold defines which risk events are to be used in calculation of the risk cost.

risk transfer: Shifting the responsibility or burden for loss to another party through legislation, contract, insurance, or other means. Risk transfer also can refer to shifting a physical risk or part thereof elsewhere.

risk treatment: Establishes and implements appropriate management responses to reduce, transfer, or accept risks.

risk treatment or reduction strategy: A set of actions that, when implemented, will reduce the overall exposure of a business to risk events. The actions are designed to reduce the likelihood that the risk events will occur and/or the magnitude of the consequences if the event was to occur.

RISQUE method (Risk Identification and Strategy using Quantitative Evaluation): A risk management process that involves assessment of risk and development of risk management strategy using predominantly financial measures.

routine decision: Determining action that will have predictable results, based on some standard operating procedure.

safe: An acceptably low or tolerable level of risk.

scenario analysis: Use of descriptions of how a risk event might arise, potential controls, responses, and consequences for a broad examination of nonstandard events or events that are hard to quantify.

semiquantitative risk assessment: Takes the qualitative approach further by attributing values or multipliers to the likelihood and consequence groupings. Semi-quantitative approaches frequently combine realistic estimates of likelihood with relative estimates of consequence. The values used in relation to consequences usually reflect the relative magnitude of the consequence and do not necessarily reflect realistic values. For example, the risk analyst may consider that the consequences of a major injury are twice as great as those derived from moderate injury. In this case, a multiplier is applied so that the estimated risk associated with a major injury reflects the degree of difference between the two consequences.

sensitivity analysis: Examines how the results of a calculation or model vary as individual assumptions are changed. Can be a form of quantitative analysis in which the results of a model are examined as one variable at a time is changed.

serious potential hazard: A hazard that is assessed as have an "extreme" potential future risk (combined assessment of the probability of occurrence and the potential consequence).

serious potential incident: An incident that is assessed as having an "extreme" potential future risk (combined assessment of the probability of recurrence and the potential consequence).

severity: The measure of the absolute consequences of a loss, hazard, or vulnerability, ignoring likelihood. In insurance terms, the absolute magnitude of the dollars associated with a single (potential) loss event.

societal risk: The relationship between frequency and the number of people suffering from a specified level of harm in a given population from the occurrence of specified hazards.

stakeholders: Individuals, groups, or organizations that may affect, be affected by, or perceive themselves to be affected by a decision or activity, or are affected by aspects of the business/project/activity.

sunny-day failure: Failure of an embankment when the river is not in flood.

threat: An action or event that might prejudice any asset, system, process, or project.

threshold method: Method predominantly used by the RISQUE method to calculate risk cost. The threshold method differentiates between occurrence of risk events on the basis of risk (the risk quotient) and assumes that the costs of the most risky events comprise the risk cost.

tolerable risk: Risk that is not regarded as negligible or something that can be ignored, but must be kept under review and further reduced.

total risk: The sum of the risk if all of the events identified as the riskiest events were to occur over the life of the project. This is the key measure of risk cost used in the RISQUE method.

triple bottom line: Extension of the financial "bottom line" concept of economic prosperity to include environmental quality and social equity.

uncertainty: Unknowns: referring to either whether an event will occur or the magnitude of consequences of an event. For consequences, uncertainty is represented by the range or spread of distribution associated with the cost of risk events, for example, by the difference between the 50th percentile and the 95th percentile confidence limits for a risk event.

vulnerability: A weakness with regard to a threat or hazard.

vulnerability analysis: A method of "completeness" checking for a defined scenario. Typically assets or critical success factors are established as well as potential threats/hazards. Each success factor is examined for each threat/hazard to see if it is vulnerable to that threat/hazard.

INDEX